REBEL
IN
HIGH
HEELS

CHARLOTTE LAWS

TRUE STORY ABOUT THE FEARLESS MOM WHO BATTLED
– AND DEFEATED – THE KINGPIN OF REVENGE PORN AND
THE DANGEROUS FORCES OF CONFORMITY

For information about this title or to order other books and/or electronic media, contact the publisher:
Stroud House Publishing
Offices in New York and Anaheim, California.
StroudHousePublishing.com
Contact@StroudHousePublishing.com

ISBNs: 978-0-9961335-1-7 (Print)
        978-0-9961335-2-4 (eBooks)

Printed in the United States of America

Cover photo by Jeremy Saffer at www.jeremysaffer.com

Table of Contents

Preface: May The Fierce Be With You   v

Part I: Rebel Against Revenge Porn   **1**

Part II: Life-Crashing   **51**

Chapter One – Stupids, Tweens and Brights   57

Sharon I: The "Hunter S. Thompson Ain't No Rebel" Theory   *75*

Chapter Two – The Battle of Atlanta   79

Sharon II: Carmageddon and the Social Media Prenup   *95*

Chapter Three – My Long, Green Pencil   99

Sharon III: Museums and Conformity   *109*

Chapter Four – The Little Atlanta Girl Who Could   113

Sharon IV: Music and Mental Health   *128*

Chapter Five – Curses and Castles   131

Sharon V: A Tennis Court Named Fido   *149*

Chapter Six – Murder, Jealousy and a Witch Hunt   153

Sharon VI: I am a Little Ball in a Boat   *163*

Chapter Seven – The Resident Heathen   169

Sharon VII: Is God a Mobster?   *179*

Chapter Eight – Jonesing and the Warthogs 183
    Sharon VIII: There's Conflict and There's Conflict 195

Chapter Nine – From Sex to Saks 197
    Sharon IX: The East vs. West on Emotion and Anger 210

Chapter Ten – Chip Chatting 215
    Sharon X: Politics and the Peeping Tom in Prison 234

Chapter Eleven – What Happens in Vegas Ends Up
    in a Book 239
    Sharon XI: Party-Crashing for the Animals 255

Chapter Twelve – Dragons and Other Strangers 259
    Sharon XII: Anchors Aweigh 271

Part III: The Troll Slayer **275**

Trial Update 297

Afterword: Rebel in a Binder 299

Conclusion: From Museum to Center Stage 301

Glossary 305

May The Fierce Be With You

WHEN IT COMES TO STYLE, format and design, *Rebel in High Heels* is distinctly disobedient. It nuzzles nonconformity and irreverence, ignoring traditional literary structure. It is, in effect, a rebel in a binder.

That which seems incompatible in this book may, in truth, be harmonious. That which appears frivolous may carry great meaning. That which jumps out as humorous and carefree may camouflage deep tragedy and struggle. In other words, *Rebel* is not predictable, and there is a unity that may not be immediately obvious.

The often-outlandish adventures of my teen and young adult years taught me about character, creativity, courage, and confidence. I learned about "character" when I was forced to rely upon my own conscience because the values of my community seemed skewed. I learned about "creativity" when I finagled a date with my longtime celebrity crush and when I sneaked my brother to visit our "brain-damaged" mom against our father's command to "forget she ever existed." I learned about "courage" when I crashed ferociously guarded VIP events (i.e., to converse with the President), and when I went toe-to-toe with bullies and racists. Success in all of these areas gave me confidence and a fiercer mindset which 30 years later, boosted my ability to fight Internet criminals and the online trolls who frolic in hate.

The seeds of my formative years comprise the center of *Rebel.* Cradled and protected in Part II, they are revealed in flashback to Sharon, a woman I have been meeting secretly for 26 years due to a bizarre set of circumstances. These seeds from my iconoclastic—and largely disastrous—youth give rise to the path that I embrace as an adult. How does a child escape, who is battered by tragedy and feels confined inside a gilded prison? How does she develop personal identity and a mission in the world? How does her dissonance with the community of her youth prepare her for a large-scale crusade in support of victims and a fight against prejudice?

Parts I and III of *Rebel* comprise the outer layer of this stylistically postmodern memoir. They detail the ups and downs—including the countless nail-biting experiences and threats to my life—in connection with my recent, public battle against revenge porn and the Internet trolls who revel in victimizing the weak and unsuspecting. I began this war to help my daughter when her private topless photo was hacked and posted on a pernicious website run by a 25-year-old who called himself a "professional life-ruiner." I soon learned that there were hundreds of other victims who needed my help. When I expanded my efforts, I became known as the Erin Brockovich of revenge porn.

This book is full of battles.

They are often uphill, sometimes treacherous, and usually energizing. They may be important or frivolous. They may make you cry or laugh. They may teach you a life lesson or not. But they are numerous, and they are always fraught with dragons.

I dedicate this book to my family who has spent the past three years—and counting—tolerating the late-night phone calls from victims, the meetings with legislators that forced me away from the dinner table, and the speeches around the country that whisked me out of town. I had to quit my "day job." Devoting one's life to causes is not always a practical choice, but it is indeed a satisfying one.

There are three pronounced themes within this book: (a) perseverance is the key to success; (b) othercentrism (helping others) is the key to happiness; and c) a person is more likely to realize success and happiness if she lives in the bold zone. The bold zone is that area just beyond the "fear zone" and the "lazy zone" where fierceness resides. It requires "showing up," taking calculated chances, going at life with gusto and becoming an accomplished, caring and relentless force of nature.

It is my hope that this book will embolden and energize readers. May the fierce be with you.

PART I

Rebel Against Revenge Porn

"*I didn't realize quite how brave Charlotte Laws is until I see her in action.*"
~ THE GUARDIAN

"*I am glad that Charlotte is sharing her story in writing this book.
It is important that we educate people about revenge porn and the
devastating effects on victims.*"
~ SENATOR ANTHONY CANNELLA, CALIFORNIA

"*Charlotte Laws single-handedly dismantled the empire of pure evil that earned
Hunter Moore the title of 'Most Hated Man on the Internet.'*"
~ MSNBC

"*Dr. Charlotte Laws became the 'Erin Brockovich of revenge porn.'*"
~ CBS NEWS

"*One mother's journey to affect serious change.*"
~ ALTERNATIVE PRESS

"We know where you live," a muffled male voice rasped. "Your life will be ruined."

Justified Fear

I had come to feel like Will Smith in *Enemy of the State*. I was being hunted, harassed, and stalked by criminals with technological expertise. I had been thrust into an unexpected war. I felt exposed, vulnerable and alone on the front line. I had awoken a hideous network of villains and saboteurs, who were in pursuit of me, hoping to ruin my life. I had received terrifying emails, backlash on Twitter, and death threats. My computer had been bombarded with viruses, and a technician had advised me to buy all new equipment because the malware was too tough to remove.

"Also, be leery of unusual cars or vans in the neighborhood," he added.

"Why?" I asked.

"If someone wants to break into your computer network, he will need to be close to your house. That is, unless he has advanced skills. Then, he could gain access from anywhere."

I hurried home from the hardware store with my all-important purchase: heavy-duty padlocks. I knew I had to secure the gates at my residence, so that an intruder or a team of intruders could not access my backyard and possibly my home.

I pulled into my driveway, glad that the suspicious white car with the young, male driver was no longer present. It had been there on the previous evening, according to my daughter, Kayla. She'd seen it when she returned from work, and she had monitored it for several hours until it disappeared. She did not report the incident to me until the next day.

"Mom, why was there a guy in a white car, watching our house last night?"

Because she had no knowledge of the "be leery of unusual cars or vans" warning from the computer technician, I could not accuse her of paranoia.

I affixed padlocks to the gates. Then the phone rang. It was like a gun. It had become a powerful way to threaten and to terrorize me. It was one of my enemy's weapons. I reluctantly picked up the receiver.

"We know where you live," a muffled male voice rasped. "Your life will be ruined." He hung up.

A caller that morning had told me that I would be raped, tortured, and killed. I glanced out the front window. The night that had once looked innocent and peaceful suddenly seemed ominous. Then I logged onto my computer to see whether the Twitter backlash against me had ceased. It had not. But there was an odd message on my feed, which read, "Please follow me. I need to direct message you."

I did as I was instructed, and the interaction resulted in a bizarre phone call. Just as *Enemy of the State* protagonist, Will Smith, got aid from Gene Hackman—an off-the-grid, former government agent—I was being offered assistance.

"Don't worry. We're going to protect you. We're computer experts," were the first words uttered by a man nicknamed "Jack," who claimed to be an operative with the underground group, Anonymous.

I knew little about the famous, decentralized network of hacktivists, who are sometimes called "freedom fighters" or digital Robin Hoods, so I conducted Google searches during our half-hour phone conversation.

"Jack" instructed me on how to protect my computer network and explained in detail how he and a buddy planned to electronically go after the man who had been threatening me and who had been urging his devotees to follow suit. He then uttered the name of the person who had become the most well-known online face of revenge porn: Hunter Moore.

"We see Hunter Moore and his followers have been attacking you on Twitter. We will go after him, and we won't stop until he stops victimizing people," he said.

I felt better after the call, but wondered if it had been a practical joke. Was this really the notorious group Anonymous or was I being duped? Did I have an ally or would the stalking and emotional harassment escalate into physical violence against my family? I would learn the truth within 24 hours...

How It All Began

My battle began a year earlier. Think Jordin Sparks music, a knotty-pine bedroom set, flowery pink linens, and my 24-year-old daughter, Kayla—an exotic beauty and actress—emulating poses in fashion magazines. She snapped over a hundred pictures of herself in the mirror with her cell phone, hoping that a few might be compelling enough to send to the *Maxim* magazine modeling recruiter.

Kayla's boyfriend, Dan, lived far from Los Angeles in New Jersey. They'd met in Israel, during "Birthright," and their long-distance romance thrived. They nourished it with phone calls, text messages, periodic visits, and social media interaction. Dan was an airline pilot, smart, Jewish and handsome. On the other hand, he was a little too controlling and way too conservative. He complained about Kayla's occasional, low-cut dress or sexy Halloween costume. She sometimes hid her fashion choices by omitting them from Facebook. Kayla's daily adventures were detailed through social media, and if a photo was not there, it meant it did not exist. Except when it came to Dan and racy outfits.

On a now memorialized evening in October 2011, Kayla took those selfies in the mirror. Some were sexy, some were goofy, and as a gag—and for her eyes only—one was topless.

That topless shot would change our lives.

I was on television that night. I had constructed a makeshift TV studio, complete with professional lighting and backdrop, in a corner of our den, where I did a weekly gig, via Skype, as a political commentator on the NBC show, *The Filter*. Three years prior, host and renowned anchor, Fred Roggin, had caught an episode of a public access program I hosted, and he had miraculously invited me to join the NBC show. Being a TV commentator was the realization of a lifelong dream.

I took my job seriously, more so than the other pundits who did not go to the expense or trouble to assemble "production facilities." Fred and staff liked to call my home "NBC's West Valley Studio." When I was on air, I placed a daunting "Do Not Disturb" sign on my front door; it said, "Beware of Mom." The word "Dog" was crossed out.

Kayla and my husband, Charles, called me "unpleasant to be around" on taping days. They were right. I was stressed, frazzled, driven, and not interested in being sidetracked. The producer typically gave me only two hours to prepare four topics. I felt compelled to come up with jokes, titillating tales, statistics and facts in addition to "my opinion." I wanted to be informative and entertaining. At the onset, the task never seemed achievable; I always felt like superwoman afterwards. One of my episodes was nominated for an Emmy.

Charles (Kayla's stepfather)—a witty, British lawyer and Oxford graduate—was on the phone in his home office on "selfie taking" night. He was discussing a bizarre case he'd won which involved grade school students whose mouths had been taped shut by their teacher. It happened in Barstow, California, and the children were "physically challenged." One was blind.

Charles is brilliant and twenty years my senior. He knows full Shakespearean plays by heart, and he has memorized countless poems. He knows dates, names and seemingly everything about history and politics. But he is clueless about American culture; he has never heard of Archie Bunker, *The Brady Bunch*, Kourtney Kardashian, *Punk'd*, The Spice Girls or the song, "Pants on the Ground." A couple of years ago, I had to explain that they make "touchdowns" in football, not "baskets."

Charles and Kayla have one long-standing complaint about me: I am always too busy. I become obsessed with a goal and refuse to relax. In fact, I am downright *down* on the idea of "down time." I feel guilty unless I am soaring at the speed of a fighter jet.

So it was not unusual for there to be a mama fighter jet pointed at the nasty world of revenge porn… only three months later.

Revenge porn (RP) is the online distribution of nude and topless photos, without consent, in an effort to humiliate and hurt victims, mostly females. A picture is uploaded by an angry ex-boyfriend or malicious hacker with identifying information about a woman, such as her full name, workplace, social media page, boss' email address or parents' phone number. Followers of the RP websites then harass the victim, often forwarding the embarrassing photo to her family members, friends and business contacts. It can lead to a loss of economic and employment opportunities, and it can strain or end a woman's personal relationships.

The most notorious revenge porn website was *Is Anyone Up?* (IAU), which had an estimated 30 million page views per month. Hunter Moore ran the site. He was an unshaven and scrappy "bad boy" who had been dubbed the "Most Hated Man on the Internet" by the BBC. He did dozens of interviews, calling himself a "professional life-ruiner." Some media outlets glorified him, giving him big-league headlines and a platform to spew hatred and misogyny. Hunter bragged about his 600,000 followers on Twitter and said, "All women are sluts... and if someone killed themselves over being on the site do you know how much money I'd make?"

In January 2012, Kayla was in a high-rise on the west side of Los Angeles, auditioning for a G-rated part—or as she put it, "a once in a lifetime role that would launch her career"—while a 23-year-old computer hacker was surreptitiously nabbing her topless shot. He worked at Disneyland, went by the fake name, "Gary Jones", and had attended high school only two blocks from our house. This was ironic because "Gary" was not targeting our community; he was randomly stealing photos from unsuspecting folks all over the U.S. and then allegedly selling them to Hunter Moore. He began his life of computer crime at age 16, according to his former pal, Annie, who I later interviewed. She and Gary shared a deep friendship—or so she thought—until she found out he was secretly stealing nudes from her computer and sending her anonymous threats.

Anyway, I can imagine Kayla innocently reading the childlike script in the high-rise, while "Gary"—a sleazy, Edward Norton-type—rifled through her emails. At the conclusion of the audition, the casting director pulled Kayla aside and gave her the good news: she would get the part.

But there was bad news waiting for her at home. She could not log into her Facebook or email accounts; her passwords had been changed. Alarmed, she came to me with "Mom, I've been hacked." I told her to alert her credit card companies. It never occurred to either of us that someone might be pilfering photos.

Kayla asked me to call the credit card companies for her, a request that launched us into another mother-daughter battle over Kayla's independence or lack thereof. Our conflicts always ended with my charge, "You're old enough to stand on your own two feet", and Kayla's rebuttal, "You're always too busy. You never do anything for me." It was routine for Kayla to stomp away and lock herself in her room. Our fights were short-lived. Despite the pain that revenge porn would bring our family, it would have one unexpected benefit: in the end, it would help Kayla transform into an adult.

Nine days following the "hack," Kayla's topless photo was uploaded to IAU, along with her personally identifying information: her name, city and social media link. I can envision the scene at Hunter's parents' home near Sacramento where the "most hated man" operated his site. I imagine he looked at his tattoos in the mirror, admiring how his skin looked like a graffiti wall, and then shifted his gaze to the gash on his upper arm, recalling when a former sexual conquest—pissed about being drugged, photographed nude, and posted in cyberspace—jumped from a van with her burly brothers and stabbed him with a pen. He regularly bragged about the "pen attack" to reporters, admitting he deserved it. I assume Hunter then wandered over to his computer and clicked on Gary's email titled "Per Your Request, Bro" to find Kayla's compromising photo.

Kayla learned about the uploaded picture at her waitress job. She got an urgent phone call from her friend, Katie.

"Kayla, I have to talk to you right now."

"I'm at work in the middle of my shift. I can't talk," Kayla said.

"This is really important," Katie replied. "You need to take a break."

Kayla knew Katie would not interrupt her at work unless there was good cause.

"Could someone please cover my tables?' Kayla asked as she headed to the parking lot with the phone.

"You are—" Katie knew the news would devastate Kayla. "You are topless on a website. It's called Is Anyone Up dot com."

9

"What?" Kayla's voice trembled. She was in disbelief. How was this possible? She had never given a revealing photo to anyone. She was confused; it had to be a mistake.

Kayla searched the website on her iPhone. She found the upsetting photo, along with personally identifying data. She erupted in tears. She felt helpless, exposed, violated, and vulnerable. Who had seen the picture? Would it be saved on strangers' hard drives? Would it spread to other sites? Kayla was frantic. The world had intruded on her private life.

Kayla stumbled through the rest of her shift, feeling disoriented. She knocked over a glass of water at table 22.

"I'm so sorry... so sorry," she said, as she wiped the spill, which seeped onto a customer's shoes.

"It's okay," the patron replied. "Are you all right?"

"There was a death in my family," she mumbled.

During a break, Kayla phoned me and uttered the four words that every mother dreads, "Something horrible happened, Mom."

"But, don't tell Charles."

"Why?" I asked.

"It's too embarrassing," she said.

I launched "Operation No Moore." This was my personal investigation of revenge porn and Is Anyone Up?. I resuscitated my skills from the past. I'd once been a detective for Proficiency, a private eye firm in Commerce, California. I'd also handled freelance work. A major studio paid me to find out whether a producer was making porn flicks on the side, and wives hired me to follow their husbands.

I'd never heard about revenge porn prior to Kayla's call, but for many months after, I would hear about little else. My daughter returned from work that night, distraught and withdrawn, and barricaded herself in her room—behavior that Charles attributed to "an actor's life of perpetual rejection," assuming she didn't get the part.

Shattered, sequestered in her room, and confronted by lewd online comments, Kayla raced to shut down her social media profiles. She was also bombarded by graphic phone calls: from strangers who called her a slut and demanded sex and from a male acquaintance who had saved her image. She turned off her phone and tossed it in the trash. Her reputation had crashed and burned; her world was falling apart.

"Operation No Moore"

Our family had many sleepless nights after the photo appeared online. Kayla tossed and turned in her bed, while I stayed up, amassing data. I perused Hunter's online interviews, printed revenge porn articles, jotted down contact information for lawyers and read the nasty comments posted by IAU followers.

Hunter maintained that his victims were sluts, asked to be abused, and deserved to lose their jobs, embarrass their families, and find themselves forever ruined. Below photos on the site, his followers posted crude and misogynistic remarks. Victims were taunted as "fat cows," "creatures with nasty teeth," "ugly whores," "white trash sluts" and "whales."

One commenter said, "Jesus, someone call Greenpeace and get her back in the water."

There were naked photos of a legally blind paraplegic, an elderly business owner, a midget, and a mentally incapacitated woman, among others. The website was not about pornography; it was about ridiculing and hurting others.

Charles woke at three a.m. that first night, curious about my whereabouts. He donned his bathrobe and came to my home office, where I quickly concealed my research. Suspicious, he jumped into "trial attorney" mode, interrogating me.

"What are you hiding?"

"What is so important that it can't wait until morning?"

"Do you realize you have a show in fourteen hours?"

I deflected his questions, adding that I cancelled the TV appearance. This was completely out-of-character, and Charles joked, "*You* cancelled? What about all those people desperate for your opinion?"

He continued, "You wouldn't be seeing another man when you have a good-looking chap like me?" I told him to stop being ridiculous and to go back to bed. He obeyed, grumbling to himself.

I *had* to cancel appointments, put work on hold, and ignore routine tasks because a naked image rarely comes off the Internet unless someone becomes obsessed with its removal. RP website operators are consumed with what they do; therefore, anyone who hopes to prevail against them must be equally consumed. I emailed Hunter multiple times, asking him to take down the photo in accordance with the Digital Millennium Copyright Act. He refused. I was not surprised.

According to his online, TV and newspaper interviews, he threw legal letters in the trash; addressed his followers as "my children," taking a page from the Charles Manson handbook; and regularly taunted victims, encouraging them to commit suicide. People claimed to be afraid of him. He had no fear of lawsuits, perhaps because he lacked assets. He knew a victim would be unlikely to sue because a civil suit would cost $60,000 and forever link a woman's name with the image she hoped to hide. Plus, if she won in court, she'd be unable to collect and feel further exploited.

On the following morning, Charles found me still anchored at my desk, surrounded by papers and absorbed in a call with an attorney. I spoke in a hushed voice when he got close, eventually putting my phone mate on hold.

"Good luck with your appointment," I said.

Charles, still suspicious, pretended to leave, but actually eavesdropped from behind the doorway. He heard me discussing Section 230 of the Communications Decency Act, the law that exempts website operators from civil and criminal penalties. More confused than ever, he left.

Under Section 230, website operators are not deemed "publishers of content," but merely "platform providers," giving the public a place to post comments and images (including nonconsensual pornography).

After Charles left for work, I found Kayla in her room.

"Aren't you supposed to be at work?" I said.

Kayla, still down in the dumps, asked if the photo was still up. I told her that Hunter refused to remove it.

"We need to use Charles' legal letterhead for leverage," I suggested.

But, Kayla responded, "Absolutely not."

I rustled Kayla out of bed saying, "It is irresponsible to skip work. It is not what adults do."

Work was humiliating and agonizing because restaurant employees passed around the now infamous topless shot. They whispered, pointed at Kayla, and giggled, plus a smug assistant manager crowed, "I could get you fired."

During a break, Kayla clicked on IAU—something she did frequently, hoping the photo would magically be gone—and she found a topless picture of her friend, Susan. She immediately phoned her.

"My husband's email was hacked," Susan said.

When Kayla told me about Susan, I realized the media had been all wrong about revenge porn. It was not only about angry ex-lovers. It seemed to be associated with theft, and I wondered if "the most hated man" was linked to a hacking scheme.

Susan had snapped the shot for her newlywed husband, Josh, a semi-famous musician in a semi-famous band. Although Susan and Josh were devastated, they had no plans to confront the situation.

"Lots of people I know were hacked," Josh told me when I called. "Asking Hunter to remove the photo will just make things worse."

"What do you mean?" I asked.

"Word of advice. Stay away from him. I know friends who know him. He's a scary guy."

I told Josh I would not stop until Kayla's photo was down, and I also planned to investigate the hacking since I had proof that both Kayla and Susan had been robbed by "Gary Jones." He had used the same email address to nab both girls' shots.

"You're crazy," Josh warned. "Do it at your own risk, but don't mention our names to Hunter under any circumstances."

Josh and Susan were not the only folks intimidated by Hunter. The Internet was flush with similar sentiments. An individual who claimed to be a victim wrote, "Don't fight Hunter if you know what's good for you… I tried to get my pictures down, and now I regret it. I will never go against him again."

Frankly, I wondered if Hunter was creating fake profiles and posting ominous comments in order to discourage complaints and takedown notices. The climate of fear no doubt helped him maintain control, build a larger base of obedient minions, and keep profits flowing. Plus, he was becoming more and more "Internet famous"; this made him seem untouchable.

The Threats Began

Hunter was periodically paid to host nightclub parties around the U.S.; the attraction was loud music and alcohol. But, according to photos, online comments and newspaper articles, the gatherings sometimes included drugs, nudity and sex. Some reporters tagged along, witnessing the (periodically illegal) behavior. A *Nightline* cameraman told me that he saw Hunter using cocaine, and a New York reporter informed me that she watched "the most hated man" have sex in the back seat of a limousine.

Violence was rare; but at a venue in New York, Hunter was arrested for physical assault. He became incensed and attacked someone. There were no major injuries, but Hunter was taken into custody. He was released a few hours later on bail to an outpouring of relief by his toadies. Hunter was their "daddy" during good times and bad.

It was troubling that Hunter had appointed himself "The Father" and named his group "The Family." It was also troubling that suicidal victims were badgered with vicious posts, such as "Go kill yourself" or "You're an ugly whore. No one wants you. Die."

But most troubling were remarks about *murder.*

"I would kill for you, Father" was a post that I saw more than once.

So you can imagine my concern when I sat down at my computer with a cup of hot chocolate and clicked on an anonymous message addressed to me, which read...

"Back off Bitch or ELSE.... Signed The Family"

I had done nothing more than send emails requesting the removal of Kayla's photo and tweet a revenge porn lawyer asking if he could help me "take down a photo on *Is Anyone Up?*" The Twitter post had been public, so I figured any of Hunter's followers could have sent me the menacing message.

A feeling of vulnerability washed over my body. I realized Hunter was not my only enemy; there were potentially dozens or thousands. An army of sociopaths could be plotting my demise. My detractors were faceless and unpredictable; they could lunge at me from any angle. Did they live near my home? Where they ex-convicts? Did they own weapons? Did they have anger issues? Maybe Josh was right. Maybe I should have been scared.

Instead, I was angry and not about to let some punk and his toxic followers destroy my daughter's life.

15

Contacting Law Enforcement

Kayla and I went to the Los Angeles Police Department, where we hoped to find sympathy and an eager-to-help attitude. We found neither. A female detective from the cyber-crimes division was more interested in condescending stares and judgmental remarks than taking a report.

"Why would you take a picture like this if you didn't want it on the Internet?" the detective blasted Kayla.

"Why would you take a picture like this if you didn't want it on the Internet?" the detective blasted Kayla.

Kayla tugged at her baseball cap, so as to partially hide her face. "I wasn't going to show it to anyone."

"People blame rape victims," I said. "You're doing the same thing right now. This is cyber rape. Would you blame Kayla if she'd taken the photo with a Polaroid and stuck it in her dresser drawer? And then a burglar had broken into the house and stolen it? Or would you do your job and arrest the burglar?"

The detective clearly dubbed us a nuisance. "I will only be looking into the hacking, not anything else. You understand that, right?"

"Of course," I replied.

When the detective went to fetch forms, I whispered to Kayla, "I'll call the FBI when we get home."

The operator at the FBI call center was not condescending or discourteous, but he also did not want to help. He said, "Just file a report online."

I knew this was code for "we are too busy with other cases and won't do a darned thing."

"I see," I replied sarcastically. "You help Scarlett Johansson when she gets hacked, but you won't help the average person." (The actress' nude picture had recently appeared online.)

The man sighed as if he didn't have the energy to fight me. "Just a moment. I will transfer you to a detective."

The FBI told me that three agents would be coming to our house later in the month.

I phoned the LAPD detective to say the FBI would be taking the case and that she could close her file.

"What? The FBI?" she was offended. "You think they're better than we are?"

I explained that there were multiple victims, and some were probably located outside of Los Angeles.

I spoke to Kayla again about the need to tell Charles. "A legal letter could keep the photo from spreading to other sites." Kayla reluctantly agreed.

Later that day, Kayla was on set with a dozen actors. She was thrilled about her film debut—and finally able to put on a happy face—but seconds later, her dreams were dashed.

The casting director approached her, "What are you doing here? Didn't you get my email?"

Kayla shook her head, explaining that her computer was hacked.

"I'm sorry, but this is a children's film. And we found this… well, this photo of you online."

Kayla left while actors galloped past her. One stopped. "Hey, where are you going?"

"The casting director says I have the wrong look after all."

Meanwhile at home, Charles returned from work, once again baffled by my odd behavior. He caught me screaming at the computer in reaction to one of Hunter's online interviews. When I noticed Charles' presence, I calmly closed the browser as if nothing was wrong and exited the room, leaving him further perplexed.

That night, supper was uncomfortable, then combative. Everyone ate in awkward silence.

Then, I turned to Charles and said, "We have something to tell you," but Kayla kicked me under the table, followed by more "quiet dining."

Finally, Kayla nodded that it was okay for me to spill the beans, but when I did, Charles made light of the situation.

"Is that what this is all about?" Charles laughed. "It's no big deal. The photo will just go away if you ignore it."

Kayla burst into tears and ran to her room. "I knew we shouldn't have told him."

"That's not how the Internet works," I explained. "You never go online, so you don't know. Things proliferate. They don't go away, especially nude pictures."

I told Charles about the FBI, but he replied, "I think they are just trying to pacify you. They probably won't take the case."

"Well, maybe you could help us with a legal letter?" I asked.

Angry, Charles left the table. "I don't want to get involved."

Revenge porn was a pack of wolves. It was tearing our family apart. Kayla was withdrawn. Charles was agitated, and I was obsessed. I contacted Hunter Moore's publicist, his attorney, his hosting company, his Internet Service Provider in France, some of his advertisers, and his mother's former workplace in the city of Davis, where associates pressed for details about Mrs. Moore's son and his venomous website. I also registered Kayla's photo with the U.S. Copyright office and spoke to nine attorneys about copyright law, right to privacy, and options for legal recourse. The consensus was that revenge porn was largely untested in the civil courts, while criminal laws were nonexistent, except in the state of New Jersey. Within days, I became an expert on revenge porn, and it was not long before lawyers were telephoning me for guidance.

My investigation file quickly expanded. The contents included personal data about Hunter and his associates, printouts from his website, copies of relevant articles and reams of information on other involuntary porn stars who were featured on his site. In other words, Kayla and Susan were no longer the only hacked victims. I'd found others, and I knew it would be difficult for law enforcement to ignore folks from all over the country, who had been violated by the same pair: Moore and Gary Jones.

Other Victims

Jill

"Please gather your things and go home," he told her while her five-year-old students watched in wonder.

Jill was a kindergarten teacher in Kansas. I knew she was going to be posted. Hunter had mentioned it on his Twitter feed—which I had been monitoring—and he asked his followers if they thought she'd get fired. They had responded with the typical landslide of loutish and smutty comments.

An hour later, her photos were visible to the world along with identifying information, including the name of the school where she taught. This was the cue for followers of *Is Anyone Up?* to bombard the principal and school board with Jill's naked shots and crude remarks, such as "Fire that slut" and "You have a whore teaching your children."

"Is Jill there?" I said to the school receptionist.

"She's in class right now."

"I'd like to leave a message. This is urgent. Please tell her to call me when she gets time."

While I was leaving my message, the principal had marched into Jill's classroom and interrupted her lesson.

"Please gather your things and go home," he told her while five-year-old students watched in wonder.

"Why? I don't understand." Jill was confused.

"Please gather your things and go home," he repeated.

Bewildered, Jill accumulated her belongings, and as she was leaving the building, the receptionist handed her my message.

"Call someone named Charlotte."

"Charlotte?" She wandered out the door.

School employees, aware of her X-rated pictures, congregated and peered at Jill through the reception area glass.

Jill called me from the parking lot, and I revealed the agonizing news. She became hysterical. "Oh, my God. No. Oh, my God. No."

I was teary-eyed myself. I could feel each victim's pain and I could imagine being in their situation. Anyone could be in their situation. It was not their fault. Making calls was depressing, and I felt like a suicide hotline. Yet, in a weird sense, it was satisfying in that I felt I was helping others. Plus, I had experience with the issue, and I could offer advice.

Jill noticed her gawking colleagues.

"They're staring at me," she screamed into the phone. "Oh my God, they all know."

She fumbled for her keys, dropping her purse; contents scattered. Bawling, she quickly refilled the bag and ducked into her car.

"Those photos were private. I don't understand how anyone got them. Wait... how do I know who you really are? Don't ever call me again."

"Hello? Hello?" Jill had hung up.

I placed Jill's information in my file titled "Unknown" because I didn't know how her shots got onto IAU. I also had files labeled "Angry Exes," "Hacked," and "Self-Submit." I was sorting victims into categories.

An hour later, Jill phoned me back. She was with her fiancé.

"I'm sorry I hung up. Please help. I have no money for a lawyer. I'm going to lose my job. How did the pictures get on the Internet? I don't understand. Could it be my ex-boyfriend? Maybe the guy at the computer repair shop?" Jill rambled. "Do you think I was hacked?"

"Maybe. Lots of people were."

I gave Jill instructions on how to send take-down notices to Google and other search engines in order to de-index her name from the pictures. I told her to beef up her online presence, joining respectable websites so the disturbing pictures wouldn't appear on the first page. I told her to register the photos with the copyright office, and I told her about the FBI investigation.

"Plus, if I get my daughter's picture off the Internet, I will tell you what I did."

Tory

Tory lived in Atlanta.

A month prior, she had been sitting on an exam table in her doctor's office. She asked a nurse to photograph her because she wanted to document the healing process. Her post-surgery breasts were bandaged; only her nipples were visible.

The nurse snapped the shot. "I will email it to you later today,"

Soon thereafter, the medical office email was hacked by Gary Jones; and the topless, bandaged image was uploaded to IAU, along with Tory's identifying information, including the name of the store where she worked.

"I'd just had surgery," Tory weeped into the phone when I called. "How could someone do this to me?"

She and her manager received troubling phone calls. Tory was slammed as a "physical retard" and "ugly stepsister with thrashed boobs."

Tory quit her job.

Carl

A nude photo of Carl was uploaded to IAU.

Carl was about to graduate from law school, and he was searching for a job.

"This is really bad timing," he whispered from a high-rise hallway. "I'm going to be interviewed by a top law firm in ten minutes. If they do a search and find that photo, I'm toast."

"Do you know how it got on the Internet?" I asked.

"Yeah. My girlfriend's email was hacked. The hacker is across the country in California. We have the IP address. I've sent DMCA notices to Hunter Moore, but he won't take my picture down."

Carl forwarded information to me about the hacking, including the IP address, so I could pass it on to the FBI.

Pam

Pam, an affluent Ohio executive, was normally in control, but that day she felt helpless. She was in crisis mode. She finished up a board meeting, hoping her colleagues would not detect her anguish.

"Cancel my appointments for the rest of the day," she directed her secretary. "I'm feeling ill."

She locked herself in her office. Her email box was full of degrading and inappropriate remarks from strangers. Pam was unsure how her nude shots made it to IAU, but she knew her career would be over if anyone found out. She had worked tirelessly to advance in a man's world, and now she could lose it all.

Tina

Tina, from northern California, was also a victim. She and a female friend had been documenting weight loss through photos. Some of the shots were topless. Gary Jones had gotten into Tina's email, nabbed the sexiest pictures, and sent them to Hunter, who posted them.

"I was horrified," she told me on the phone. "I was at a restaurant, and a total stranger came up to me and said, 'I've seen you naked.'"

Tina had been stalked online, and she was seeing a psychologist because she no longer felt safe in the world. I put her in touch with the FBI.

Cathy

Forty-year-old Cathy was divorced, and she feared losing custody of her two children. She had taken extreme measures to dodge the graphic photos depicted beside her name, city and social media links. Cathy had quit her job, changed her phone number, moved to a new town and gone back to using her maiden name. She was freaked out when I located her, because she thought she'd erased all traces of her existence.

"I don't understand how you found me," she bawled into the phone. "If my ex-husband sees the photos, he will petition to take my kids away. I'm gonna lose my kids. What am I going to do? I can't lose my children."

Cathy had not been hacked; her photos had been morphed. In other words, she had never taken a nude shot. Someone had Photoshopped her head with an unknown nude body in highly acrobatic and embarrassing poses. It made Cathy look like a vulgar and veteran porn star.

"I've emailed Hunter Moore twenty times. He knows it isn't me, but he won't take the pictures down," she wailed. "Please help me."

I said I would.

After the call, Charles asked if I wanted to rent an after-dinner movie.

I bargained, "I will if you provide a legal letter."

He became furious that he had to bribe me to have fun and that there were headshots of victims all over my desk staring at him.

"Who are these people?" Charles picked up the headshot of Cathy. "You're letting strangers into our home. Stop with this nonsense. You're disrupting our life. You're not a private investigator anymore. That was twenty years ago." He marched away.

I looked out the window and saw Kayla in her "sad spot" in the yard, cuddling the dogs. It hurt me to see her in pain. I joined her and dove into a private conversation about going public. I asked permission to reveal the hacking to the media because they had been reporting that revenge porn was only about disgruntled exes.

"If I go public, you do, too," I said. "Your name will be out there."

Although Kayla was concerned that Dan would find out about the photo and break up, she agreed to let me talk to reporters if it could help others.

"I will withhold my identity for as long as I can."

Kayla asked about the other victims, and I relayed the harrowing tales.

"Some jobs are in jeopardy," I said. "All worry that friends and family will find out. Some people are suicidal, and I have to jump into the role of crisis counselor."

I listed some of the other victims: a photography business owner, two real estate agents, a bank executive, a Pizza Hut employee, three actresses, a boutique shop owner, two waitresses, three teachers (including Jill), a Nordstrom manager, a public speaker, a stay-at-home mom, a social worker, a car salesman, a yoga instructor, a college student, a mathematician, a social worker and a police officer's wife, among others. And then there was an accountant named Mandy.

Mandy

Mandy was a special victim. If I were Sherlock Holmes, she was my Watson. She was from Iran, had been hacked by Gary Jones, and was as feisty as a tornado.

Under her topless photo, there were posts such as, "I hope she gets stoned to death."

Although Mandy was Catholic, not Muslim, she had highly religious relatives who would ostracize her for this sort of transgression. Most women in her family dressed like nuns; they considered it sinful to show too much skin. Although Mandy was not expected to don a hijab, burqa, or habit, her family demanded that she wear modest attire. Plus, if news of the photo leaked, she could never return to Iran. It would simply be too dangerous.

Mandy's boss called her into his office.

"Strangers are emailing a topless picture of you to company employees."

"What are you talking about?" she was bewildered.

"Get it off the Internet right now, before a client sees it," he barked.

Shocked, confused, and horrified, Mandy dashed to her computer to search for the humiliating shot. She was all sobs and frantic mouse clicks.

I called her that evening. She was in the midst of conducting robo-Google searches with hopes that the photo had not spread. Her traditional, hijab-wearing sisters and mother—unaware of her situation—were nearby in the kitchen, cooking. Mandy ducked into a private hallway to speak with me.

She whispered into the phone, "Who are you? How did you find me? That photo was stolen. I've sent five emails, but he won't take it down."

A few days later, Mandy's dad said, "We have to visit your grandpa. He's dying."

Mandy—terrified because a topless picture in Iran can mean death—launched into every excuse in the book.

"I can't get off work."

"I think I have jury duty."

"My passport is expired."

Her dad, a militant patriarch, ignored her song and dance, saying, "You are coming to Iran with us. Period."

Mandy knew she *had* to get her photo down.

"I can't go back while my picture is up," she told me. "It's too dangerous. You have to help me."

She explained how a woman can be killed in parts of the Middle East over minor infractions, such as showing too much skin or holding hands with a man not her husband. Mandy told me about Mina, a female friend, who was nabbed by Iranian officials after holding hands with a male acquaintance. She was tortured in jail and killed.

"The authorities didn't initially tell her family the truth. Her relatives got the run-around. They went to visit Mina after her arrest, but were told she was transferred to different prison. The family went there. Then the authorities said she was sent to yet another prison. They went there, but nothing. This happened again and again... until her family gave up. The authorities did not want to reveal the truth... that she had been dead for years."

Although Mandy had never been a private eye, she was very smart. She knew how to finagle information, find clues, look outside of the box, and compile information for "Operation No Moore." Although she was afraid of "the most hated man on the Internet," she worked tirelessly behind the scenes, helping me to compile evidence for the FBI.

"Is that Mandy again?" Charles stood at my home office doorway, watching me on the phone.

"Mandy? I'm not sure who you're talking about," I joked, but he knew it was her because it was *always* her.

"I've decided this is a worthy cause," Charles continued. "I will help you get Kayla's picture off the Internet. I will write a legal letter."

"Thank you," I jumped up and gave him a hug, glad that we now had a top lawyer on our team.

"Not all victims are so lucky," he added, "to have an ex-private detective for a mother and an attorney for a stepfather. Hunter Moore will regret the day he messed with Kayla Laws."

My Shocking Survey Results

By this time, I had spoken with dozens of victims from around the country, and my findings were astonishing. A full 40 percent of victims had been hacked only days before their photos were loaded onto *Is Anyone Up?* In most cases, the scam began through Facebook and ended when Gary Jones gained access to the victim's email account. Another 12 percent of my sample group claimed their names and faces

26

were morphed or posted next to nude bodies that were not theirs; and 36 percent believed they were "revenge porn victims" in the "angry ex-boyfriend sense" (although some of these folks were on good terms with their exes and thought the exes might have been hacked). Lastly, 12 percent of my sample group were "self-submits." "Self-submits," of course, are not victims at all; they are individuals who willingly sent their images to Moore. In the end, it was disturbing to realize that over half of the folks from my informal study were either criminally hacked or posted next to body parts that were not theirs.

I wanted to circulate this information, to alert the media and the public; yet I didn't want my name to be linked. So I went to a resort in Las Vegas (I was on a three-day vacation there), and created a Blogger. com page under the fake name, "Cassie Freedom." I wrote a post about the suspiciously high percentage of stolen photos that appeared on IAU and published it.

The blog was immediately hacked… clearly by someone who got a Google alert on the phrase "Hunter Moore" or *Is Anyone Up?* because I did not advertise the online journal or entry.

Plus, a video virus was planted on the blog; it carried the message: "Hey, Click here."

The hacker also changed my password for the blog, and the only way to access it again was through the Gmail account tied to it. I suspected this person was trying to ascertain my identity. Gmail accounts identify the IP city at log on. Las Vegas had been listed as the first location. In order to further confuse the hacker, Mandy logged in at a Starbucks in Phoenix. I could imagine Hunter wondering who was in Nevada, and then suddenly… in Arizona.

An Alliance with Facebook

"Hunter's back on Facebook," Mandy revealed. "We need to wait until he gets a few thousand friends, then pow. Kick him off."

I was in daily contact with a number of victims from *Is Anyone Up?* Although they felt helpless and exploited, they shared a minor joy, a feeling of power that could be exerted at will. We could kick Hunter Moore off Facebook anytime, any moment, regardless of how much effort he expended to compile "friends." This is because I had created an alliance with the executives at the popular social networking service, a feat which seemed remarkable itself.

I had initially contacted Facebook to request that they fund a civil suit on behalf of victims. They had banned Moore from their site and sent him a legal letter because he had violated their terms of service by linking victims' photos with Facebook pages. Hunter responded to their letter with a copy of his penis. He had also put a bounty on their lead attorney; in other words, he wanted nude photos of this man. Facebook executives mulled over my "civil lawsuit idea," but ultimately decided against it, thinking it would lead to a slippery slope in which everyone would ask them to finance lawsuits.

The victims and I repeatedly kicked Hunter off of Facebook. He would sneak on, create a new page and tirelessly build a huge network of friends and followers. We would wait patiently. Then, I would make the all-important phone call and poof, his page would disappear. The victims would phone me, elated. Also, one person from our group knew the CEO of Paypal and got Moore banned from the e-commerce site, hindering his ability to collect donations.

Serving Moore and Going Undercover

Charles was watching television when I presented the ready-to-be-mailed legal letter, which demanded that Kayla's photo be removed immediately or face a costly civil suit. Charles reviewed the document and signed.

"Maybe you could talk to Hunter Moore's attorney? I've spoken with him twice, but I don't think he's taking me seriously. You could have a conversation lawyer to lawyer."

Charles shook his head no.

I sent the document certified mail because I knew Hunter was crafty about avoiding service. In fact, I spoke to Ray, a process server who had been hired by a victim. He'd spent 72 hours staking out Hunter's parents' house. When the "most hated" man finally emerged on his way to get pizza, Ray sprang into action.

Hunter was climbing into his car when he noticed Ray and sprinted back to the front door. Ray chased him. Hunter was served.

Mandy also wanted to serve Hunter; and I suggested the perfect place: one of his DJ gigs. I knew it could be costly paying a process server to wait outside of a house, hour after hour, day after day.

Mandy was not affluent, but she'd exhausted her $10,000 savings account on legal fees because getting her topless photo off the Internet was a priority. Her attorney hired a process server, who handed Moore legal documents at a northern California nightclub where he was hosting a party. Moore became incensed, tearing the papers into shreds and throwing them in the air. Later, he denied being served at all.

"You don't think he saw my name, do you? Do you think he read the paperwork? Oh my Lord, what if he saw my name?" Mandy was terrified.

I called Mandy's process server.

"Hunter was in such a fit of rage, ripping apart the documents," he told me. "I don't think he saw her name."

The process server also said there were club employees who witnessed everything. "So his denials about not getting served don't wash."

Because Mandy was scared that Hunter or one of his cronies would retaliate, she halted further legal action.

Another hacked victim wanted to serve Hunter and asked me to play witness. I agreed to go undercover at his DJ gig in Long Beach, California.

Before and After

"Undercover," in this case, meant dressing like a freak with pasty white make-up, sunglasses, a black wig, a beatnik beret and a tacky velvet jacket. I looked hideous.

"What do you think?" I asked Kayla, who snapped a photo.

"Don't let Charles see you. He'll lock you in the basement," she said.

"We don't have a basement."

"He'll dig one just for you."

Suddenly, Charles walked by, catching a glimpse of my crazy attire. He shook his head; he no longer had words.

Hunter's party was held at a large Long Beach motel where there were bands at various locations on the premises. I climbed out of my car in the darkened parking lot, locked the door and whirled around to find myself face-to-face with my nemesis: Hunter. It was freaky. He was accompanied by three other scene kids.

I locked eyes with Hunter for one brief second. Then he and his friends continued on their way.

I took a deep breath, trying to contain my anxiety, and scurried to an outdoor stairway, monitoring the foursome, who climbed into a nondescript van. The van remained parked in the lot, and I wondered what they were doing.

Later, I stood in a conference room with about 100 people while Hunter hung out on a podium at the front of the room, ready to assume the role of disc jockey. I was surprised there were so few attendees because Hunter was popular on Twitter. The other conference rooms were packed.

One of Hunter's friends, hanging with him on the stage, was Mr. Curious; he eyed me suspiciously. I tried to act nonchalant.

It was time for the music to begin, and Hunter—in a less-than-brilliant move—threw a cup of beer into the air. The liquid landed on his laptop, ruining it. The songs, which were designed to play from his computer, sputtered and stammered for the rest of the evening. I tolerated the on-again-off-again music while I waited, and waited, and waited. Nothing happened. Finally, I ducked into a quiet hallway and called the victim on my cell phone.

"Where's the process server?" I asked.

"I cancelled him," she confessed.

"Why?"

"I don't know what Hunter Moore might do. What if he has me killed?"

"That's ridiculous," I replied.

"People tell me stuff," she said. "He's dangerous."

I wandered back into the conference room and caught Mr. Curious scrutinizing me again. Then he whispered to Hunter.

I panicked and ran for the exit, periodically checking to make sure I wasn't being tailed. As I climbed into my car in the parking lot, I saw Mr. Curious in the distance peering at me. I screeched out of the parking lot.

Inside the car, I tried to contact Mandy on her cell, but was forced to leave a message.

31

"Mandy, Oh my God. Where are you? I think one of Hunter's friends may have recognized me. I am getting out of here as fast as I can. I hope he doesn't follow me."

"Operation No Moore Nonsense"

Kayla's photo was still online. Hunter had been inundated with appeals to remove it: from me, Kayla, Charles, his advertisers, his publicist, his attorney, his website technician, and his hosting company, among others.

"You need to take down Kayla Laws' picture."

"Just take down that Laws girl."

"It's in your best interest, Hunter, to remove her. She's causing way too much trouble."

Hunter ignored the requests, so I jacked up the intensity and moved on to "Operation No Moore Nonsense," which required Charles' assistance because we had to be ready, willing, and able to sue. I contacted Jeffrey Lyon, the president of Black Lotus Communications—Moore's Los Angeles-based, Internet security company—and asked for his help. I mentioned the hacking scheme and the FBI.

"I doubt you want to be complicit in illegal activity," I said on the phone.

"Does Hunter Moore know about the FBI?" Jeffrey asked.

"Probably. I told his attorney."

"I need to talk to my tech guys. We might be able to block Kayla's page. Although it would technically still be there, no one could see it."

"That would be great. Then maybe you could do the same for the other victims."

Kayla was cuddling with the dogs on her bed when I burst into her room.

"The Internet security company has blocked your page. No one can see it."

Ecstatic, Kayla grabbed her laptop and pulled up the website, but her smile faded when she saw that her photo was still there.

I was baffled. "It's supposed to be gone."

I called Jeffrey, who told me that Hunter had circumvented his efforts and maliciously created a new page for Kayla. Her topless photo was visible again, and we were back to square one.

"Maybe we should try blocking the photo instead of the page," Jeffrey said. "I will talk to my tech guys and see if it can be done. Give me a couple of days."

Charles returned home from an appointment. He searched the house for me and Kayla. A fax was arriving; he studied it.

It read, *"Hey, Ugly Bitch. Get off Hunter's dick. If you don't we'll rape you and put a shotgun down your throat."*

Charles peered out the window and saw me, Kayla and the dogs at the pool. He glanced at headshots of victims on my desk and then back down at the fax. He studied my computer, which was open to *Is Anyone Up?*, and he read a post about a girl who Hunter claimed had AIDS. The allegation was printed above her embarrassing nude shots.

Charles finally became enraged. He marched into the backyard.

"What's the number for that asshole's fucking attorney?"

Hunter's lawyer was Reza Sina, who was based in Los Angeles. I had spoken with him twice. He'd expressed sympathy for the victims, yet claimed to have no control over his client.

My intuition told me that Reza had more control than he acknowledged. I also felt he did not take me seriously, so I was glad Charles was willing to have a stern chat with him, lawyer to lawyer.

"We have talked to the FBI," Charles said to Reza on the phone. "They will be coming to our house. Plus, I am walking into court and filing papers in thirty minutes if that photo is not down. Period."

Charles, Kayla and I waited in the living room in stiff silence, eyeing a clock and anticipating the photo's removal. The countdown began.

Thirty minutes turned to twenty. Twenty minutes turned to ten. Tick tock, tick tock. Suddenly, it was time. Kayla searched the website on her laptop, and joyfully announced, "It's down!"

I ran to phone the victims, to tell them the secret to getting their pictures removed, but Charles restrained me.

"What are you doing? It's time to stop."

He showed me the "rape threat" fax and added, "You're a target. The FBI will be coming. They probably won't do anything, but you have to let *them* make that decision."

I broke away from him. "The victims are counting on me."

Two days after Kayla's image came down, Jeffrey and his tech folks were able to block photos of many victims from our group, although it was unclear whether Hunter could bypass the cyber-barrier.

Meanwhile in Kansas, the teacher Jill's high heels went clippity-clop as she walked into a classroom, set up "inquisition style" with a lone chair facing her authorities, an intimidating school board. Jill was hammered with "Your photos have been emailed to all of us multiple times, to the teachers, to the parents… Do you think it is appropriate to take pictures like this, Miss Jill?"

Jill emitted a barely audible whimper.

The FBI

Three young FBI agents from the Los Angeles Internet Crime division appeared at our door. They were professional and supportive. Unlike the LAPD detective, they never pointed an accusatory finger at Kayla or other victims.

"I am normally against the Patriot Act," I joked. "But, in this case, I say 'Go for it.'" They chuckled.

Lead agent Jed said that the bureau only has time for cases that involve large losses of money; therefore, he probably wouldn't get approval to proceed. Plus, the FBI would only be looking into the hacking, not Hunter's website, unless he were found to be complicit.

As a topper, he added, "These investigations usually take at least a year to complete."

Despite the barrage of bad news, the agents agreed to search Kayla's computer and cell phone while I brought out the big guns: my 12-inch pile of research, complete with victims' names, contact information and proof of the hacking scheme. The agents were flabbergasted by the vast amount of data.

"I have phone numbers for hacked victims all over the country," I said.

Charles joked, "The FBI should hire Charlotte. It's her calling."

An hour later, the agents finished up. Jed struggled to carry my cumbersome stack of research to his car, adding, "If our boss gives us the green light, we'll be back tomorrow."

They came back.

The second visit was much the same. Jed and the other agents spent hours copying files and questioning Kayla about the hacking. I told them that I had disclosed the complicated and detailed story to a reporter named Camille Dodero with the *Village Voice* because it was important to clear up misinformation. The media had been inaccurately reporting that photos on revenge porn websites stemmed from disgruntled exes. There had been no mention of hacking or Photoshopping.

"Also, Hunter Moore lies about living in San Francisco," I told the FBI. "I'd like to put his home address on the Internet, so victims know how to serve him with legal papers."

"I can't tell you what to do," Jed said. "But we would rather you not put his address out there yet, and we'd prefer the *Village Voice* not publish anything at this time, because we don't want Moore alerted to the investigation."

"Unfortunately, he probably knows about it," I said. "We told his attorney and the president of his security company. I'd be surprised if they didn't relay the information."

I asked Camille to stall the *Village Voice* story.

The FBI agents stopped by our house a final time. It included a "victims meeting," designed to discuss the possibility of a civil lawsuit and give the agents an opportunity to interview multiple victims in one location.

Present at the meeting were Kayla, three other hacked victims with their spouses or significant others, Charles, Michael Fattarosi (another lawyer), two FBI agents and me. Four other hacked victims were accessible by phone.

Michael Fattarosi specialized in adult entertainment cases. "The porn industry is against revenge porn," he said. "It gives them a bad name and hurts their bottom line."

Then, Michael glanced at the solemn and emotionally battered victims in our living room and offered the following advice: "Leave porn to the professionals."

The comment drew a big laugh.

Computer Viruses

A week later, I was having breakfast when I heard a bizarre dinging. I moved slowly toward the noise, baffled. The sound seemed to come from my home office. My unattended computer was going haywire. It was being bombarded with viruses. How could this happen? I hadn't touched anything. It was freaky, and I was unsure what to do. Plus, I sensed that someone had turned my desktop into a spy device. Was this person peering at me through the camera? I placed my hand over the hole while I frantically shut down the contraption.

Seconds later, the house landline rang. I answered it to hear creepy breathing.

"Hello? Hello?" I said. There was no response, so I hung up.

Then my cell phone rang. Then the landline rang again. It was chilling. I seemed to be the target of a tech attack.

That afternoon, a repair technician came to the house and removed the viruses from my computer. He said, "You need to be more careful. Your computer is old. It might not clean up next time."

The harassment got worse. One particular member of "The Family" named Evan tormented me relentlessly online. Weeks later, there were posts on Hunter's Twitter feed that he had died of a drug overdose.

In addition to Internet trolls like Evan, there were hang-ups and threats of violence, plus someone seemed to be trying to hack into my main phone, unaware that it was a landline.

I had been exposed—loudly and clearly—as an enemy of Hunter Moore and of revenge porn.

The FBI Raid and Threats

He added, "I will literally fucking buy a first-class plane ticket right now, eat an amazing meal, buy a gun in New York, and fucking kill whoever said that."

Moore would soon learn it was me.

Hunter unexpectedly took down *Is Anyone Up?* selling the domain. Some of his followers were distraught. Some were baffled. Others were furious, calling him a sell-out. Hunter claimed that he got tired of looking at nude pictures and that the site became too much of a hassle. But I knew the real reason: he was worried that law enforcement might be closing in on him.

They were.

Federal agents stood outside Hunter's parents' home with their walkie-talkies—while another set of armed federal agents jumped from official vehicles and broke down the front door of the residence.

Hunter, astounded, put his hands in the air. He was presented with a search warrant; and his computer, cell phone, and electronic equipment were confiscated.

The alleged hacker was raided at the same time by FBI in Los Angeles. Like Hunter, he was shaken and cooperative.

A few days later at *Village Voice* headquarters, the editor strolled into Camille's office. "We need to run the Charlotte Laws story now. Call Moore for a statement."

I can imagine Hunter eyeing his "boarded-up" front door when he answered the phone. Camille mentioned the FBI, and Hunter went ballistic, cursing and making threats.

"Honestly, I will be fucking furious, and I will burn down fucking the *Village Voice* headquarters if you fucking write anything saying I have an FBI investigation," he screamed into the phone.

He asked who had supplied her with the FBI information, but she refused to say.

He added, "I will literally fucking buy a first-class plane ticket right now, eat an amazing meal, buy a gun in New York, and fucking kill whoever said that."

Moore would soon learn it was me.

Camille hung up and stared at her article. This was a pivotal decision-making moment because she knew her actions could lead to retaliation against me and the paper.

Her editor appeared at the door with "Is the story ready?" and Camille made an on-the-spot-decision to move forward.

"I just need to add the last two quotes."

The *Village Voice* article came out, creating a huge stir from Hunter's supporters, the media and the public at large.

The repairman returned to my house, revealing that I now had *21 viruses.*

"Are you going for some sort of record?" he asked. "I suggest you buy a new computer. It's old and not worth fixing."

He also told me to beware of unusual cars parked on the street because someone might try to hack into my computer network.

"Unusual cars?" I was alarmed. "My computer network?"

Relaunch of IAU and Posting Moore's Home Address

Hunter must have felt invincible because out of the blue he publicly announced that he would relaunch *Is Anyone Up?* with all of the original photos, plus the site would be more insidious than before because it would include the addresses of victims along with driving directions on how to get to their homes. This terrified the people in our group, especially Mandy.

When reporters questioned Hunter about alleged hacking (per the *Village Voice* article), he denied it, boasting that he received way more content than he could use.

"I get 150 submissions a day. I don't need to hack," Hunter said to a news magazine show.

Hunter also wrote to a Twitter fan, "The FBI would have arrested me by now if they were going to."

I feared Hunter was right.

Too much time had passed. It had been almost a year. In fact, Jed no longer returned my calls. I took this as a bad sign.

Maybe law enforcement had moved on to other cases, but I—well, I had to stay focused. I needed to work on getting anti-revenge porn legislation passed. Plus, I wanted to post Hunter's home address with hopes it might halt the relaunch of the site.

"No. Don't post his address," Mandy begged. "You don't know what he'll do to you."

I walked through my house in a quandary. I looked out the window. I glanced at Hunter's Twitter feed. I poured a glass of juice. I looked out the window again. Finally, I drummed up courage and although shaky, I managed to write a Twitter post revealing Hunter's home address. I pushed the "tweet" button.

Within seconds, "the family" exploded with a cascade of hatred, vitriol and death threats against me; the venom came at me via Twitter, Facebook and email.

Hunter sent me a tweet, "Btw when you and your daughter get my dick out of your mouths you will realize how hard I troll you @CharlotteLaws."

Then he sent me a second tweet, "Posing [posting] your daughter's nudes tonight @charlottelaws I am Internet and seo genius I'll ruin your life and your daughters the fun way."

His threat to repost Kayla's photo alarmed me. Then, the phone rang.

A male caller said, "We're going to rape and kill you. We've ordered a body bag in size Charlotte."

He laughed; then click… he hung up.

Kayla came out of her room on her way to work and sensed I was rattled. She asked if something was wrong, but I said no. The phone rang again.

Kayla said, "Aren't you going to answer it?"

"No. I'm getting lots of sales calls."

Kayla shrugged and left.

A jittery Mandy arrived at the airport with her sisters, mom and dad. She once again launched into "excuse mode" because she was worried that her photo would reappear online.

Her father blasted her, "Shut up, Mandy. I don't want to hear about it again. You are coming with us."

In a desperate final attempt, Mandy pulled her mother aside for a private conversation and confessed the truth. Her mom, normally a calm and submissive woman, became panicked… and then uncharacteristically tough.

She confronted her husband, "Mandy's *not* going to Iran with us."

"Yes, she is."

"No, she's *not*."

Mandy's mom shooed her daughter away. "Hurry. Hurry. Get out of here."

Mandy grabbed her belongings and fled.

The Stalker, Anonymous and The Creepy Letter

When Kayla came home from work, she noticed a white car parked in front of our house. This was uncharacteristic; our cul-de-sac street was normally empty.

An hour later she settled at the dining room table to study for her real estate exam and noticed the suspicious white car was still present.

Kayla had changed her mind about career. Now she wanted to be a Realtor rather than an actress. She hated the negative attention that revenge porn had brought. She despised criticism and had come to realize verbal attacks are common for folks in the spotlight. It comes with being a public figure. Kayla wanted a private life.

On the following morning, Kayla mentioned the suspicious white car to me. Charles was out of town, but I could imagine his scathing words.

"You are bringing danger to the house. Who cares if the website goes back up? It's not your problem. You've got psychopaths after you. It's been a year, and the FBI has made no arrests. If they can't do anything, what makes you think you can?"

Maybe he was right. What made me think I could do something if the Federal Bureau of Investigation couldn't?

I looked around. The house suddenly seemed unsafe and spooky. I contemplated potential hiding spots on my property and formulated a mental strategy should Mr. White Car return. I thought about booking a hotel room for Kayla and me, but I could not leave my animals. They were the most vulnerable beings on the property. My two dogs could have been boarded at a kennel, but I also had hens. Finding overnight accommodations for a bunch of chickens–frankly, I didn't think it was possible.

So I got in my car and drove to Home Depot.

There was tension and a trace of paranoia as I scrambled to find padlocks at the store. While hurrying to complete the purchase at the checkout counter, I thought I saw an indiscernible man peering at me through the store front, but in a flash, he was gone. I figured it was my imagination.

It was dusk when I nervously exited with my purchase, searching for shadowy figures. I saw none.

I drove, checking my rear view mirror for suspicious vehicles. The road was clear.

When I got home, I made sure my animals were okay and then launched "Operation Lockdown," affixing padlocks to the side gates. The phone rang, jolting me like a bullet.

A mysterious male caller said, "We know where you live. Your life will be ruined."

Charles had wanted me to inform the police about the death threats. I hadn't, because I figured I'd have to get them up to speed, an onerous and time-consuming task. Plus, I knew police departments were better equipped to handle physical crimes as opposed to virtual ones.

But, I decided to make that call. I spoke to a male officer on the phone; he was irretrievably confused.

"I've never heard of revenge porn. Could you explain it again?"

I mentioned Hunter Moore and "the family."

"What family?" he asked.

I spoke about my grueling battle against a website. I am pretty sure he thought I was a nutcase.

He said he couldn't send a patrol car, but suggested, "If you feel threatened, you should leave."

"I can't. I have animals," I explained.

"You shouldn't be worried about them," he said. He clearly didn't put much value on their lives.

"You're welcome to come down to the station and file a report. Be sure to bring the letter and anything else you have."

I thanked him and hung up. I glanced at the backlash on my Twitter feed and noticed the odd message from someone named "Jack." We spoke on the phone.

"Jack" had a southern accent and claimed to be with the underground group, Anonymous. It comforted me when he said, "Don't worry. We're going to protect you." It felt like I had backup. I hoped he was real, not a practical joke.

Two hours after the Anonymous call, Kayla was studying real estate near the front window, and saw something suspicious for the second time.

"Mom, that white car is outside again," she yelled.

"What?" I was in disbelief.

I was tired of having my family victimized. I was more furious than afraid and fully prepared for a mother-to-stalker showdown. I marched out of the front door, unsure whether I was stepping into danger.

Kayla tagged behind, yelling, "Mom? What are you going to do?"

There was a blonde, curly-haired, 20- to 30-year-old guy in the white car. He was fiddling with something in his lap.

I stood in the street and yelled, "May I help you?"

He looked up at me and flew into panic mode. He quickly started his car and screeched away, almost barreling into my neighbor's stucco wall. I got five digits of his seven-digit license plate.

On the following day, I learned the truth about "Jack." He was real. He was my Gene Hackman. Anonymous launched a technological assault on Moore, crashing his servers and publicizing much of his personal information online, including his Social Security number.

Hunter retreated, becoming oddly quiet. He stopped speaking with the press, probably on orders from his lawyer because the FBI investigation was pending.

The Indictment and The Aftermath

On January 23, 2014, there was astonishing news. In the middle of the night, a team of federal agents descended on the alleged hacker's residence in Studio City, California.

And, in northern California, another team of federal agents apprehended the unshaven and sleepy Hunter Moore after riling him out of bed.

Both men were handcuffed, read their rights and taken into custody. They were charged with conspiracy to hack, unauthorized access to a protected computer, and aggravated identity theft. The trial was initially set to begin in the spring of 2014. Each faced a maximum of 42 years in prison.

Ironically, Hunter's last post on Twitter was "@justinbieber I'm comin to bust you out lil nigga." (Justin Bieber had just been arrested in Miami for DUI.)

I was the first person to be informed of the arrests. Jed called me on January 23 and said, "How are you?" in a coy, upbeat way.

"Fine," I spoke slowly, unsure whether he was calling with good news. "How are you?"

Then he came out with it. "Hunter Moore and the hacker have been arrested."

"What? You're kidding? I can't believe it." I was overjoyed. "What's the hacker's name?" (I only knew him by "Gary Jones").

"Charlie Evens," Jed said.

"Why does that name sound familiar?" I asked.

"You spoke to him on the phone two years ago."

"Oh…. The comedian?" I asked.

"Yep."

When calling victims, I had phoned a guy named Charlie Evens, who billed himself as a local comedian. Charlie had posted his own nude picture on IAU, but told me he had no idea how it got there.

"It's possible my ex-girlfriend posted it," he said at the time. "But she's not really the type."

"Do you think she might have been hacked?" I asked.

"I don't know."

"Are you upset about being on the website?" I continued.

"No, not really."

I did not trust him and withheld information about the FBI investigation.

"Thanks for your time. Sorry to have bothered you." I hung up.

Jed told me I could inform the press and public about the arrests. I did so on Twitter. My tweet said; "News Alert: Hunter Moore & his [alleged] hacker Charlie Evens have been arrested by the FBI..."

Victims, reporters and anti-revenge porn advocates immediately phoned.

Some members of "the family" were incensed and lashed out at me on Twitter. One mentioned my name and wrote, "We need to put a hit out on this bitch."

A few days later, everything was back to normal... or so I thought. My family was having breakfast.

Frustrated, Kayla thumbed through paperwork, "I need to buy new health insurance, but it's so complicated."

"Do you want me to help?" I asked.

Kayla looked at me like I had three ears. "No, Mom. I can do it myself."

Things were not back to normal. Kayla had matured.

Suddenly, levity turned to heaviness when the phone rang. The three of us froze. Charles and Kayla looked at each other with an "Oh no. Not again." look on their faces. The phone continued to ring.

"It could be a victim," I said in a meek and hesitant voice.

Charles and Kayla groaned.

I took that call and many others. I continued to serve as a hotline, helping victims of online harassment and revenge porn. I have assisted over 300 people to date.

Legislation

Although *Is Anyone Up?* was down, there were other disturbing sites and other desperate victims. I began pushing for legislation to protect victims, connecting with politicians on the state and federal level. I met with Senator Cory Booker, Congressman Adam Schiff, Senator Anthony Cannella, Assemblyman Mike Gatto, Congressman Brad Sherman and former Senator Chris Dodd.

I met with aides for Senators Barbara Boxer, Dianne Feinstein and Fran Pavley; as well as staff for Congressional representatives, Janice Hahn and Tony Cardenas. I had multiple phone conversations with the offices of Representative Jackie Speier and Senator Jeff Merkley, among others.

I also testified in favor of anti-revenge porn bills, including SB 255 and SB 1255. They passed. And I became a boardmember for the Cyber Civil Rights Initiative, a nonprofit designed to help victims of online harassment which was started by RP victim, Holly Jacobs. Boardmembers who serve alongside me include professor Mary Anne Franks, attorney Carrie Goldberg and non-profit guru Christina Hartman. Professor Danielle Citron is a board advisor. These fearless women—Jacobs, Franks, Goldberg, Hartman, and Citron—are staunch advocates for victims of nonconsensual pornography.

As of the writing of this book, sixteen states have laws against non-consensual pornography: New Jersey, Virginia, Alaska, Hawaii, Delaware, Pennsylvania, Illinois, Texas, Idaho, Utah, Colorado, Arizona, Georgia, Maryland, Wisconsin and California.

Bills have been proposed in many others: Washington, Massachusetts, Florida, New Mexico, Missouri, Pennsylvania, Kansas, Kentucky, New York, Rhode Island and Connecticut.

Representative Jackie Speier of California plans to introduce a federal law in mid-2015.

Interest outside of the U.S. has also soared. Israel, the United Kingdom, Germany, the Philippines and the Victorian state of Australia have passed laws; and bills have been introduced in Canada, and Brazil.

Today, there are an estimated 3,000 revenge porn websites in the world. There are thousands and thousands of victims.

My years as an "Internet troll slayer" have been bizarre and difficult, to say the least. Sometimes I look back and wonder what would have happened if Hunter had removed Kayla's photo when first asked. Would his site be up today? Would "Gary Jones" still be hacking into emails? Would politicians have taken up the issue, and would there be laws in 16 states with the possibility of federal legislation? But most of all I wonder if Charles was right.

Does Hunter Moore regret the day he messed with Kayla Laws?

Charlie Evens Arraignment

It was arraignment day at the Edward Roybal Federal Building in Los Angeles for the 25-year-old alleged hacker, Charlie Evens. The Feds said he'd victimized folks from Maine to Oregon, and from Florida to Arizona—while residing at his grandparents' property, which was only 1.4 miles from my office. His former high school, Notre Dame, located in Sherman Oaks, was a scant two blocks from the home where I'd raised Kayla. I'd walked and roller skated regularly past the school, which placed me only 100 yards from his classroom in any given direction. It was coincidental and a little eerie.

Today was my first time inside a criminal courthouse, and I was unsure what to expect. An army of reporters, with their news trucks, cameras and tape recorders, were huddled around the perimeter of the structure. I knew this human corridor needed to be penetrated if I wanted to access the proceedings. When I stepped near the courthouse, I became the media's go-to gal for sound bites. Microphones were jammed in my face. I tried not to disappoint as I spoke about the destructive nature of revenge porn and the need for justice. No doubt reporters would have preferred a pithy comment—or even a wisecrack—from Evens or his parents, but I was all they had.

Inside, the hearing room was empty, except for arrestees in handcuffs sitting behind a glass partition. I entered—unaware that I had gate-crashed—and sat in the audience area, preparing my pad and pen for note-taking.

Evens, sitting in the middle of "handcuff row," wore a light blue T-shirt and beige pants. His hair was unkempt, and his face was unshaven. He flashed an overconfident expression in my direction; he seemed oblivious to his sticky predicament. Ten minutes later, I was approached by a uniformed court officer.

"How did you get in here?" he asked. "No one is permitted in the room yet."

I joined the hallway crowd, which included members of the media and Evens' parents. Evens' mother was mobilized next to Evens' father and stepmom in what seemed to be part strategy session and part "Oh my God, is this really happening?"

I was rearranging my purse when I was confronted from behind.

"Who are you?" Evens' mother, Jackie, inquired.

I whirled around and immediately felt a spark of sympathy. She seemed like a nice lady who had been through an emotional obstacle course. Her son had saddled her with an unexpected burden. I figured "the whole truth and nothing but the truth" might instigate verbal battle, so there was no point in going that route. Instead, I opted for an incomplete truth.

"I'm a mom...." I said.

She stared at me suspiciously. There was awkward silence. A nearby NBC broadcaster—aware of my true identity—held his breath. Other people stared at us, anticipating a mother vs. mother brawl.

"And I write articles from time to time," I added, hoping to diffuse the tension by mentioning my role as a part-time reporter. I often wrote op-ed pieces for newspapers and magazines; and I planned to write about the trial.

Jackie exhaled, as if I had given her the right answer. Then she tried to convince me and others in the hallway that her son was not all that bad.

"He's a really good person who made some bad choices," she declared. "He volunteers with the Special Olympics every year."

She looked at the NBC reporter, "I can't believe this is newsworthy." Then, she paced the hallway, saying "Why? Why? Why? Why? It's one shock after another."

The doors opened for Evens' trial, and I entered with others from the hallway. The courtroom filled to capacity. I sat next to two sketch artists, and the formalities of the arraignment began. I jotted down the rapid back-and-forth conversation between the judge and attorneys.

I learned that Evens was on probation due to a "driving under the influence," that he had a substance abuse problem, and that there was a warrant for his arrest on a misdemeanor.

Evens responded to the judge with "yes, your honor" and "no, your honor" and eventually entered a plea of "not guilty."

He was released into the custody of his mother, Jackie, on $60,000 bond, and told he could not contact any of his victims or access the Internet, except at Disneyland where he worked. His hacking seemed to be compulsive because he had brazenly continued to break into people's emails *after* the FBI raid.

The prosecutor told the judge that law enforcement was stunned when Evens hacked into "...up to another 300 emails through October 2012, even though he knew he was under investigation."

This was not altogether surprising to me in light of posts on Evens' Facebook page, which I had read from start to finish. Evens had written the following status update: "I think part of me actually likes a bit of drama. I've worked hard these past few months on having a somewhat normal, steady, stress-free life but let me tell you, I'm starting to get a little bored."

Perhaps there is a bright side to being under federal indictment: a person is rarely bored.

When Evens left the courthouse that day with his mom, he blundered.

KTLA news reporter, Mary Beth McDade, put a microphone in his face and asked him, "What do you want to say to the victims? Are you apologetic for what you have done?"

Evens replied, "Of course," in what seemed to be an admission of guilt.

His expression, however, did not signify contrition. It was a look of smugness and defiance.

PART II
Life-Crashing

"[She is] a crusader…"
~ NBC News

"She is such an amazing and inspiring woman."
~ Buzzfeed

"Never underestimate a former Buckhead debutante."
~ Atlanta Journal-Constitution

"This book is two for the price of one. 'Rebel in High Heels' provides a gripping account of Charlotte Laws' dangerous battle against revenge porn. But it also details Laws' roller-coaster early years: dating a superstar, dealing with suicide, hobnobbing with celebrities, fighting racism and being thrust into the glitzy world of 'sex for sale.' By following Laws' bold, life-crashing adventures, the reader learns how to become a rebel and a relentless advocate for victims. This memoir is about persistence, leading an active life and helping others. Laws invents her own recipe for success. She reveals her secrets in this mesmerizing tell-all book, tidbit by tasty tidbit."
~ Every Way Woman Show

"When Charlotte gets something in mind, nothing can stop her… She has embarked upon lots of activities in her life, but with one purpose: to fight for her beliefs."
~ Stylist Magazine

"My goodness, she does a lot!"
~ LA Talk Radio

FTER THE CHARLIE EVENS trial, I searched the hallways surrounding the courtroom, and I found her. It was Sharon, my guardian angel, my ally, my longtime confidant. She stood at the end of the dimly lit corridor like a gallery portrait, regal and reassuring. She wore a soft blue frock that resembled the figure in Renoir's *Young Woman With a Japanese Umbrella*. Her brownish-green eyes penetrated, yet welcomed. Brown curls framed her symmetrical face. I'd once remarked on her resemblance to Elizabeth Taylor, but now that she was older, her timbre was more "Jacqueline Kennedy Onassis" minus the prim reserve. With Sharon, there was a touch of tomboy and a sprinkle of childlike enthusiasm. She could not be bothered with manicures or makeup. After all, beautification was time-consuming, and life was meant for more important matters.

Sharon was my secret.

Few knew about her. She was a pleasure in my life, like a locked armoire filled with designer dresses and stilettos. Our furtive get-togethers—which sprang from a bizarre set of circumstances—were infrequent, usually once or twice a year. I looked forward to them; Sharon was my extra Christmas.

I expected her that day. She'd left a message about a three-day visit to Los Angeles. I'd returned her call with the address of the Charlie Evens arraignment. She traveled 2,300 miles from her home near the White House and Pentagon with her husband, Ricky.

Maybe Ricky was jealous. He was attached to Sharon. Perhaps he had no interest in sharing her with others. This was Sharon's theory as to why he flew into a rage when he learned about me 26 years prior.

He did not normally explode like this. It was uncharacteristic. I had triggered panic.

"If you meet with her, we are getting a divorce," Ricky yelled at Sharon as he stomped out of their two-story home.

His anger confused me. Why was he so possessive? My relationship with his wife was not romantic.

Ricky expected Sharon to cut ties with me, swiftly and mercilessly. Maybe he thought I was a bad influence. Or maybe he was upset that she had kept me under wraps for so long. They had been married for years, yet Ricky knew nothing about me. Perhaps this would anger any husband. Perhaps he was within his rights.

Sharon did not agree to kick me out of her life; she did not disagree either. She dodged the issue. She did not want to lose her marriage, so our get-togethers became clandestine and calculated. Ricky did not mention me again. Maybe he wanted to avoid the truth. Ignoring reality can be a way to cope.

I moved toward Sharon in the courthouse corridor, and we shared the usual warm hug.

"How did it go?" she asked.

"He was released on bond," I replied.

"It's horrible what happened to Kayla and all those victims," she said. "I am glad you're getting justice, especially after the years of effort you've put into this cause." She put her arm on my shoulder and led me to the elevator. "Where's Kayla and Charles?"

"Kayla is out of town, visiting her dad. And Charles is in San Francisco."

Sharon told me that she was in Los Angeles for three days with Ricky. He was attending a medical industry convention for his company. Ricky was a universal healthcare expert and what I call a "man on the go." He had an adversarial relationship with rest. He needed to be on the move: working, camping, hiking, skiing, and attending events, such as lectures and jazz festivals. Sharon did a pretty good job keeping pace with him, but she often felt like the straggler in the race.

"I only have four hours tonight," Sharon said. "Ricky doesn't know where I am right now. I need to be in the hotel room when he gets back."

I nodded. I understood her predicament. The "cloak and dagger" game was intact, and I had no intention of blowing the ruse.

"Let's get some dinner," she suggested as we headed out the front of the courthouse toward my car. "Did you bring it?"

"It's right here." I presented her with a coil-bound booklet of pages. It was my partially completed memoir. "This is the first 22 years of my life."

"Oh good." She took the manuscript. "You've told me a lot about your life over the years, but never the whole story. Do you mind if I read it aloud on our way to dinner?"

"That would be fine," I smiled.

As we settled in my car, Sharon began reading from the booklet. My tale began in 1976. It was a day of blood and horror. It was a day that would change my life.

Stupids, Tweens and Brights

WAS AT THE MALL that Thursday when Mom slashed her wrists. The birds were silent as if they had a dark secret. The trees did not sway. They stood like soldiers, frozen and stiff, hoping not to be reprimanded for moving out of line. The skies were "Gun Metal Gray" or number 10–12 at the Dunn Edwards Paint Center. A toxic shadow seemed to reach down and swallow up our modern estate on River North Parkway in Atlanta. It was 1976, and I was 16 years old.

School let out early that day due to teacher meetings. My 14-year-old brother, Buddy, had to hitch a ride home with a friend because Mom had asked me to go to the mall to buy tennis shoes. This was peculiar. She rarely asked me to go shopping because she knew how much I liked clothes; the credit card bill could be high.

At two p.m. that afternoon, Buddy opened the front door.

"Mom, I'm home."

There was silence.

"Mom, where are you?" he searched the kitchen, the living room filled with plastic-covered couches, the antique-appointed dining room and the study.

There was no answer. It was odd because Mom was always there. In her worldview, home was where a wife and mother belonged. She had no extracurricular activities or friends, beyond a couple of ladies with whom she spoke every few months. Housework and grocery shopping were handled by our servant, Richard Baker. Now that I was 16 with my own car, I drove Buddy and myself to and from school, sports practices and parties.

My brother made his way to the master bathroom door and noticed the carpet was damp. He could hear flowing water.

"Mom, are you in there?" he shouted. "The rug's wet. What's going on?"

There was no response. He struggled with the doorknob, but it would not budge.

He figured she'd gone to do an errand and forgotten to shut off the tub faucet. He didn't want the carpet to be ruined, so he dashed to the utility room and rummaged through a drawer for a screw driver. Then he sprinted back to the bathroom door and jimmied open the lock.

Mom lay unconscious in the tub, immersed in crimson-colored water, wearing a pale blue nightgown. There were gory gashes on her wrists and neck, a razor blade on the tile floor and blood on the designer wallpaper. It was a ghastly sight. Water poured over the sides of the porcelain tub because the drain could not handle the heavy flow from the faucet. Mom was a rag doll, her head tilted backwards, barely above the water line. Although the room looked like a grisly crime scene, it was clear that Mom's wounds were self-inflicted. In addition to cutting her wrists and neck, she had popped pills.

Buddy staggered backwards. He was paralyzed and nauseous. Then he stumbled from room to room in search of a phone. This no longer felt like his house, like his neighborhood, like his life. It all seemed alien. He could not cry because Dad had taught my brother and me to resist tears and "unnecessary displays of weakness."

The incident was traumatic for Buddy who was devoted to Mom. It would have been better if I had found her. She and I had always been distant.

Buddy called an ambulance and Dad at work. Then, he hunkered down on the brick steps in our front yard and waited for the commotion to begin.

I visualized yelling parents as I parked in the driveway at seven p.m. that night. I had overindulged on clothes and shoes at the mall. I entered the house with shopping bags behind my back.

"Where have you been?" my father barked at me.

"The mall. Mom told me to..."

He interrupted. "Your mother tried to kill herself today."

My world shifted at that very moment. My excessive purchases would never be mentioned. Dad filed for divorce.

Thursday was the suicide (attempt), but by Sunday, my father seemed to have forgotten Mom ever existed. Dad had always called her "his anchor," but I realized she had been nothing more than a raft tied to his luxury liner. When she started taking on water, he cut her loose. Even though she drifted in his sightline during those first few weeks in the hospital, he was able to point his ship in the opposite direction. Eventually, she was an inconsequential speck on the horizon, and then the raft sank.

"We should go visit her," Buddy suggested.

"You are *never* to mention your mother's name in this house again," Dad roared before marching back to his ham radio room in the basement.

His tech hub was not just a place to hibernate in the winter. It was his year-round sanctuary. It looked like the control room at NASA.

Dad also forbade us to visit Mom in the hospital where she was hooked up to life-support machines or later in the convalescent home where she lay in a semi-conscious state as a quasi-vegetable for the next ten years until she died.

"She can't recognize you anyway," Dad said.

But this was a lie. It was true she had brain damage and no control over the left side of her body: her movements were spastic and erratic. She slurred her words to the point that it was sometimes impossible to know what she was trying to say, and her short-term memory was damaged. For example, she did not seem to remember her self-destructive actions. But she clearly knew who we were and recollected many events from the past.

I had no trouble disobeying orders, whether they came from my school, my friends, Atlanta society, or my dad. Buddy was too young to drive, so I sneaked the two of us to visit Mom every week. Mom had always chided me for being a "sneaky child," and lucky for her, she was right. Buddy was grateful for my chauffeur-related assistance because he cared about Mom much more than I ever did.

I felt bad for not visiting her more, but the stench and sickness in the convalescent home was difficult for me to bear. I left for college two years later and never lived in Atlanta again. She had no visitors for most of her remaining days, and died without a funeral. My father did not even telephone to tell me when she did, in fact, perish. I suppose in his mind she was already gone on that fateful Thursday.

Thursday was Richard Baker's day off. Richard was our "man maid" as I liked to joke. He was an elderly black man who would spiff up the house six days a week, vacuuming, preparing dinner and mowing the lawn. He snacked on banana and mayonnaise sandwiches, and he regularly poked his fingers through lamp shades, afterwards trying to hide his mistake. When questioned, he would blame it on mysterious little critters called lampshade moths.

"Them lampshade moths are everywhere," he'd say.

I'd just laugh and play along with his tale.

Richard was my pal. I bestowed on him the highest accolade: that of honorary teenager. Our gossip sessions took place in the kitchen when nobody was around. I revealed my mishaps at school—including bad test scores and the stupid things I said to boys—and he would tell me about his girlfriends. I found it incredulous that this homely, married, senior citizen had a bunch of fillies on the side, yet I never questioned his veracity.

There was one incredibly embarrassing fact about Richard: his ancestors had been slaves to our family, generation after generation after generation. He was the first actual employee. My mom advertised this as if it was normal, even enviable. Perhaps it was a way for her to tell the world that she sprang from aristocratic roots. The slave thing also did not seem to bother my friends. I was left alone with my horror, but I was used to being alone. My views were always outside the Atlanta mainstream.

I was a black sheep.

Dad was a clever and jocular fellow. Two of his signature quips always put me in stitches, partly due to his southern drawl.

"There are three types of people who own motorcycles: those who *have been* busted up, those who *are* busted up and those who are *gonna be* busted up."

"I'm ugly, and I'm proud of it."

He was right. He wasn't the most beautiful bud on the bush with his hairless head and constant battle with weight. He wore black-rimmed glasses and liked to say, "I'm blind in one eye and can't see in the other." He had stolen Mom's affection from an opera singer. Mom and Dad were 25 when they married.

Although Dad came from a family of money, he was proud of the fact that he plodded upward based on his own initiative. His father was a doctor and had the same aspiration for his son, but Dad had no interest in medicine and instead became a laborer and field office clerk for a company called Beers Construction. Six years later he started his own successful business. His company built hotels, stores and restaurants throughout the United States. Wal-Mart, Coco's, Winn Dixie and Days Inn were clients.

Mom mostly had to go it alone because of Dad's workaholic ways. Although Dad was protective and a good provider, Mom hated that he was rarely home. When Buddy and I were little, we didn't even know we had a father.

"You wanted to know who the stranger was," Dad liked to say.

Mom tried to be strict, but at the end of the day, became a "wait till your father gets home" parent. Dad's philosophy differed: it was "let her learn the hard way." The "hard way" meant his daughter would have to fail before she could succeed. I appreciated his tendency to offer advice, and then step back and leave the decision-making to me. Because of his authority in the home, I was raised in a hands-off, lenient environment, which blended perfectly with my independent, nonconformist nature. I regularly sought his counsel on matters because I considered him smart. I never valued Mom's opinion and rarely asked for it.

When Mom got really upset with me, she whirled around and struck me erratically with a belt or her hand. Dad never hit me; he would ground me or send me to my room, but then fail to enforce the isolation.

When I was 13, Dad scolded me, "Never say anything except 'yes daddy, no daddy, yes mother, no mother.'"

I looked at him and joked, "Yes, mother."

He grounded me for three weeks.

I went directly to my room, but ran away from home that night to sleep with our horses in the barn, which was located on an adjacent street. It was itchy and uncomfortable on those bales of hay, so I returned the next morning at six a.m. to find no one had noticed I was gone. Three days later, Dad had forgotten about the grounding so I went on with my life.

The only other time I ran away was when I was 17, but this time it was more of a vacation rather than an outward statement of discontent. It was after the attempted suicide, so Mom was in the convalescent home. I told no one but Buddy about my travel plans to Chicago and New York for a week because I wanted to see if Dad would notice my absence. He didn't.

The disconnect between Mom and me stemmed from the fact that the two of us were opposites, like two piano notes that produce a grating noise. She was like an obedient government worker, while I was the anti-government protester. Mom followed rules while I bucked the system. She was proud of the fact that her high school classmates had voted her "most ladylike," a distinction I would have loathed due to its sexist connotation. "Biggest tomboy" would have been my preference.

I was a jock, competing at every sport offered in school: track, tennis, basketball, cheerleading, cross country, field hockey, soccer and softball. Yet, Mom had never done more than take a few swipes at a badminton birdie. Her life revolved around making the family work, yet it had been in hopeless disrepair from the start.

For an exercise in my ninth grade English composition class, I wrote a poem, describing my family life and my feelings towards my parents:

- Kinship gives no certain loving connection to a being. It can give nugatory trash and decayed concern in return for care, containing the fumes of putrid, poisonous air and always the impatient desire for fleeing.

- Artificial interest and nonexistent regard can be a family's only assets. Since self-love prevails over all, antipathy is dumped on all within. So look outside your kin for love from other men, while shielding from ancestral debts.

◆ I have escaped from these filthy flies who surround me. I entrust my love elsewhere to a family of no relation, but who feels when it comes to care. And here I pray I'll always be… while the trash is buried in my past miles away from me.

"Rewrite the poem when you are not angry," my English teacher suggested.

But I had not felt any anger. I was calm when I wrote the poem. That was simply how I felt. When I spoke of a "family of no relation," I was referring to the parents of my high school sweetheart, with whom I had become close.

Our home was like a boarding house; everyone did his or her own thing. Rarely did our lives intersect. That was fine with me. I especially liked being home alone so I could twirl my long, green pencil in the air like a baton and catch it behind my back while dancing to loud music. I liked hitting tennis balls against our house, an activity prohibited by my parents because I had once broken the front window. I liked turning the heat up to ninety degrees and donning my bathing suit. I could be free and have fun as long as my parents were not chaperoning the coop.

When Dad was not building restaurants and hotels, he was in the basement schmoozing with his radio pals. Buddy and I would come home from after-school sports and head straight for the TV. Buddy watched television from the black, vinyl arm chair in the family room, and I planted myself on the yellow, tweed couch in the study. I would do my homework while watching my favorite programs. The only time the family merged was during the evening meal. However, Dad was obsessed with the sound of silence.

"Shut up and eat" was my father's favorite command, and he followed up with "Dinner is for eating, not talking."

Buddy and Mom obeyed the "no conversation" rule, but I would chatter about the events of the day while my father scolded me. He eventually termed me "motor mouth." Dad would finish eating first, then jump from the table and head to the basement. I would finish second and my brother third. We would leave Mom—who was highly emotional and who could cry at the slightest transgression—at the table alone. It was callous, but it was routine.

Mom's (attempted) suicide shocked me, but, on the other hand, it didn't. I could never figure out how she could be happy. She would putter around the house, glance through the occasional book, and watch cartoons and *Mister Rogers' Neighborhood* on TV. Maybe she had a secret crush on Fred Rogers. She did not buy fancy clothes, work for nonprofit causes, have intellectual discussions, enjoy eating out or even know how to bake. On Richard's day off, opening cans was her idea of a meal.

Although she was quite convincing in the role of satisfied housewife and mother, I was her Tony Robbins or life coach, regularly encouraging her to adopt hobbies, to make friends, to find a goal or to become enthusiastic about something. But enthusiasm was not in her DNA. My pep talks never produced pep.

Mom had only given me one piece of advice in all her years, and it appalled me, even at age 13.

"Don't buy a mink coat until you are old," she said, "or you won't have anything to look forward to in life."

It's ironic that I am now an animal rights advocate who lectures about the fur trade: about how 33 million living beings are murdered each year for their skin and about how one coat can be comprised of as many as 400 dead animals. Mom and I clearly had different values.

Mom had cut her wrists and neck at 11 a.m. that Thursday, but at nine a.m. that morning, my father had been the second Tony Robbins in her life.

"Why don't you get out of the house for a change?" he said as he headed to work. "You've been cooped up for way too long."

Maybe that prompted her to get into the tub that last time. Or maybe her nervous breakdown had to do with the hysterectomy she'd endured months earlier, which my father claims was unnecessary. There was a spike in hysterectomies in the 1970s. These procedures were performed for reasons that would not be considered valid today, such as for preventative care or to do away with the inconvenience of menstruation. Depression and mood swings after hysterectomy were common.

Mom left three suicide notes: one for each of us, which my father claims he never read. He says he instructed the police detective to destroy them. I regret not knowing her thoughts: maybe her words would have been inspirational or pointed to character defects in myself that I could have fixed. I called the Atlanta police department 25 five years later in search of my note, but was told suicide files are tossed after a decade. Her comments were probably not ladylike.

Mom had two fur coats when she died.

For years, I had nightmares about Mom. It was always a dreary Atlanta day. Mom wore a demented, even sinister, expression as she fanatically moved her rocking chair back and forth, to and fro at a frenzied and frightening pace. She was on the front porch with a homemade, crocheted blanket draped around her head and body as if to conceal her derangement. It reminded me of the reveal scene in *Psycho*.

I never told anyone, but I did not want Mom to come home after the attempted suicide. I was scared of her. If she could cut her own flesh, maybe she could cut mine. I envisioned locking my bedroom door at night and keeping my escape route through an open window and onto the roof prepped at all times.

Prior to this, Mom had always seemed sane, perhaps with the exception of some tearful outbursts with broken dishes—which I attributed to her overly emotional nature—and the "blue car incident." My father had given me a powder blue Oldsmobile Starfire to drive on my sixteenth birthday. When I came home from school one afternoon, Mom shrieked and flailed like a mental patient from the Danvers State Asylum.

"What were you doing home today?"

"What are you talking about?" I answered. "I was at school."

"I saw your blue car parked in the driveway," she raved. "Then when I got in the house, it was gone. What were you doing here? Tell me. Tell me. Tell me."

I had no idea what she was talking about, and even suggested that she call my school to confirm attendance. She never did. But she went berserk over my blue car for days.

It seemed odd that someone in a car like mine would venture up our long, winding driveway and park, and then disappear when my mother came home. I chalked it up to a door-to-door salesman or burglar, although I figured both were less likely than a temporary kink in Mom's brain.

Mom was weak, and it is likely the attempted suicide confirmed that for Dad. Maybe this is why he was able to erase her existence in one abrupt stroke, like removing an old Band-Aid that no longer had functionality. Mom today, gone tomorrow. Dad had no respect for weak people, and he did not want them in his life. His brother Tween was a case in point.

It was a decade prior to Mom's attempted suicide. My Uncle Tween was 28 years old and sprawled out in the hallway at the YMCA in Atlanta where he lived.

"He's not breathing. I think he's dead," a dorm mate bellowed, unsure how to administer CPR.

It was an unsuccessful suicide attempt. Tween had taken an overdose of sleeping pills. He was rushed to the hospital, treated at taxpayer cost and released with no long-term side effects. He was, however, required to join a substance abuse program for drug addicts like himself.

Tween was red-haired and eight years younger than dad. Both boys had attended boarding school, but Tween eventually transferred to a public school: Northside High. Dad lived in the freeway's fast lane, so to speak, while Tween was the guy hitchhiking on the interstate shoulder. Dad viewed himself as a leader and his brother as a follower. Dad was strong-willed and unemotional. Tween was mushy and sensitive. Tween was a lot like Mom.

After the suicide attempt at the YMCA, Dad put a cancel stamp on Tween's file. He was no longer allowed to be part of Dad's life. Tween had proved himself weak and unworthy.

"Lie down with dogs. Get up with fleas," was a phrase Buddy and I heard over and over like a song refrain. It was my dad's national anthem. He was ultra-worried that his kids would follow the crowd, but he did not need to worry about me. I was the type who intuitively deviated from the norm. If everyone was doing A, my immediate reaction was that there was something wrong with A, and I should do B. Dad didn't want his children to be average; they had to be leaders. They had to be willing to buck the trend.

Dad first preached about "bucking the trend" when I was eight years old. He said he would give me flying lessons when I got older because pilots are leaders, and it would set me apart from others. However, this never came to pass; in part, due to the "near death" ordeal we faced that very day.

Dad suggested the family go up in his private plane, which was technically owned by his company. This was to be a scenic flight over Atlanta and parts of north Georgia. The company's Cessna 310 provided convenient transportation for executives and other employees to get to building sites around the nation.

Dad was an experienced pilot; he had been an air traffic controller in the Air Force for nineteen months. He was drafted on D-Day. Upon leaving the armed forces, he obtained his pilot's license and completed 2,500 hours of flight time.

The plane was kept in a hangar for a hefty monthly fee, but that morning, it was waiting for us in the open air. Dad conducted an exterior preflight inspection. As we climbed into the red and white plane and strapped on our seatbelts, Dad brought out a checklist, which had been compiled from the approved flight manual for the aircraft; and he continued his rigorous inspection of the systems, settings and instruments. Everything seemed normal.

"Clear," Dad yelled out the window to alert anyone standing near the propeller that he would be starting the engine.

He turned the key and called the tower to get permission to proceed to the runway for takeoff, while still studying the controls and gauges. Flying was serious business. Even a minor error could be deadly.

"Cessna November 5066Q cleared for takeoff. Runway 16/34," a male voice blasted through the radio system.

Moments later, Dad pushed the throttles forward and the twin-engine plane barreled down the runway. My six-year-old brother, Buddy, was in the co-pilot seat; I was in the back with Mom.

Dad's happy-go-lucky smile turned to heaviness when the controls went haywire.

"The plane's going to crash," Mom nervously bit her bright pink lipstick.

"Hold on tight," my always calm dad said, but I could tell the skin behind his neck was damp from panic and apprehension.

I was frightened and moved towards Mom's hand, but she slid it from my reach. Mom wasn't the affectionate type, and she had an aversion to germs or what Buddy and I called "cooties." Being touchy-feely did not comport with her "most ladylike" image, a standoffishness I assumed was normal at the time. Mom and Dad rarely hugged or touched us kids.

The aircraft seemed eager to topple into a fiery crash. Dad's emergency maneuvers were quick and decisive, but his expression told me he was silently calculating the odds for emerging from the situation alive. I was too young to understand that small planes could be dangerous, but I was not too young to sense when my parents were afraid.

Dad quickly realized he had a "son problem" rather than an "engine problem." My six-year-old brother had decided he wanted to fly the plane himself. For some unexplained reason, he had taken both hands and thrust the throttle closest to him back into its original "off" position.

Dad was horrified as the aircraft began swerving to the right, a dangerous condition that pilots call "adverse yaw." While attempting to keep the plane stabilized, he had to make a split-second decision about whether to abort the flight, knowing the tremendous speed of the plane could propel us into a more catastrophic situation or keep going forward. He decided to jam the throttle back into the "on" position and continue onward, hoping there would be enough runway to recover. Luckily, there was.

We did not crash. The rest of the flight was without incident. Dad never took the family up in his plane again.

Every moment spent in Atlanta felt as perilous as that small plane, and I imagine Mom felt the same way. This was my connection with her. Although we clashed, on some level, we shared a desire to escape.

Mom was a ball of clay, directionless, waiting to be molded into the expectations of others. Her aim was to please Dad and Atlanta society; but in so doing, she lost herself. She ended up a distortion, a blur, a maze of confusion, a purposeless form without identity. I was a ball of clay as well, but I was stubborn. I refused to let others leave their imprint without full permission. I was determined to forge ahead, alone, if necessary. My identity would belong to me, while Mom's identity belonged to everyone else.

Although I was scared of Mom immediately following her suicide attempt, a few years later, I began to see her as a victim. She was not a weakling as Dad intimated, but merely a product of cause and effect, prey to forces stronger than her. They swallowed her. It was not her fault, and I suddenly felt a deep compassion. In my early twenties, I decided that if she snapped out of her semi-conscious state, I would invite her to live with me. I would take care of her because she had no one else.

Mom never regained full consciousness.

Five years after the plane ordeal, I faced another near-death experience. A twig possibly saved my life at Gwynn Valley Camp in North Carolina. This is not the reason I feel plants have interests and are worthy of public policy consideration, but it could certainly root a gal in environmental awareness.

Gwynn Valley was my delightful summertime retreat for three years. Most camps were too regimented for my outlaw nature. One, in particular, mandated stiff uniforms with nerdy neckties and treated campers like youth detention center inmates. It was also "all girls" which was frankly a big drag. I wept a lot and begged Mom and Dad to let me come home; they refused. At another camp, counselors thought they *were* Mom and Dad. I was told to always stay within thirty feet of my "buddy" (or supervisor). I dared not defy the invisible tracking device, or punishment would be imminent. Detentions at camp seemed the height of absurdity, so I cried a lot there as well.

There were no tears at Gwynn Valley, just lots of soccer. I chose to spend all day, every day kicking that black and white ball, while other kids hit the archery field, arts and crafts hut, volleyball court, tetherball pole; or participated in some other activity or combination thereof. Teens and preteens were grown-ups at Gwynn Valley; we got to plan our own day. At night, campers would sing together in the lodge—that is, with the exception of me and whichever friend I could drag into a life of crime. Together we would sneak into the empty kitchen and raid the refrigerator. We did this not because we were hungry, but just to see if we could.

Twelve-year-old Andrea asked me in the midst of a caper, "Why are we going to the kitchen?"

"Because it's there," I trumpeted as if we were great explorers.

We never got caught skulking around the cookhouse, nor did we get snared when we embarked upon our next mission: spying on the boys' cabins after dark. All campers were supposed to be in their bunks, but my daredevil cabin mates and I tiptoed past the sycamore trees to eavesdrop on the boys. On the following day, we feigned psychic powers by relaying verbatim what they had been discussing during bedtime.

The two-day canoe trip was the best thing about Gwynn Valley because Bo was the counselor in charge. Just about every female camper had a crush on him. He resembled a hippie with stringy, long hair and round spectacles. He was a taller and better-looking version of John Lennon, and he was probably 30 years old. Why a bunch of eleven-to-thirteen-year-old girls thought he was bee's knees was as inexplicable as Colony Collapse Disorder.

The boys were not invited on the girls' canoe trips, so it was only some female counselors; plus the "hot" Lennon lookalike and a bunch of little girls fighting for his attention. Specifically, the competition was to see who could give Bo a back rub that night after making doughnuts and roasting marshmallows on the campfire and before crawling into our sleeping bags. Bo would take off his shirt, lie on the ground, face down; and suck up the pleasure as he received one massage after another. On the night prior to my near-death experience, I stretched my magic fingers across his deltoids and shoulder girdle.

The next morning, I was hiking with twenty campers on a narrow path. We were walking single file. The craggy cliff adjacent to us was bare except for a lone branch sprouting up from the ground; it clearly hoped to someday grow into a tree. But on that day, it would be my hero.

I lost my footing and tumbled down the embankment towards a rocky ravine. That is when the humble twig caught my eye. I grasped it at exactly the right moment. It seemed quite hardy considering its scrawny structure and lack of foliage. It held firm in the ground as if to say, "I'm as mighty as an oak."

With my legs dangling downhill, I lay there suspended like a flag on a pole. It was at least sixty seconds before Bo and another panic-stricken counselor could pull me to safety. I did not understand the severity of the situation until I reached the bottom of the cliff and looked up to realize that my fall would have been quite sizable, possibly deadly.

Above the rocks, I could see that lone twig, still secure in the ground. It looked regal and valiant. It was a little prince to me then; it is surely a tree today, as well as king of the hill.

My Uncle Tween—who had attempted suicide—was addicted to amphetamines, Dexadrine and Dexamil, which he had stolen repeatedly from my grandfather's medical office. Samples were kept in giant paper sacks in the supply room, and he would abscond with them every chance he could. At least, this is what he told me on the phone in 2012. It was not the story Dad offered.

When I was 13, my father lectured me about the perils of marijuana. He insisted Tween had gotten a bad batch of pot when he was in the Navy.

"It made him go crazy," Dad said. "He had to be admitted to mental institutions. He's out now, but messed up."

The lesson was: Don't ever try marijuana. I never did. In fact, I have never tried a cigarette, an illegal drug or a glass of alcohol.

"Tween was the sort of person who would go along with anything," Dad told me.

This conjured up the familiar image of lying down with dogs and getting fleas.

"He was into glue-sniffing and alcohol. He's a loser, and his life has been wasted. He is not a deep person, went to public school, and was brought up as if he is stupid."

Mark Clifton used the word "Tween" in his 1953 science fiction book, *Star Bright*, to refer to those who are between a Stupid and a Bright. My dad was a Bright. He attended boarding school through eleventh grade, and then Emory University.

Like Tween, my mother was not a Bright. When I asked her homework questions, she never knew the answers. Dad always knew the solution. Rummaging through the attic at age 13, I found Mom's old report cards: Science D, Math D+, English C-. Let's just say she dug into academics in the same way she dug into sports. I have always put a high price tag on brainpower, and to this day, I have an inferiority complex.

My life has been a constant struggle to learn and retain, and my continual academic efforts highlight my insecurity. Some people think I have "degree collection disorder" or more degrees than a thermometer. I have five: a Ph.D., two master degrees and two BAs. I usually feel like a Stupid, sometimes like a Tween, but never like a Bright.

"Guess I'm the black sheep of the family," Tween said to me during that 2012 phone call.

I replied, "You and I have something in common."

SHARON I

The "Hunter S. Thompson Ain't No Rebel" Theory

With Sharon, Los Angeles 2014

After reading a little about my early life, Sharon and I decided on the perfect location for the evening's furtive meeting: Hugo's restaurant in Studio City, a Los Angeles hot spot and a 45-minute drive from the Charlie Evens trial. Afterwards, I planned to drop her off at her hotel so her conference-going husband would suspect nothing.

As we entered the eatery, Sharon seemed pleased with the brown and green motif, Chinese lanterns and hi-tech recessed lighting. She was even more pleased when a server seated us at a table next to actor, Jon Voight, and his son, James Haven.

"Wow, that's the actor from *Midnight Cowboy*... Angelina Jolie's father. And he is with Angelina Jolie's brother," Sharon said. "I guess you run into all sorts of famous people living in L.A."

"Yeah," I replied. "It's pretty common."

I studied the menu and announced that I would be a nonconformist diner.

"I feel it's important to be a rebel whenever possible," I smiled. "Would you like to be a rebel, too?"

75

Sharon laughed, "I guess so."

"See the create-a-plate option on the menu? You can make it completely vegan if you want," I said.

"I almost never eat meat," Sharon replied. "It's not good for you. I am very interested in health. The pigments in bright fruits and vegetables are powerful antioxidants."

I opted for grilled tofu, garlic spinach and zucchini while Sharon's create-a-plate was a combination of colorful veggies.

"You call yourself a rebel, but that's not really true… since you've never tried a glass of alcohol, a cigarette or marijuana. You're not exactly Hunter S. Thompson."

"Ah, but your theory is wrong," I smiled. "Most people drink alcohol… up to 87 percent, according to studies. And a large percentage of Americans have at least tried tobacco or illegal drugs. Therefore, these activities represent conformist behavior. Someone who abstains… well, she might be called a rebel."

Sharon laughed, "I guess you're right. Your Uncle Tween took drugs, so he wasn't a rebel. By the way, where is he now?"

"I tried to call him six months ago, but his number was disconnected. Then I found his obituary online. He died last April of pneumonia. I phoned my father, thinking he didn't know. I was wrong."

"He knew?"

"He not only knew; the hospital phoned him when Tween was brought in and placed on life support. My dad ordered them to disconnect all machines immediately. I got the sense Dad also regretted keeping Mom alive all those years."

"Do you think it had anything to do with your mother and Tween being black sheep?" Sharon asked.

"Black sheep stand out from the rest of the flock. It can make survival more difficult. But to give my dad the benefit of the doubt, maybe it was about expense, not wasting money on what he thought might be a poor quality of life."

"Your dad seems to be traditionalist, operating from a sense of duty," she said. "But he clearly lacked a sense of duty with his own brother."

I studied the interaction between our restaurant-mates, Jon Voight and his son, while Sharon took out the manuscript.

"I think we should read another chapter," she said and dove back into my bleak and airless days growing up in Atlanta in the 1960s and 1970s.

Two

The Battle of Atlanta

OM AND DAD WERE NOT my biological parents. Natural children were impossible for them due to Dad's bout with mumps as a youngster. He had become sterile.

"You were returned twice before we adopted you," Dad told me when I was eight.

"But you adopted me at two months of age," I said.

"See what a rotten baby you were," he chuckled.

I have hand-written notes from my childhood in which I try to figure out why two separate couples would return me to the adoption agency. It was as if I was a smashed parcel from the post office or an unwanted blouse from a department store. I wondered if I was a loud crier or more trouble than the average infant. However, today I have come to the conclusion that Dad invented this tale so I would be more appreciative of him. It was probably his way of saying, "You're lucky to have me."

Evidence suggests Dad was not truthful. According to a 1960 *Atlanta Journal-Constitution* article, adoption demand exceeded supply that year. There were four requests for every available child. The Child Service Association, which arranged for my adoption, paid foster parents forty-five dollars to sixty dollars per month to care for an infant. Fifty-five couples were providing such assistance. There had been 160 children adopted in 1959, the year prior to my birth. This suggests each foster family was tending multiple children. Any so-called returns were likely made by those who could no longer continue in the role of foster rather than by adopting couples who had received a child at the expense of so many other applicants.

I was actually born in the backseat of an Oldsmobile. My birth-mother was in labor for 15 minutes, not long enough for my birthfather to drive us to Grady Hospital in downtown Atlanta. I popped out during the Drifters' song, "There Goes My Baby"; and moments later, away I went. In the emergency room parking lot, I was whisked away by a nurse, complying with a prearranged adoption pact. She was under the assumption—as were most adoption "experts" in 1960—that cutting ties should be done in an abrupt and swift fashion. I would not see my natural parents again. At least, that's what everyone thought.

My adoptive family always had the appropriate number of cars, boats and country club parties. They were skilled at complying with "old money" standards. Those who had "new money"—such as show business folk or overnight get-rich schemers—were naturally inferior to us, or so I was told. By adopting me, my parents were on track for procuring a suitable number of children for a respectable family: two. Buddy was adopted a couple of years later.

To the neighbors, everything looked primed and painted, but I was well acquainted with the wood filler and industrious termites beneath the surface. Our family was a hip storefront window for a shop with no merchandise. Mom and Dad did more than keep up with the Joneses: they were the Joneses. But when Mom attempted to kill herself, all that changed. She exposed the ruse. She blew our disguise as the perfect family. Friends and strangers could no longer be bluffed. Mom became an informant, a stool pigeon, a snitch. Her existence was a reminder of an irreparable crack in the foundation. Perhaps that is why Dad cut ties. He may have wanted an unmarred life, rather than maneuvering forward with a blemished wife.

Partly, my negativity stemmed from this charade. But partly it came from a perception that I was an outsider with an entirely different value system. If I did not qualify as the black sheep of the family, it was for only one reason: sheep tend to be followers. I was more like an independent, black cat, who went my own way. My first recollection of forging my own path was at Lake Burton.

Lake Burton is located in Raburn County, Georgia, which is in the northeastern corner of the state. As a child, one of my few fond memories involved regularly visiting my family's rustic, seven-bedroom, vacation cabin there. I never complained that it was without television, air conditioning or telephone. It was like gliding onto the set of *Little House on the Prairie.* I took delight in the long gravel driveway, the hammock cradled in the forest and the wood floors that gave me splinters on my feet. Swimming, water skiing and boating were daily adventures.

I remember Buddy and his friend, Jeff Rogers, singing "the birds and the bees and the flowers and the trees and that thing called love" on the cabin porch, while my friend, Anne Morris, and I eavesdropped from behind a tree, giggling because the boys seemed so effeminate. I was twelve, and Buddy was ten.

On the following morning, I rose a little later than usual and wandered down the winding dirt path to the dock where I found my father, mother, brother and our schoolmates fishing.

"Why are you murdering fish?" I asked in a genuinely curious way.

"Why don't you join us?" Mom cast her line into the water.

"Nah," I wandered back up the hill alone.

I felt empathy for the fish, and the word "murder" seemed appropriate. Although I ate meat, had never heard of vegetarianism and had seen actors in movies fishing and hunting, this was the first time I had been confronted with the actual killing of another creature. I had an immediate distaste for the idea.

I grew up empathizing with underdogs regardless of whether they were people, animals or plants. For example, I would insist on buying the ugliest or most straggly Christmas tree because I figured it would never have a chance to find a home. A psychologist might say this behavior stemmed from the perception of myself as an outsider or underdog. Perhaps she would be right.

I felt like a stranger in Atlanta, so I never completely unpacked my bags and made myself at home. My things clashed with their things anyway. Mine were bright, flashy and adventurous. Theirs were demure, tasteful and conservative. It seemed like I was by nature different, like a shelter animal who had lost her natural home and who was now living in a place she could not comprehend. The rules confused me, and I abhorred the value system that Atlanta society had embedded around my throat like a too-tight turtleneck. The climate multiplied the problem. Atlanta weather—which resembles that of Seattle—is overcast and rainy much of the time, a death sentence for someone like me whose happiness is linked with sunny skies.

Alienation can have a profound effect upon self-reliance; it made me stronger. It became easier to trust my own values and beliefs rather than those of my parents and peers. Television was my telescope to the world; it gave me an awareness that alternate views existed. Remote objects became close, and my dream to escape seemed possible. Every family vacation in our motor home was an opportunity for me to find the place I would live when I was no longer under my parents' roof.

I may have felt like a cornered animal as a child, but I did not view Atlantans specifically as my foe. My real enemy was prejudice. In fact, I came to believe my life's mission involved working towards its eradication. At the time, I was unaware of speciesism—or the false belief that humans are superior to nonhuman animals—but I was fully aware of racism. In the 1960s and 1970s in Georgia, it was as prevalent as peach trees.

Lynching was once a way to control African Americans in the South. From 1882–1964, Georgia had the second highest number of recorded lynchings: 458. Only Mississippi had more with 538. Georgia's capital, Atlanta, was Ku Klux Klan headquarters in the early 1920s. The organization had great sway with key Georgia politicians and the white masses because its tenets were largely accepted back then.

But even in the 1960s and 1970s when I grew up, racism was pervasive. It was a dark, depressing and inescapable factor in my life. Grady Hospital, where I had been born, had been constructed as a segregated institution. One section served whites, and another served African Americans.

The Piedmont Driving Club—an elite country club in which my parents held membership—did not permit black or Jewish members. This institution was the center of controversy on a number of occasions, such as when an Opera Company event was outright cancelled upon learning African American soprano, Leontyne Price, would attend.

The Driving Club was located inside a Tudor-style mansion about five miles from the mall at Lenox Square. The initiation fee was $4,500 with annual dues of $450. Atlanta mayors were automatically given membership until 1969 when a Jew was elected into office, and then the practice was abolished. I swam and played tennis with my schoolmates at the club during the summer without any knowledge of its exclusionary policy.

The Lovett School, the private prep school I attended from first through twelfth grade, did not approve racial integration until 1966, when it issued a statement that it would accept "those applicants deemed best qualified... without regard to race." The school claims the first black student was accepted in 1967, but when I look at yearbooks, the first picture of an African American appears in 1974. This also conforms to my recollection of a conversation outside French class.

"Now, they're letting coloreds in the school," I heard a classmate shout. Students groaned. "They let the Mayor's kids in."

Maynard Jackson, who was the first African American mayor of Atlanta, had just been elected into office. I never verified whether this classmate was correct, but there are several dark-complected kids with the surname "Jackson" in school yearbooks in the late 1970s.

Lovett was more progressive than many Atlanta schools. In fact, it was one of the first private schools to desegregate and hire a black teacher, which it did in 1974. It had been the target of earlier protests due to its whites-only policy. In 1963, Reverend Martin Luther King, Jr. asked Lovett to accept his son, but the school refused on racial grounds. A number of benefactors said they would withhold funds from the institution unless the educational institution remained closed to blacks.

In 1960, when I was born, the population of Atlanta was 62 percent white, but today it is 68 percent minority. The shift is noticeable. In well-to-do Buckhead, where I grew up, one can find a tremendous number of elegantly dressed, black professionals driving Mercedes and BMWs, something that would have been unthinkable when I was a child.

Buckhead is called "the Beverly Hills of the South," and according to *Forbes Magazine*, is home to the ninth wealthiest zip code in the U.S. where the average household income tops $341,000 per year. Stunning, colonial homes on gracious-sized lots are common in residential areas; and there are upscale shops in commercial zones. In the 1960s and 1970s, Buckhead was stomping ground for the "haves," while the "have nots" resided in the southern sections of town.

My family lived on River North Parkway in 1974. It was located in an affluent area just outside Buckhead. This was two years before Mom's (attempted) suicide, and I was fourteen years old. I came downstairs to find my parents had guests—four members of the Patterson family—in the living room. This was uncommon as my mother did not like to entertain.

"What do you call a barn full of niggers?" Pete Patterson snickered. "Farm equipment."

My parents and the four members of Patterson family roared with laughter. Luckily, Richard Baker was out of bigotry detection range. He was preparing fried chicken and mashed potatoes in the kitchen.

"What do you do if you see a nigger rolling around on the ground?" Pete continued. "Stop laughing and reload."

"Could I speak with you in private, Dad," I towered over my father who was sitting in the green print armchair. "I have a problem."

Dad seemed annoyed that I was plucking him away from the party, but he followed me to a hallway.

"I am not going to tolerate that kind of language in my house." I said.

"This is not your house. You're just a guest here," my father replied. "If you can't be civil, go to your room."

"They know how I feel, and they still talk this way. I can't believe you're gonna take their side."

"Go to your room. Now," he ordered.

I stomped upstairs and slammed my bedroom door with the bluster of an aerial bomb. I did not reemerge for dinner.

The Pattersons were different from the majority of Atlantans I knew because they flaunted their racism. Most Atlantans were more discreet, concealing their intolerance in corners, closets or drawers; and extracting it as needed to bolster an argument or beef up social status. This was the first time the Pattersons had been to our house, but my parents had dragged me to their place many times. I had politely voiced objections to their bigotry, but I had never been too forceful because I was a guest. This time they were the guest, and I felt wholly justified in throwing a tantrum.

If tantrum-throwing is a skill, I was clearly inept. Although I had plenty of practice, I never seemed to convince my parents to side with me against my opponent, especially when it was my brother. Buddy had an offensive tendency of bursting into the study after dinner to recite racist jokes. I would rage with disapproval and stomp out of the room to fetch Mom and Dad. Buddy would follow closely behind, guffawing like a sinister clown. To this day, I am not sure whether he was racist or simply got pleasure agitating his big sister. I would guess the latter. After all, it is a brother's job to make his sister miserable whenever possible.

Tattling never did anything more than earn me the nickname "narc." Mom and Dad would take Buddy's side, tell me to relax and often chuckle at the joke, after Buddy repeated it. This was my family's warped after-dinner ritual, which occurred for about two years—from when I was fourteen until the day of Mom's (attempted) suicide. Buddy lost his sense of humor when he lost Mom.

Mom would denigrate blacks from time to time, but to my father's credit, when I was young, I never heard him make a racist comment. Of course, he laughed at others' jokes; but at the time, I figured this was chiefly an attempt to be hospitable. Dad liked to play the part of jovial host. Eventually, I asked him what he thought about African Americans.

"Some things from the black culture tend to lower our culture. Like the degeneration of marriage. That comes from the blacks," Dad said.

"All four of your grandparents were prejudiced," he added. "They considered poor blacks a threat because of their values."

Dad went on to say that the family unit is of primary importance and anything that hurts that unit, including homosexuality, is inferior or wrong. To my amazement, he said that Mormons and Muslims have stronger family units than Christians and are therefore superior in that area.

He added, "It is perfectly acceptable for a man to have more than one wife if the social situation calls for it. This happens in places where there are too many women."

I never would have suspected these bizarre ideas to be floating around in Dad's head.

Dad was a mixed message in the area of sexism. He believed men were more adept than women outside the home, but at the same time, he thought a woman could accomplish anything she wanted, even become a company CEO or get elected to the U.S. presidency. Although I am normally bothered by discrimination, I appreciated this schizophrenia because it alleviated a whole lot of pressure. It was like I was a factory worker and my supervisor was saying, "It's okay if you're not good at your job. After all, you're only a woman. But if you put your mind to it, you can beat every guy in this joint and end up boss."

This was a win for me, but produced ceaseless stress for my brother. As a male, my father's expectations for Buddy were high, and I tended to prevail in the daily competitions that Dad devised, largely because I was older. It was not just about grades and sports; everything was a contest in Dad's world. Even when he was not explicit, he was sizing us up and judging a champ. Buddy and I felt an urgency to these exercises because, in Dad's view, winners sailed down the freeway in a swank convertible, while losers were like Tween, broke and limping along the shoulder of the road. Winners were independent. Losers were leeches. Winners were high society. Losers were low class. Winners earned Dad's respect. Losers could be ousted from his life like scrap paper.

"Your sister's beating you," was one of Dad's most common phrases. What always followed was Buddy's dejected face and his clear feeling of inadequacy. It reminded me of the "agony of defeat," as showcased on

ABC's Wide World of Sports when I was a child. Buddy must have felt like the Slovenian Olympic skier whose failed jump was played over and over on the network. I was conflicted. I felt sad for my brother, but at the same time wanted Dad to be proud of me.

"Let me help you, Buddy," were the words that marked the first time I swindled my little brother.

I was eight years old and plucking Easter eggs out of his basket and placing them in mine so I could win the grand prize, a piece of chocolate cake that grandmother had made. We were in the mani-cured, quarter-acre front yard at Mom's parents' house, and I wore my perfectly tailored little, pink coat and matching bonnet. Buddy did not try to stop the overt theft; his gorgeous brown eyes stared hypnoti-cally. I didn't even need the eggs. I already had the most. Snap, snap, snap. The grown-ups took photos and chuckled. Maybe they were impressed with my savvy nature and competitive spirit, envisioning me as a corporate executive. Or maybe they just thought my brother and I looked so darned cute with our wee baskets. This incident was evidence of my burgeoning sneakiness, my mom told me a year before her attempted suicide.

When Buddy and I were very young, I was bigger, which largely attributed to my success with Dad's daily competitions. But Buddy sprouted up to a muscular six feet by his early teens. Side by side, we looked like a lamp post and a fire hydrant. To this day, I am sort of like a fire hydrant. Dogs are attracted to me. The eventual difference in size meant I had to rely more on brainpower.

"Rub for two hours, and you will get three wishes," I said to Buddy when I was fifteen and he was thirteen.

I gave him hand cream to massage onto a miniature, plastic Aladdin's lamp that I had received as a toy at a fast food joint. He didn't know it sprung from such ordinary beginnings. He believed it was magic and had been found in a rainforest. I wanted Buddy to waste a bunch of time rubbing so I could finish my school assignment first and announce to Dad that I had won the "completed homework contest" that evening. My plan succeeded. It took Buddy an hour to realize he had been duped.

"You're gonna miss this shot," I announced during our regular basketball game of "H-O-R-S-E" on the driveway. I knew if Buddy *believed* he would lose, he *would*. He came to think I had special powers to predict the future. I was a pain-in-the-butt, older sister who knew how to manipulate my little brother, but, of course, he had learned how to upset me with his racist jokes, which gained him parental approval and a "win" of sorts.

Mom considered my mental manipulations and natural ability to view situations from an alternate angle as "sneaky," but as a child, I called it common sense or "smart talent." It was my closest link to natural intelligence. When someone announced a rule, I was proud of the fact that I could quickly find exceptions like a good philosopher or lawyer might. To this day, my favorite compliment is, "You are a philosopher."

Buddy was not the only victim of my "smart talent." When I was eight, there were pink banners, balloons, confetti, party favors, colorful cupcakes and a bunch of little girls in the banquet room at an International House of Pancakes. It was my classmate's birthday party, and an illusionist named Magic Marvin performed tricks at the head of the room with assistance from various audience members. He plucked a fan from his pocket, opened it and showed us kiddies that it was wholly intact. Then he tapped it on his wrist twice and called up eight-year-old Leah to open the fan. She did, and the fan was suddenly broken. The kids laughed, and Leah retreated back to her little, plastic chair. Marvin struck the fan again twice and opened it to show us that it was indeed whole. He struck it twice again, and then called me to the stage. But

I had already figured out that tapping was the key, so when I took the fan, I tapped it twice before opening it. It was flawless.

"You can't be my assistant again. You sneaky little kid," Magic Marvin snatched the fan and hurried me back to my seat.

I had mixed feelings. On one hand, I felt bad that I had embarrassed this nice man and ruined his illusion. On the other, I felt clever and could hear Dad bragging, "My eight-year-old daughter outsmarted Magic Marvin." After the show, parents asked how I had figured out the trick. I viewed it as a form of praise.

My "smart talent" bore no correlation with standardized test results. In the mid-1970s, my Latin teacher, Ruth Wells—who was like a mother to me—revealed that my Lovett entrance exam IQ score was substandard.

"But your brother Buddy has the highest score in the history of the school."

This increased my already colossal inferiority complex. I tried to compensate for my lack of innate intelligence by trying harder and further fine tuning my common sense. In the end, my grades were mostly As, which won me affiliation in the National Honor Society. However, a significant portion of my class received the same accolade. It was a highly motivated group. Buddy did not study; and because he failed to put his natural smarts to use, he stumbled along as a C student.

I never wanted to reveal my upper-class Southern roots. When strangers asked where I was from, I would muffle my mouth with my right hand and garble the answer, "Georgia." The word came out as if it had been through the "liquefy" setting on the Vegematic. I was embarrassed. The stereotype of the backward, lazy and intolerant southerner was perpetuated by mainstream media and Hollywood. But it was not just the stereotype that haunted me; it was the actual experiences that I wanted to escape. Even in Atlanta, which is a relatively sophisticated city, the emphasis back then seemed to be on beer, Bibles, sports, guns and the Confederate flag. I wanted to make it clear to anyone who was willing to listen that I was not really that person who grew up in the South in the 1960s and 1970s. My body had been there, but my soul had been elsewhere. The fact that I didn't believe in mind-body dualism was irrelevant.

After a stranger determined I was from Georgia, he would grin and ask, "Are you a Georgia peach?"

"No, I'm a Georgia potato," was my standard reply.

"Potatoes don't come from Georgia." He'd look baffled.

"I'm adopted."

By revealing I was adopted, I was distancing myself from my Atlanta upbringing and my family's genes. I did not have preppy DNA. I was an outsider, probably even a northerner or westerner. I did not think like Atlantans, pray like them, vote like them, eat like them, or dress like them.

If the stranger asked whether I had siblings, I would mention Buddy, plus the thirteen dogs we had, who were like brothers and sisters to me. From there the conversation would twist into a goofy comedy routine about my assortment of dogs.

"It's a pain waiting in line for the bathroom," I'd say. "We only have one tree. Every week my dad takes us to the park, but there is always slobber on that tennis ball. Then he follows me around with a pooper-scooper."

If I could get the stranger to laugh, he might forget about the "Georgia birthplace thing."

Life in well-to-do Atlanta was all prep, all the time; think Brooks Brothers, argyle sweaters and *The Breakfast Club*. Like a chameleon, Buddy blended into this conservative backdrop, while I stood out like a UFO.

According to *The Official Preppy Handbook*, my high school is listed as the fifth most preppy, coed, day school in the nation, and the nickname my parents had given me, Missy, is regarded as the second preppiest girl name after Muffy and just before Buffy, Bitsy and Bootsy. It was as if my parents read the book and arranged our lives around it. We went on ski vacations in the winter and visited Sea Island in the summer, just as the book said we should. Mom forced me to wear my hair short before I was ten, although I dreamt of having it long. I wore white cotton socks, Oxford shoes and lots of navy and khaki, and never "hooker colors" like black. My childhood was one big bundle of prep.

My rebellion against "preppy" started one afternoon at the mall.

"Gawdy, gawdy, gawdy," my friend Carol pushed her nose into the air. I'm not saying she had a big snout, but it always looked large when she was in her snobby place.

It was my friend Sherie's turn. "Gawdy, gawdy, gawdy."

I could not bring myself to mimic the usual words and instead blurted out, "Oh God. That's nice."

I was staring at a silver, sequined evening gown; it was as ostentatious as a Christmas tree and as sexy as *9½ Weeks*.

As usual, my pals and I were at the mall, judging whether the mannequins' outfits in department store display windows were sufficiently preppy or conservative. I always participated with my own version of "gawdy, gawdy, gawdy" until the day I had the epiphany. I suddenly realized I was different from my friends. The sequins were like little mirrors into my soul. I liked flashy clothes; they did not. It was a tangible distinction that provided the framework for establishing my own identity. My support for civil rights and my disdain for "old money" snobbery were bricks that I affixed to that sequined structure. I was on the way to discovering who I was and would become.

"That dress is vulgar. Only a vain person would wear it," Carol stared at me in horror. I shriveled.

Like a guilty binge-eater, I snuck back to the mall on the following day when my friends were not around and bought that $700 sequined gown.

As I moved through high school, my outfits became less and less conventional by Atlanta standards. I spoke with my former math teacher, Sandra Sturgeon, who told me it was apparel that first signaled to her that I was different from other girls in my class.

"Everyone would buy their dress for the dance at Regenstein's. They would look the same, only different colors. But not you," Sandra said.

Regenstein's sold preppy evening attire for high society Atlantans. To me, their gear was drab. It was equivalent to watching television snow in the days of bad reception, and I naturally wouldn't want to wear television snow to a dance.

I was more of a high-definition wardrobe gal. I mostly shopped at Rich's, Lord and Taylor, and a boutique at the Phipps Plaza mall called Snooty Hooty. This boutique had opened in 1966 under a different name, but when a customer complained that the sales clerks were snooty, the store changed its name to fit. Although I despised the rude, uppity clerks, I shopped there for their big city, fashion-forward designer lines.

Lovett was a uniform school, but I was voted "best dressed" by a group of classmates. I was also voted "shortest" at four feet eleven inches, although another girl was technically smaller at four feet ten inches. It was disheartening to know that I *looked* shorter. I wore glitzy belts and multicolor knee socks to class, although the rules permitted only white or navy. Instead of saddle shoes and loafers, I wore high heels so I could look taller, and I never even owned the approved, powder-blue blouse with a Peter Pan collar. Once a month we had a "wear what you want" day in which students paid a quarter to dress out of uniform. Some students didn't remember or refused to participate, which was considered nerdy. I never forgot. Fashion was foremost on my mind.

When I was 17, I was sent to the principal's office by Alice Cheeseman, a high school English instructor. She had come upon me in the hall and was floored by my fern-green blouse, my raspberry-colored belt and my green and gray striped socks.

At the principal's office, I was blasted: "You're out of uniform. Go home and change…. Now."

"I've been at this school for twelve years. I've never even owned the uniform," I said. "And I graduate in two months."

The principal floundered, "Well… then go back to class."

I tended to be buddy-buddy with my teachers and figured this was why I had averted the uniform police for so long. I had never been a student in Mrs. Cheeseman's class, so we lacked that chumminess. I did not dress to rebel. I just wanted to look pretty, plus unconventional clothing by Atlanta standards had become my calling card. It was not that I disliked preppy clothes, but they were merely one type of fashion in a closet of many.

If I had to pinpoint a clothing style that most captured my essence, it would be that which singer, Tom Jones, wore offstage: in other words, outfits that were tailored, high-quality, a bit flamboyant, and kind of sexy.

SHARON II

Carmageddon and the Social Media Prenup

With Sharon, Los Angeles 2014

"It's really funny that you were voted best dressed at a uniform school," Sharon laughed.

It was after dinner at Hugo's. Sharon and I were in my car, tackling what could only be described as a dense forest of cars, exhaust and pavement, also known as traffic.

"This is almost as exciting as Carmageddon… or as frustrating, depending on your perspective," I said.

"What's Carmageddon?" Sharon asked.

"It was the annihilation of civilized society due to the improvement of the 405 freeway in 2011. It was traffic congestion of biblical proportions," I replied. "Actually, I'm exaggerating; it wasn't that bad. But I thought it was cool when people put lawn chairs on top of their parked cars. They sat there on the freeway watching the construction. It was a form of entertainment."

"Really?" Sharon laughed.

"That's what I call thinking outside of the box, being unconventional," I continued. "Have you ever achieved joy and eternal peace by watching a pulsating jackhammer? "

Sharon chuckled. "Nope. I guess I've missed out. People in Los Angeles seem to have some unusual hobbies."

"Well, what else is there to do? It's not like we have a big ball of twine," I joked.

My cell phone rang; I glanced at caller ID and recognized the name. It was a woman who feared her new boyfriend with a "vindictive personality" would someday retaliate against her should they break up. Although I wondered why she was dating a guy like this, I had agreed to help her with a preemptive strike.

"Who's calling?" Sharon asked.

"Someone who needs me to draft a social media prenup." The call went to voicemail.

"A social media prenup?"

"Yeah," I replied. "It's a document that says a couple can't post unflattering or embarrassing information online about each other."

"That's a really good idea," Sharon said.

"The 'no nudity' provision is really important. You can incorporate steep financial penalties for noncompliance."

"Are they paying you for this service?" she asked.

"No. It's part of my role as a victim advocate."

"What does your man-maid, Richard, think about your activism? He must be very proud of you."

"Dad told me he died years ago, but I don't know any details."

"Sorry to hear that," she replied.

"He was in his late eighties or early nineties. Dad also told me a funny story about Richard."

"What's that?"

"As you know, Richard did everything inside and outside of the house, from cooking and cleaning to mowing the lawn. Dad wanted to make his life easier, so he bought him a leaf blower. Apparently, Richard had never seen one. He didn't know what it was…. Dad came home from work and found Richard leaf blowing the living room couch."

Sharon laughed. "How old is your dad now?"

"Eighty-seven," I said. "He says he can never die because the Lord doesn't want him and the Devil is afraid of him."

I glanced at the clock on the dashboard and became anxious. "Yikes, I hope I can get you back to your hotel before Ricky notices you're gone."

"We've got almost an hour. It should be all right," she said. "Let's continue with your book. You wrote about Tom Jones and fashion. I'm sure there's a reason you mentioned him instead of Calvin Klein, Michael Kors or Donna Karan."

"Okay, but it's getting dark," I said. "Are you sure you can read?"

"I brought my key chain flashlight," she pulled it from her purse and dove back into the experiences of my youth, some 38 years ago.

My Long, Green Pencil

F ATLANTA WERE A CLASSIC antique brooch tucked away in a safe, then singer, Tom Jones, was the Hope Diamond. He was flashy, larger than life and on public view. His humble beginnings in a Welsh mining town and ensuing success provided hope for those without means. Tom, who was "new money" or nouveau riche, was judged as a trespasser by Atlanta "old money" gatekeepers. This was not a criticism of Tom specifically, but a judgment in general about show business folk. Although things have changed a bit in the twenty-first century in that entrepreneurs are appreciated for their work ethic and drive, in many circles there still lingers an attitude that those with inherited wealth have greater cultural sophistication and moral superiority than those with achieved status.

A carefully constructed "old money" web stretched over the upper-class Atlanta community where I lived during the first eighteen years of my life. Outward escape was not an option, so I escaped inward into the television. Those on TV seemed to lack the racist attitudes I originally thought were standard practice throughout the world. Those on TV donned showy, sequined gowns and ignored stupid dress codes. Those on TV did not seem bent on getting dead presidents (or money) from dead relatives in order to lead a dead existence. Those on TV seemed open-minded and full of life. I never subscribed to the view that a hefty bank account (or a fur coat, as Mom would say) led to happiness. I also didn't think that "new money" folk, like Tom, were of low pedigree. I was impressed by self-starters, and I was especially impressed by what I had learned about Tom from media interviews and watching his 1969 ABC show, *This Is Tom Jones,* when I was nine years old.

Kissing the television set during Tom Jones' weekly variety show was an embarrassing habit. Not only did Buddy catch me puckering up, but so did my parents and a couple of their friends. I learned the hard way: never let anyone see you doing something really stupid that they can reveal to their friends. My brother and his classmates teased me.

"Missy's got a boyfriend. His name is Sony…. Don't you think your boyfriend is a little square?"

"Missy got mononucleosis from the boob tube. Eww, gross. That's obscene."

As comical as it may sound, I thought I was in love with Tom who was twenty years my senior. I was obsessed with him, chattered about him constantly, and asked for his record album for Christmas. When I was nine, Santa left me a child's version of a motorcycle, which cost a heck of a lot more. I rode it once and gave it back to Dad. He sold it. Finally two years later, I sprinted into the living room alongside Buddy on Christmas morning to find Tom's *Funny Familiar Forgotten Feelings* album. A home movie captured the glorious event. I wore my bright pink bathrobe that zipped up the front; and I rocked back and forth, elated, squeezing the record to my chest. For the following decade, that Tom Jones album was the only music I owned, but I played it constantly. My green pencil and I loved the beat.

My fixation on Tom did not falter as I matured; by sixteen, I was reading articles, interviews and biographies that could give me greater insight into his personality and interests. Before nodding off to sleep each night, I would invent detailed dramas in my head about the two of us. They were not sexual because sex was not part of my world or awareness, but they were romantic. Tom would hold me in his arms, and we would have conversations. I would say A, he would say B, and then I would say C, and so forth. I believed I could predict his words and reactions.

When Tom was handed the *This is Tom Jones* variety show, he wanted rock-and-roll icon, Jerry Lee Lewis, to be a guest. This did not bode well with program executives, who considered the "Balls of Fire" performer too radical for Middle America, but Tom got his way in the end. I learned all of this from a newspaper article at age 16, as well as that Tom's favorite musical performance of all time was one by Jerry Lee in 1962 at Sophia Gardens Pavilion in Cardiff, Wales. I had no inkling who Jerry Lee was and had never attended a concert by any artist, but Tom's "recommendation" was sufficient: I headed to Jerry Lee's concert at the Great Southeast Music Hall in Atlanta one night that summer.

There was an insufferably long line that curled around the Great Southeast Music Hall, and a patron told me the show was "sold out." I had come a long way, so rather than head back to my car with dashed dreams, I taught myself how to gate crash. Actually, it took no planning or fore-thought. My "smart talent" immediately kicked into gear.

"I am here to apply for a job," I told a ticket taker, who was preoc-cupied with the concert-goers at the door.

"Go inside to the office on the left and ask for an application," he said.

I entered the building and veered right instead of left. Then, I plopped down in a front row seat inside the auditorium. The show was spirited and entertaining; and I especially liked Jerry Lee's fancy fingerwork on the piano.

Before the concert, I may have been a sassy rule-breaker, but I was insecure. I saw myself as unattractive, as overweight and as not all that intelligent, except for my infamous "smart talent." When I glanced in the mirror, I saw what entrenched self-doubt wanted me to see. Dad and Buddy regularly called me fat, even though I was only ten pounds heavier than I should have been. No one at school ever said I was overweight, except one popular girl who zeroed in on my lower legs one afternoon at cheerleading practice and criticized, "Your calves are fat." I remember being disappointed when a female coach chuckled at her words with approval.

Neither family members nor schoolmates ever offered me a compliment, with the exception of a couple of boys in my class and my mom. I remember them vividly. Steele Hawkins told me, "Your teeth are blinding me" while I was cheering on the football field; and Robin Loudermilk put his fingers around the area above my elbow one day and said, "I can get my hand around your whole arm." Steele had implied I had nice teeth, and Robin had implied I was thin. The boys at my school were not rude, but they seemed to think it uncool to compliment females. This also applied to David Hart, the only boy I was attracted to during my many years at Lovett. David—who looked like a Scandinavian version of Tom Jones—focused on sports. Girls were not a priority.

"Take off that dress. You look too sexy," Mom said when I was 16.

This is the only compliment she ever gave me. I was in the dining room modeling an outfit for the school dance. There were two interesting facts about this remark. First, this "compliment" was actually meant as an insult. And secondly, the outfit belonged to Mom. I was clothed in a cocktail dress that she had worn in high school. Because my chest was fuller than hers, my cleavage was playing show and tell, something she never had to confront. As an adopted child, my genes clearly came from a different test tube. Mom was tall and lean. I was short and curvaceous.

My "most ladylike" mom thought I looked like a slut, and when Dad entered the room, he agreed.

"You need a chest reduction. You've never looked classy," he said. "You'll soon be a debutante, and debutantes don't have big chests."

This became one of Dad's routine grievances, but I never considered plastic surgery because I liked my chest. To my parents, a large chest meant lack of class. And "lacking class" was analogous to harboring a hideous deformity or moral defect. It was a wholly unacceptable condition for an "old money" Atlantan like I was supposed to be.

Directly after the Jerry Lee Lewis concert, a white-haired man named Jerry D. Sullivan (or JD) intercepted my exit from the row and provided the inciting incident for my life. In screenplay jargon, an inciting incident is that which jumpstarts a story into action. My life was jumpstarted that night by JD.

"I'm JD. Would you like to go backstage to meet Jerry Lee?" he asked. "I think he might like to meet you,"

"Sure. Why not." I figured there was no harm.

JD led me up steps to a makeshift dressing room located in the rear stage area. The "walls" consisted of heavy curtains, and Jerry Lee sat in a chair, removing his shoes. He introduced himself, and we briefly exchanged niceties.

"I need to change my clothes," Jerry Lee said to me. "You can either stay here or wait outside."

"I'll wait outside. Thanks."

I left the "dressing room" and perched back down in the front row of the now empty auditorium. A few minutes later, JD emerged and sat next to me.

"Mr. Lewis would like to be in your company this evening," he said.

"Thanks, but I'm not interested."

"You're kidding? All the girls want to go out with him."

"No, thanks."

"Really? Well, who would you want to go out with?" JD asked. "What about John Travolta, Robert Redford, Sylvester Stallone…."

As he listed popular sex symbols of the day, I shook my head after each. JD seemed amazed, yet he was determined to pinpoint a celebrity I found attractive.

"Well, isn't there anyone?" he asked after exhausting two dozen names.

My rattling on about Tom for the previous seven years had done nothing but earn me embarrassment, snickers and badgering. I was reluctant to be vulnerable again.

"Well… there is one person."

"Who?" he asked.

"Tom Jones," I said.

JD did not laugh or mock me. He reared back in a bold way as if he was my mentor and warmed me with a huge smile.

"You could go out with him, young lady," he said. "You are beautiful, sweet and smart. Of course he'd be interested. After all, Jerry Lee is interested, isn't he?"

It made perfect sense. If Jerry Lee was interested, maybe Tom would be as well. My confidence boomed upward from a two to a ten. For the first time, I felt pretty. I was able to embrace my inner peacock. I gave JD an exuberant bear hug.

"Thank you so much. I'm gonna do it. I'm gonna get a date with Tom." I bounced up the aisle.

JD shouted, "Wait. Don't you want to go back and see Jerry Lee?"

"No, I'm gonna get a date with Tom."

I dashed out of the concert hall with spunk, self-assurance and a mission. I lacked a road map, but was confident that with a little common sense, I could devise one along the way.

Days after the Jerry Lee Lewis concert, I had what could only be described as an epiphany or spiritual moment in which I suddenly had an understanding about life. This time my revelation did not occur while gawking at a sequined gown. It happened while sitting on a mountaintop with my beloved Amy.

Amy was a Hungarian sheepdog called a Puli, and she was the most important being in my life. She looked like a cuter and curlier version of "It" from *The Addams Family*. Her long, white, corded coat covered her playful, yellow eyes. She was my favorite of our many dogs. Two or three times each week, Amy and I would traipse through the hills of the partially developed neighborhoods surrounding the River North subdivision, often sneaking into half-constructed homes through unlocked windows and doors. Once inside, Amy would watch me sing and dance; sometimes I would baton twirl with my trusty, long, green pencil. I was pretty darn good: I could catch it behind my back and in my toes. When I was not performing for Amy, I was reading philosophical works, including the Bible. Although I did not consider myself religious, I was open to insights from any source.

On epiphany Saturday, Amy and I sat in the dirt among weeds. Weeds are, of course, nothing more than socially unacceptable plants that somehow got stuck in the nuisance column of botanist guides. Amy and I watched the sun fade on the horizon. From our vantage point, we could see my parents' two-story house, the Smith's Colonial estate and advertising executive Richard Heiman's Tudor mini-manor located at the end of a short cul-de-sac. He somehow got that street—which was not much longer than my green pencil—named after him.

A Bible rested in my lap. I had been analyzing the text and criticizing passages that contained racist or sexist content. I generally viewed the Bible as a detrimental work, partly for its objectionable sentiments and partly for the powerful (and negative) way it had impacted society and the masses throughout the ages. Think mass murder and heretics burned at the stake. Bertrand Russell and Christopher Hitchens would understand. Suddenly, poof. There seemed to be a burst of energy or flicker of light that temporarily surrounded Amy and me. Perhaps it was my imagination, but at that moment I came to the realization that I should undertake a mission to try to make the world better, and the mission was to be centered on the elimination of prejudice. Studies show that one-third of all people in the world believe they have a mission in life, and I had now joined their ranks.

Because racism was an "in my face" problem, it became the starting point for my anti-discrimination pursuit. Since I was underage and could not secretly join a civil rights organization without my parents' knowledge, I decided to be an example of tolerance.

The teasing began shortly thereafter. I unwisely mentioned my "epiphany" to a group of Lovett students, who laughed at me. One girl embarked upon a crusade to harass me as a "negro lover" week after week, month after month, until graduation. In an attempt to avoid her, I would alter my path through Lovett hallways and steer clear of her table in the lunchroom. I was willing to set an example of open-mindedness, but I hated personal attacks. Fighting back had always felt uncomfortable, unless directed towards those I knew best: Mom, Dad, and Buddy. When it came to peers and strangers, there was only one thing I hated more than being taunted: actual confrontation.

I came home from school one gray afternoon a few months after my spiritual moment on the hill.

"Amy?" I yelled as I entered the front door. "Amy? Amy?"

Amy did not come running like she always had. I had a high-pitched way of summoning her that only I could do.

"Where's Amy?" I asked Dad who was sitting in the family room recliner watching television.

He replied in a matter-of-fact way. "She died today."

"What?" I panicked. I could not contain my tears, even though I knew my father thought crying was weak.

"Our horses were stolen this morning. I called the police to fill out a report. The policeman ran over Amy in the driveway."

Dad was apathetic. I was devastated.

"Where is she?"

He was fixated on the TV. "I buried her in the backyard."

Crying, I sprinted out the sliding glass door to the yard, but there was no sign of disturbed dirt. He had lied to me about the burial. I figured he had asked the cop to dispose of her body. It was the sort of thing he would do. Dad could not be bothered with digging a hole for a dog.

"She's not out there. You didn't bury her," I said, wiping my eyes.

"Yes, I did." He chuckled. "Amy never liked you anyway. She liked your mother better."

Although Dad's cruel remarks were routine, they always caught me off guard. It was as if a truck had veered in front of me, forcing me to slam on my brakes emotionally, regain my composure and move in a new direction.

But the sting from Dad's hurtful comment was nothing as compared with the torment I felt over losing my beautiful Amy; and to this day, I still feel the pain of her loss. She was a life boat on the rough and dangerous sea called Atlanta. I loved our other dogs, but never felt as connected to them as Amy. I also worried about the fate of our two stolen horses who were never recovered. Bad things seemed to happen at River North Parkway. If I'd been so inclined, I might have reckoned there was a curse on the place.

Not long after Amy died, Mom's sister, Aunt Helen, stayed with us at our River North Parkway home. She liked to call herself a "floozy," but she did not sleep with just anyone. She had a particular affinity for truck drivers. While I was obsessing over Tom Jones, she was obsessing over Ned, a partially toothless Oklahoman who steered an eighteen-wheeler, and Barney, a 40-year-old, former construction worker who rarely bathed and who barreled his truck through her neck of the woods once a month. Helen would meet them at truck stop diners, and then fool around with them in their rig or at run-down motels along U.S. Route 10 just outside Houston, Texas where she lived. She bragged that they were younger men.

Helen had not always been this way. For thirty-five years, she had been married and even raised two children. When her husband died, she went wild. She was ten years older than Mom and anything but ladylike. Helen was brash, smoked like a chemical factory and lived in a trailer. She had narcolepsy and almost killed herself falling asleep at the wheel. She wore glasses and only had one breast because her cancerous growth had been removed prior to routine reconstructive surgery. Helen's breast grossed me out; I had mistakenly caught a glimpse of it when I was 14 at Beech Mountain, North Carolina where Dad's company had one of its many vacation homes. She would sometimes join us when we went on holiday and periodically visit us in Atlanta.

Despite her obvious lack of class, Mom and Dad treated her like an accepted member of the family. She was a lot more fun than them, and like my "man maid" Richard, she was my buddy. She detailed her seedy escapades. Frankly, I considered both the men and the affairs disgusting, but highly fascinating. I reciprocated by confiding in her about private matters, such as the pivotal moment with Jerry Lee and JD and my desire to somehow meet Tom. She offered interest and enthusiasm, a rare commodity in the Laws household.

"I'm going to Caesar's Palace in Las Vegas," I burst into the guest bedroom. "That's where I will meet Tom."

I was 17 years old and finally ready to get my fantasy underway. I was explaining how Tom would be performing at the venue when Dad appeared ominously at the door. He had overheard our girl talk.

"Why would *he* want to go out with *you*?" He gestured as if I were a pathetic little creature and disappeared down the hall.

I was confused. Dad had always condemned "new money" entertainment folk. He painted them as inferior. It seemed he was not even willing to waste paint on me.

S H A R O N   I I I

Museums and Conformity

With Sharon, Los Angeles 2014

My car turned into the portico at Sharon's hotel. It was only five minutes before Ricky was scheduled to return from the convention. Was he early and waiting in the room? Was he suspicious about her absence and wise to our scheme? If so, what would be Sharon's excuse? She was not a mendacious person. It was one thing to withhold information from her husband, but it was another to lie.

"Pick me up here at ten in the morning," Sharon said to me as she hurried out of the car and into the hotel lobby.

If caught, I knew Sharon would be truthful. It was her nature. I also knew I would not find out if there was a blow-up until the next day. Sharon was not the type to phone me about marriage troubles, even if I was the cause of the friction.

At ten the following morning, I waited at the hotel entrance. Sharon appeared with a smile and climbed into the car.

"Was Ricky in the room when you got back last night?"

"Nope. He came back pretty late."

I was glad we had averted the napalm bomb. Our secret relationship would be intact for at least one more day.

"I'm looking forward to seeing the Getty Museum," Sharon said.

She loved art museums. I hated them, despite the fact that I felt safeguarding pieces with historical significance was an important task for society. I was cynical and viewed museums as airless tombs where pretentious elites showcased personal taste. There was nothing objective about art, yet many critics pompously anointed one item to be "masterful" and another to be "rubbish." I liked the line from the movie, *The Thomas Crown Affair,* in which the Denis Leary character calls museum pieces: "swirls of paint that are important to some very silly rich people."

"We should go to an outdoor art show sometime. They hold them in the local parks," I said. "I love seeing regular people showcasing their creations. Plus, it's outdoors in the sunshine."

I had once told Sharon my opinion, that I considered museums claustrophobic and that I abhorred the conformist rules: do not take photos, do not eat, don't wander away from the docent, and don't go beyond the ropes. But art was her passion—almost a religion—and she seemed to think I would eventually convert. In her mind, it would only take one more glass case, one more inscription, one more stroll over a marble floor. I wanted to please Sharon, and I liked spending time with her, so I always agreed to tour another cavernous room filled with super old stuff.

Sharon had once taken me to see newer stuff at the Museum of Modern Art in New York. We saw the imprint of a person's thumb on a canvas and a can of Campbell's soup on a pedestal. I was flabbergasted when visitors stared at the pieces with furrowed brows and serious expressions. I overheard a man say, "Look at the colors on that tin can." Hadn't he ever been down the soup aisle at Safeway?

There was also a red circle printed on a white background, hanging on an otherwise bare wall—no doubt a creation by the Target Store ad team.

I approached a museum guard. "I really like that bench. It screams post-structuralism; it entreats us to relax in a hurried world. Who's the artist?"

"That's just a bench for the public, ma'am. It's not art." He had a straight face.

"I beg your pardon," I replied. "It's way better than that ridiculous red dot."

Now we were in Los Angeles, pulling away from Sharon's hotel and heading for the Getty Museum.

"Yesterday, we left off with your aunt who dated truck drivers," Sharon said and pulled out my manuscript. "Let's find out what happened next. I'm especially curious about Tom Jones."

Sharon went back to reading about my tumultuous life in the late 1970s.

F O U R

The Little Atlanta Girl Who Could

S MY PLANE DESCENDED into McCarran Airport, I could see the red and black billboard boasting "Caesars Palace Proudly Presents Tom Jones." I hoped it was a good omen. A nervous feeling rippled through my gut.

After a short cab ride, I dragged my suitcases up the steps into Caesars Palace, eyeing the imported, $100,000 marble statues that seemed to be guarding the front entrance. On second thought, maybe they were the ones being guarded. I was 17 years old, and the casino was overwhelming. There were clanking slot machines, blackjack dealers wearing solemn looks and cocktail waitresses in Roman-style, gold-and-white garb. Straight ahead was an oval gambling pit with an onyx-colored ceiling; to the left was the front desk and around the corner was the Circus Maximus Theatre where Tom performed two shows each evening.

I had paid $50 per night, the lowest price for a room; but was pleased with the two double beds, table and chair. These wooden pieces would be my confidants during my stay. I was 2,000 miles from home and had no one else.

I pulled a $20 bill from my purse and scurried to the bellhop desk.

"Hey," I signaled a friendly-looking bellman, "I need to know which room Tom Jones is staying in, what time he goes to his dressing room for the show and what path he takes."

I guess $20 was a lot in those days because he jammed the bill into his pocket and checked the computer. He gave me the room number, and then led me up an elevator to an empty hallway.

"Tom Jones walks past here every night at seven thirty," he said. I smiled and thanked him.

I purchased a ticket for the late show which began at 12:30 a.m., but my impatience was overwhelming. I slipped into the first show when the maitre d' was preoccupied. I plopped down in an inconspicuous back corner. Tom was as much a hunk in person as he was on television, and his voice was flawless. My heart was a runaway train. I was jittery and insecure. Was I too fat and ugly? Maybe Tom would agree with my father and brother. I knew I would have to "get in Tom's face" just to find out if he thought I was attractive. This would probably involve crashing past security. Oh God, could it be done? Jerry Lee was a far cry from Tom Jones. Maybe JD had not wanted to hurt my feelings. Maybe I was a dud. Maybe he figured I would move on with my normal, little life and forget about Tom. He could not have anticipated I would become such a focused and determined lass when I dashed out of the Southeastern Music Hall that night.

When the second show rolled around, I was naïve about ringside seat protocol, and got stuck in that darn back corner again. But I refused to take rejection for an answer and watched how others got put in the front: the secret was a hefty tip to the maitre d', whom I later learned was Angelo. I figured Angelo had to be a gazillionaire by now. Since it was too late to tip, I eyed an empty front row seat and when the warm-up comedian finished his act, I scrambled into it. Moments later, the curtain rose, and Tom burst onto the stage.

It was not only that the show was 8,000 times more amazing close-up, and Tom's looks and sex appeal sucked the breath right out of me, but he showered me with attention. At first, I thought this was just part of his shtick, but as the show progressed, it seemed extraordinary. People around me agreed.

A lady behind me seemed bothered, "Do you know him? Why does he keep looking at you?"

A blonde next to me whispered, "Wow, you are lucky."

Indeed, I felt lucky. It was customary for women to throw under-wear at Tom or stand for a kiss between songs. I thought the "lingerie thing" was low-class, but decided to stand for the kiss, even though it would make me look like a fan. I knew acting like a fan could be a fatal mistake.

"I'm only 17," I told Tom when he approached me with his mike.

"You're 17? I didn't know they let them in so young," he spoke to the crowd. They laughed. "So, where are you from?"

"Atlanta, Georgia."

He slid into a routine joke he'd recite when bantering with a southern gal.

"I like southern girls because they don't say 'You can.' They say 'Ya'll can,' and we travel in a group." He motioned to his band members, and there was a drum beat. The crowd laughed again.

Prior to the trip, I had learned several sentences in Welsh, thinking this would somehow impress him. Due to the pressure of the moment, I could only remember one and blurted it out, even though it had no relevance to the situation.

"*Ffarwel, fy annwyl Gariad.*"

Translated it meant, "Goodbye my dearest love." Tom looked baffled. "That's Welsh," I added.

He replied, "Oh, I don't know any Welsh."

I felt like an idiot. Then he reached down and gave me a kiss and moved on to the next song. Each night during my stay, I watched the second show from a ringside seat and to my surprise, received the same special attention and kiss from Tom. I never had to rely upon tipping because Angelo became my buddy and would automatically place me in the front row.

I sneaked, trekked and crawled, while trying not to get sweaty or stain my white, silk blouse. I pulled on a door; it was locked. I tried another; it opened. I moved to a new passageway where I found a miniature ladder which led to an undersized doorway. I moved through it like Catwoman, and then skulked down another hallway, hoping there were no hidden cameras. All the while, I was calculating which direction would most likely result in success.

It was my second night in Vegas, and it was two hours after Tom's late show. I had spent a ridiculous amount of time in the back hallways and tunnels behind the coffee shop at Caesars Palace, trying to figure out the secret access to a particular door that I knew opened onto the stage adjacent to Tom's dressing room. I had found the portal earlier that day when scoping out the backstage area.

Suddenly, it all clicked together, and I swung open the sought-after black door. The good news was I found myself on the stage. The bad news was I was staring at Alma Davis. Alma was part of the security staff at Caesars Palace, but acted as a private bodyguard for Tom when he was performing in the showroom. She was a lean, tall, black woman with a buzz haircut. She wore a uniform and a scowl.

"You're not allowed back here," she said, grabbing my arm and towing me into the empty showroom. She deposited me there and returned to her post.

This was not my only confrontation with Alma. On the following night, I was again watching the show, and one of Tom's pant seams seemed to have separation anxiety. Directly after the performance, a lady sitting next to me in the audience accompanied me to report the news. Alma was guarding the backstage entry.

"Tom's pants are starting to rip," the lady said to Alma.

"I think you should let Tom know," I added.

Alma replied, "So what? I'm not telling him anything. Isn't that what you guys want anyway?"

"That's rude and disgusting," I said in a huff. Alma was oblivious.

Angelo told me that Tom's parents were visiting; so on the following day, I bought a sizable bouquet of flowers for Freda and Thomas Sr. I wrote their names on the card and knocked on the suite number given to me by the bellman. Tom's mom answered the door. Like me, she was a petite, blonde woman. She was warm and receptive.

"These are for you and your husband, Mrs. Woodward," I handed the flowers to her. (Tom's real last name is "Woodward.")

"Thank you," she replied with an appreciative grin.

It became common in ensuing years for me to give a gift, often something handmade, to the parents of any guy I liked. A handful of men fit the bill at some point in my life; their parents were benefactors of my affection for their son.

Day five of my six-day visit arrived, and I still had not met Tom, apart from being a measly audience member. It was time to get serious, so I donned a provocative, flamboyant dance costume, which I had intuitively packed. I'd had it made in Atlanta by a seamstress, partly for a local dance production and partly for use on the trip. I looked like a Vegas showgirl, despite my miniature size. The outfit consisted of a silver-sequined, one shoulder leotard, fishnet stockings, silver boots and a blue-and-silver feather headdress that brought my height line up a foot. My plan was to pass Tom "coincidentally" in the hallway while he was traveling from his suite to the dressing room.

At seven that night, I planted myself in position. Several male passers-by stopped to flirt, which increased my self-confidence. Although I was glad they approved of my looks, I frantically worked to get rid of them. Tom's guitarist, Mike Morgan, passed by and stopped for a minute to chat.

I was alone when I heard Tom's voice in the distance. I walked slowly and nonchalantly towards the sound, although my heart was beating like a maniac. First, I saw the dreaded Alma and turned my head towards the wall, hoping not to trigger another confrontation. She moved past me without saying a word. Tom was behind her. I glanced at him and he glanced at me.

"I remember you," he said. "What's your name?"

"Missy," I smiled.

This was my nickname. I was not called by my actual first name "Charlotte" until years later.

"You look really good," Tom seemed attracted.

"Thank you." I was ecstatic, but trying to appear relaxed.

"What are you up to?" he asked. He seemed to like my sexy outfit.

"Dance rehearsal," I replied.

Alma, who was unaware Tom had stopped, was now at the far end of the hall and breezed back.

"We have to go, Tom." She sent me a stern look, like a bully who could not hit me because the teacher was present.

"See you later," he beamed.

He and Alma disappeared around the bend. I did petit jete leaps and pirouette spins all the way back to my room, blissfully rehearsing my dance routine as I had promised.

On my final night in Vegas, I stood at my ringside seat and told Tom I was leaving the next day. He gave me the usual "audience-member" kiss. After the show, I went to my room and telephoned the dressing room to ask if I could come backstage.

A gruff man answered. I later learned it was Lloyd Greenfield, Tom's no-nonsense manager who was based out of New York, but who traveled with the singer on the road.

"This is Missy and I was wondering…" Lloyd hung up before I finished my sentence.

I broke into tears, even though I knew the hang-up was nothing personal. Lloyd had no idea who I was. I went to Tom's suite and sat on the floor outside sobbing until a hotel security guard found me and ordered me back to my room. I returned to Atlanta without a date.

Despite my failure, I still chattered on about Tom. I probably heard the words "stop dreaming" more times than there are days in a year. I was teased a lot, twice receiving love notes in my desk at school signed "Tom Jones." Classmates exploded in laughter. It was embarrassing, but I had no plan to give up the dream. Even at 17, I knew perseverance was key.

A couple of months following my failed attempt to get a date with Tom and my unpleasant tussles with Alma, Aunt Helen wanted to experience Las Vegas for the first time. She invited me to share her hotel room at Caesars Palace. I agreed, although I knew Tom was no longer in town.

I looked like innocence in a pit of debauchery. Sporting pink bows and pigtails, I bopped through a sunken blackjack table section at Caesars Palace one afternoon.

A 60-year-old man approached me. He was a graying Fred Flintstone with a bulbous nose, friendly black eyes and unkempt hair. His black-and-orange, animal print top was either a Hawaiian shirt gone wrong, an early Halloween costume or threads left over from the Stone Age. On the other hand, I looked like "the midget miler," as I was routinely called by Lovett track team enthusiasts, with my jogging shorts, tank top, tennis shoes and waist pouch. I had just completed a two-mile run down the Las Vegas strip. We surely looked like the odd couple.

"I just won $13,000 gambling and want to buy you a diamond bracelet. No strings attached," Fred said to me.

"What?" I said.

"I don't have any kids or a wife. Let me spoil you." He took my upper arm and led me toward the hotel gift shop. I wondered why he had no Dino or Wilma, but chose not to pry.

"This is my friend," Flintstone introduced me to a plainclothes Caesars Palace security guard, another senior citizen, who was escorting us.

Would Mr. Security eject me? I was clearly underage. And what was his purpose? Was he there to protect Flintstone from swindlers? Fred carried a drink and seemed to have fallen off the sobriety tightrope into the abyss of intoxication. Mr. Security flashed a knowing smile in my direction as if to say, "I know you're a youngster, but I am gonna look the other way."

At the gift shop, Flintstone bought me an $800 diamond bracelet. The stones were microscopic, but I was astonished and wholly appreciative.

"Now, let's gamble," Flintstone tugged at my upper arm and led me back into the casino. Mr. Security scampered behind.

At a blackjack table, Flintstone took chips from his pocket and placed bets. When he won, he shoved the winnings into my waist pouch. When he lost, he purchased additional chips. Mr. Security was obsessed with keeping Flintstone's glass filled to the brim, which made me think his real aim had something to do with padding casino coffers rather than watching out for swindlers.

"What are you doing?" I questioned in semi-protest each time Flintstone stuffed chips into my pouch.

"I want to get you some clothes." He turned to Mr. Security, "Where can I do that?"

"There's a boutique around the corner from the gift shop," he said.

Off we trotted, but Mr. Security did not follow behind like he had before. He sprinted ahead. When Flintstone and I entered the store, Mr. Security was whispering to a sales lady, and I had a bad feeling.

"Go to the dressing room," the sales clerk commanded. "I will bring you some pretty things."

Moments later, she appeared in the dressing room with a stack of silk garments draped over her forearm.

"You're not bringing any of this stuff back. Got it?" she said in a threatening tone. "You're lucky you haven't been arrested for gambling as a minor."

My jaw hit the dressing room floor, "I wasn't gambl…"

"Try these on," she interrupted.

In shock, I slowly slid the first dress off its hanger, now convinced there was a kickback deal between Mr. Security and the clerk. Flintstone was so intoxicated by this point that alerting him to the scam would do nothing but land me in trouble. I walked out of the store with $4,000 in merchandise.

"Well, it was nice meeting you, young lady. But, I'd better be going," Flintstone said when we reached the casino area.

"It was nice meeting you, too. Thank you so much." I hugged Flintstone and headed toward my aunt's hotel room. I could feel Mr. Security's eyes on me.

Aunt Helen was stretched out on the bed, engrossed in a television program. I thought about my family's ridiculous tradition of going on a trip only to stare at the TV day after day. Dad was famous for taking us to exotic places, and then becoming mesmerized in front of television weather reports.

I dumped my loot on the bed and counted the chips. My two hours with Flintstone was like winning a game show. Cash and prizes totaled $7,700.

"I wish I was young again," Aunt Helen sighed.

I wondered whether this generosity was a common occurrence or a fluke. Did people just give away money in Las Vegas or did the gambling-town gods have a temporary crush on me?

My answer came a few days later when I was again cutting through the casino at Caesars Palace. A man named Craig asked if I'd like to gamble. He was determined to hit the jackpot and stalked a row of slot machines, popping coins obsessively into one, then another and another. I agreed to play an adjacent row with a bucket of his coins. An hour later, I said good-bye, and Craig handed me a hundred dollar bill for my time.

"If I'm ever poor, I'm moving to Las Vegas," I told Aunt Helen. "People just give money away."

That same year, I invited actor Burt Reynolds to my prom. It involved a bet.

One afternoon, my best friend, Sherilyn Evans, and I created a list of possible escorts for the Lovett junior-senior prom. As usual, classmate David Hart was my first entry. I had taken him to a full 90 percent of the dances and parties in the past because, with the exception of Tom, he was the only guy who interested me. David fell short of 100 percent only because I wanted to give him breathing room, freedom and an opportunity to accompany someone else. I didn't want him to feel smothered. It was quite calculated on my part.

Every dance to my recollection was "girls ask boys," a formula that blended well with my assertive, "I know exactly who I like" nature. I was inflexible on the subject of my heart. If I was not attracted to a guy right off the bat, then it was "no" forever. I was not a candidate for conversion.

When it came to inviting David to dances, I was quick. Other girls would dilly-dally with their date choices, consulting with girlfriends or checking the calendar, but I'd quickly drop the dice on David's table. He always said, "yes." To this day, I am grateful for his receptiveness, not only because I enjoyed his company, but also because he lifted me a few more notches away from my ever-present inferiority complex.

I was not part of the "cool crowd," yet the popular boys—of whom David was one—were quite friendly. In fact, many were my close friends. On the other hand, most of the cliquish girls treated me with disdain. Sherilyn and I decided it might be interesting to bring famous escorts to the dance, partly as an adventure and partly to outdo those cruel girls who clearly deserved to be outdone. We decided our choices had to be realistic. The men had to be single and had to live in or visit the Atlanta area. She chose Falcon quarterback Steve Bartkowski, and I chose actor Burt Reynolds.

Burt was the number-one box-office attraction in 1977–1978 and helped catapult Georgia to the third most popular filming location during those years, after California and New York. He was committed to making movies in the South and frequented the Atlanta area. Although I had no romantic interest in him, I thought he'd be an ideal date.

"I'll ask Burt if you ask Steve," I offered my hand to Sherilyn. We shook.

Sherilyn never contacted Steve, but I immediately telephoned NBC in Burbank, California to get contact information for Mr. Reynolds' representatives. I was given a phone number for Dick Clayton of Clayton Enterprises. A person at that office told me to contact manager David Gershenson, who was doing publicity with Burt in New York and staying at the Waldorf Astoria. I figured that might mean Burt was staying there as well, so I called the hotel and asked for Mr.

Reynolds' room. To my surprise, the call was not screened. The phone rang and rang. There was no answer. I phoned thirteen more times that day without success.

If Mr. Reynolds would agree to go, my plan was to turn the prom—which was slated to be held at the opulent, mosque-like Fox Theatre—into a fundraiser. A "Save the Fox" campaign was already in the works because the building was set to be demolished. I figured Mr. Reynolds would favor keeping the landmark intact. In the end, the Fox Theatre mortgage was paid off six months ahead of schedule in 1978. The structure still stands today.

At seven the following morning, I called the Waldorf Astoria again. Buddy was listening secretly from the study phone, unconvinced I could get the actor on the line. He had eavesdropped during some of my failed attempts on the previous day, but I'd scolded him, and he'd promised to stop. I figured he would blurt out something sophomoric and spoil my plan. The phone rang and what sounded like a groggy Burt Reynolds answered. I was flabbergasted, tongue-tied and worried that I had awoken him.

"Mr. Reynolds?" I asked.

"Yeah?"

I told him there would be a benefit for the 'Save the Fox' campaign in conjunction with the Lovett prom. I asked if he might be in Atlanta at that time and wondered if he would like to be my escort. I gave him the date. He was silent for thirty seconds.

"I was just trying to remember my schedule...I have to be in L.A. then. Sorry," he said.

Buddy was silent during the call, but sprinted into the kitchen seconds later.

"How'd you do that?" he asked. It was one of the few times he seemed impressed with his big sister.

I still lacked an escort for the prom, but I would find a handsome actor suitable for the role a week later when I landed my first movie part.

Farrell's Ice Cream Parlour and Restaurant at Cumberland Mall in Atlanta was an upbeat, balloon-filled eatery with shiny, red booths and a well-stocked selection of colorful candies for sale. I worked there part-time when I asked Burt Reynolds to the prom, and I still own the uniform, a black-and-white striped, high-collar, cotton top and a black skirt. It was not my first job. I had worked for a low hourly wage, along with another kid named Ralph, at my dad's company where we made copies of documents in an eight-foot-by-eight-foot room. I got peeved when, by the end of each day, I had Xeroxed three times more than Ralph, but got the same pay. It was unfair, so I quit.

In addition to my duties as candy counter clerk and cashier at Farrell's, I was expected to answer the phone. This proved advantageous. The phone rang one afternoon, and a man asked for a dishwasher named Hal. Employees were not allowed to take calls during business hours, so I asked if I could take a message.

"I'm working on a movie in town. Tell Hal to be at the audition tomorrow at 1:00 p.m. It's the Thataway Production office at I-75 and Howell Mill Road," the man said.

He gave me details which I scribbled onto two napkins: one for Hal and one for myself.

I had never before skipped school, but at noon on the following day I slipped into the Lovett parking lot, popped into my car and sped off campus before the school security officer could put down his coffee cup. I knew a detention would be forthcoming, but figured my debut in a movie, if I could nail the audition, would be worth the punishment.

The production office waiting room looked like boot camp. There were three dozen men in army uniforms. There were no women other than me and a receptionist. My smart talent emerged.

"I'm here about the movie. My agent told me to come," I feigned confidence, but actually had no agent and knew nothing about the audition process.

She cocked her head. "The women came in this morning. Only the men are supposed to audition this afternoon. Are you sure you've got an appointment?"

"Yes, of course."

"Oh, maybe you've already been cast?" she ventured. "Could that be the case?"

"Yes, that's probably it." I nodded.

"Honey, are you one of the party girls?" She asked.

"Yes, that could be it," I lied.

"You're shooting today. Hurry over to the set. See wardrobe when you arrive.... You're late." I was excited, but worried I'd be spotted as an intruder.

Filming was at a sumptuous Colonial estate at 281 Blackland Road, owned by Saudi Arabian Prince Faisal M. Saud Al Kabir. It was two houses away from where my classmate, John O. Mitchell, lived. The home had been the setting for a Clark Gable and Carole Lombard photo shoot during the premiere of *Gone with the Wind*. Dad's mom, whom I called Nanny, was close with the author of the book, Pulitzer Prize-winner, Margaret Mitchell. Today, I have correspondence between them, as well as the original costume drawings and fabrics used in the 1939 film.

Confusion was in the air, as is often the case on movie sets. When everyone is in charge, no one is in charge. Disarray was good news for me. It meant there was less chance that my infiltration would be detected. I acted as if I belonged, which is a fundamental precept to "crashing."

I also discovered the movie in question was *They Went That-A-Way and That-A-Way,* starring Tim Conway.

The wardrobe mistress wore jeans and sunglasses. She was organizing dresses in a light brown trailer.

"I'm supposed to be the party girl," I announced.

"You're late," she replied.

She outfitted me in a yellow, floor-length, polyester dress, and then pinned the hem to suit my height. She applied makeup, sculpted my hair into a stiff bun, and pointed me to the top of the hill where there were dozens of females in gowns and males in military attire. The men were dressed as soldiers from different branches of the armed forces: army, navy, marines and air force. There were also cavalrymen, mounted on horseback.

I was paired with a handsome actor, who became my "date" in the movie and later evolved into my escort for the prom. Multiple times, the two of us, along with other actors, screamed and ran down a hill to where Tim Conway threw money in the air. A man with a script marched in my direction. I assumed the worst.

"Here, learn these three lines," he said and handed me a paper.

These were my only lines that day. I was a "featured extra." At lunch, I was asked to fill out paperwork so I could get paid. At six-thirty, it started to drizzle, and everyone was told they could leave. Although I was drenched and embarrassed by the style, fit and cheap fabric of my dress, I decided to introduce myself to Tim Conway. I assumed correctly that he was inside a trailer parked along the road. The door was open, but the metal screen was closed. I knocked at the metal.

"Who's there?" I yelled.

"Who's that?" a voice came back.

"Me. Is that you Mr. Conway?" I said.

"Yeah. Come on in," he replied.

I found him reclining on a built-in sofa, still wearing his clothes from the set. We chatted for ten minutes, and then I headed home. The detention I received a few days later was relatively painless. The actor who became my junior-senior escort may not have been as famous as Burt Reynolds, but he stirred up some serious whispers at the prom. The rebel in me was pleased to create controversy.

I would leave for the University of Florida three months later. But catastrophe seemed to be stalking me. It would come hammering at my door and force me back to Atlanta, the city I had been trying to escape for so long.

Music and Mental Health

With Sharon, Los Angeles 2014

Sharon and I roamed the massive complex of structures called The Getty Museum, located on a sprawling hill in the western part of Los Angeles. An outdoor patio provided a sweeping view of the city, but the powerful wind made it seem like I was standing on an airplane wing in a skydiver suit.

Sharon and I ventured from room to room, viewing hundreds of "collectibles." We agreed that Vincent Van Gogh's "Irises" with its curved silhouettes was the nicest piece.

"Let's check out the furniture," I said.

Sharon and I moved toward the "decorative arts" rooms on the Plaza level.

"You've been very active in your life," Sharon said. "Maybe that is why you are not fond of museums. It's a passive hobby."

"True," I replied. "I'd rather paint than look at artwork. I'd rather play sports than be a spectator."

"Do you like listening to music given your early interest in a singer?" Sharon asked.

"Tom has an amazing voice. There is no one better in the world, and I love his songs. But honestly, I've never thought of myself as a music person. I don't go to concerts, keep a playlist or even listen to songs on the radio. I barely know what an iPod is."

"You're in the minority," Sharon laughed.

She was right. According to a study on music and mental health, I was in the minority. There was a team of psychiatrists who—like art critics—hoped to impose their view on others. They invented a new malady, suggesting that folks who are lukewarm about music have "bad brains" and a form of mental illness called "specific musical anhedonia." Although music does not aid in survival or success, these "therapy gods" insinuated that I—and the one to five percent of the population who are similar to me—are mentally unstable because of our "take it or leave it" attitude about sound.

"There's nothing wrong with being in the minority," Sharon added.

"I doubt many psychiatrists would agree," I said. "They tend to value that which is 'normal' and 'normal' is, by definition, majority behavior. A world full of robots would do very well in psychological evaluations. They could be programmed to be identical. There would be no pesky deviants or radical thinkers in the mix."

Sharon laughed, "You don't have a very high opinion of psychiatrists."

"I may not be a Scientologist," I replied. "But I jump on the same couch as Tom Cruise."

Sharon chuckled, holding an atrium door open for me. "Psychiatrists are experts. They play a valuable role in society."

"What if I told you I've been in the presence of a *floating pink elephant,* and I realize this pink elephant loves me?"

"I would say you're a little cuckoo," she laughed. "You'd need one of those psychiatrists."

"Really?" I replied. "Well, what if it was God and not a pink elephant?... In other words, what if I said, 'I've been in the presence of *God,* and I realize he loves me?'"

"That's a very good point," Sharon replied. "You'd be like lots of people."

"It's all about conformity and what society thinks is acceptable," I said. "Let's get some lunch before we look at furniture."

We stumbled upon a café and ate: a burrito for Sharon and a vegetarian burger for me.

"Why don't we drop by your house later today? I've never seen it," Sharon suggested. "Ricky won't be finished with the convention until six."

"Okay," I replied. "How are your art classes coming? Did you bring your drawing book to L.A.?"

"No, I forgot," Sharon said. "But this trip is for me to learn about you. I want to know about the catastrophe that you said was coming. Let's read another chapter before we look at furniture."

Sharon pulled out the manuscript and flashed back to 1978.

F I V E

Curses and Castles

UDDY WAS BORN ON Friday the thirteenth. According to the Stress Management Center and Phobia Institute, it is estimated that 17 to 21 million people in the U.S. fear this day. It's not that there was a black cloud suspended over Buddy's head, but there was definitely a mottled one. It was the color of clumsiness. It is the color created when a can of paint is spilled mistakenly onto a canvas. Buddy was gifted when it came to breaking things or hurting himself. At eight, he tumbled off the kitchen counter onto his head. At 12, he got tangled in a bee nest and sustained multiple stings. At 14, he ran through a glass door. Each incident required an ambulance ride to an emergency room.

On the other hand, I was Miss Careful. I have always been overly conscientious when it comes to handling objects. It pains me to see things break. I cringe at car crashes in movies because I say to myself, "what a waste of manpower and materials." I think about the suffering in the world, the lack of resources and how money spent to build a new car could have gone to better use. My diligence is multiplied twentyfold when it comes to clothing; I treat my outfits as if they are my children, ever cognizant that one grape juice spill could prove fatal. My good clothes hang untouched unless I have a pretty darn good reason to wear them.

As for self-protection, I am obsessive and usually have a predetermined escape route from any situation. As a child, I established a route from my bedroom window onto the roof, and then into a tree, which could take me safely to the ground.

My most pronounced memories of Buddy include his fixation with Twinkies and comic books, and his tendency to peel the wrapper off a stick of butter and eat it as if it were a banana. When we were young and had both been punished and sent to our rooms, we delighted in trying to pull each other out into the hallway, tug-of-war style, with a rope. Our rooms were directly across from each other. When Buddy succeeded, he tattled, "Missy's out of her room." I did the same when I prevailed. Other rituals involved eating Cheerios one at a time and calling them "hiccup pills", and being bombarded by Buddy's favorite sendoff, "good riddance," whenever I left the house.

My brother's real name was Arthur Powell Laws, Jr. The nickname "Buddy"—which only our family used—was created to differentiate him from Dad. My brother's friends and schoolmates called him "Arthur."

Buddy was a frictionless sort. Before entering Lovett, he graduated junior high from the one-classroom school at Trinity Presbyterian Church, which was much less pricey than Lovett. On the other hand, I complained on my first day at Trinity. My parents immediately switched me to Lovett, where there was constant stimulation, such as fancy classrooms, sports fields, a theatrical stage, and art rooms. I remained there until graduation.

Buddy thought I was grandiose, although he never used that actual word. He'd caught me rehearsing for pretend television interviews in my room, something I did quite regularly as a child. At the time, I believed my dream to be a well-known TV star and interviewee stemmed from my mission to be a positive influence in the world and from a desire to be loved and noticed.

"Missy thinks she's gonna to be famous and important," I heard him tell his friends. "Not gonna happen."

Buddy was a brown-eyed, young version of actor Aidan Quinn. His droopy puppy dog eyes were deceiving. He was relatively lighthearted prior to Mom's attempted suicide, even though he had to endure the stress of Dad's daily competitions. He had not enlisted in a battle with Atlanta as I had. He was at peace with the notion of growing up in the South. But after Mom was carted off to the convalescent home, he changed. It was as if the mask of normalcy was removed: he was filled with worry, despair and animosity towards Dad. He had no support system. He did not recruit teachers to be parental figures, as I did; and he must have felt alone.

I'd finished high school, and I'd been studying at the University of Florida for three months when a priest came looking for me at my dorm. He delivered the news.

"Arthur is dead."

I was shocked and close to speechless, but managed to ask, "My father or my brother?"

Although I had fond feelings for my 16-year-old brother, I prayed Dad was not dead. It was frightening to think of fending for myself without parents.

"Your brother," the priest replied.

I flew back to Atlanta. When I entered the house, I found Dad in the kitchen. He spoke words which I will never forget. They are painfully seared into my flesh like a malignant wound.

"You were always the bad one," he said. "Buddy was the good one. You're the one who should have died, not him."

Dad collected classic Ford Mustangs. He had seven when Buddy died. He made me drive a white one; Buddy drove a red one. I use the word "made" because I complained constantly that they were dangerous, that they were difficult to keep on the road. They were featherweight and seemed to get a surge of air under the body, and then skip around like an incalculable breakdancer. My father's girlfriend, Linda, agreed. She possessed another of Dad's Mustangs for a time.

Linda was a 20-year-old interior designer who took up with Dad a few months after Mom's (attempted) suicide. This infuriated Buddy who already resented Dad; he blamed Dad for Mom's self-destructive actions. Plus, he felt that anyone who was not Mom was unsuitable. My reaction towards Dad and Linda's relationship was entirely different: I was apathetic. I was friendly with Linda, even though she was only four years my senior, but I agreed with my brother that she was more interested in Dad's Mustangs and fat wallet than him.

Linda was a rattlebrain and a disaster of a person. She crashed one of Dad's Mercedes. I was in the car; neither of us was hurt. She was also a jewelry and underwear thief, a not-so-flattering tidbit I learned during the summer of 1977 when she and Dad went on vacation. I was asked to care for her cat. My friend, Sherilyn, and I entered her apartment to find my emerald ring signaling me like a long-lost friend. It was resting on a living room table. Dad had given me this ring, and it had gone missing. I was enraged, so Sherilyn and I scoured her apartment to see if she had pilfered anything else. That is when we found my four pair of pink pansy panties in her bedroom dresser. I stole it all back, but later noticed the ring and panties had again disappeared. By this time Dad was no longer dating her, so I never reclaimed my property.

Buddy loved driving the red, convertible 1964 Mustang that crushed him to death. He never called it perilous. It was hip. On November 27, 1978, a typical rainy day in Atlanta, Buddy and his friends, Jeff Rogers and Preston Stevens, had just finished working out at the Lovett gym. They were heading home when one of the Mustang's tires veered off the curvy road. The tires went into an indentation in the dirt. Buddy was not an experienced driver and rather than stop, he tried to steer the vehicle back onto the road. The car hydroplaned and spun to the right. Buddy was hit by an oncoming car on the driver's side. The door crumpled like a piece of cardboard and pierced my brother's body.

Jeff was relatively unscathed in the back, and immediately evacuated the car. Preston was in the passenger seat and had been knocked unconscious, but woke soon after without major injuries. Two nurses, who had just gotten off work at Paces Ferry Hospital, stopped to help. An ambulance and fire truck appeared on the scene and gave Buddy CPR. He was temporarily revived, but died en route to the hospital. He had massive internal injuries.

Although I did not shed tears over Mom's (attempted) suicide, I wept at my brother's funeral, but only for short period. I didn't want to be weak, and I never saw Dad cry. I'd learned to be strong and plod forward, despite tribulations. There had been many tribulations. Buddy was a good kid, and I think we would be close if he were alive today, despite the competitions we were thrown into as children. Jeff told me that Buddy was struggling terribly with Mom's (attempted) suicide, and he was drinking alcohol to excess. Twenty years later (in the 1990s), Buddy's natural mother would find our family and tell me that my brother's birthfather had been an alcoholic, and had committed suicide. Buddy's funeral was on November 29, 1978 at Trinity Church. Many students from Lovett attended.

The summer before his death, Buddy had found his first girlfriend, Liz. She lived near Dad's vacation property in Lake Lanier, Georgia. They went to the movies and boated together. She was a precious bauble in Buddy's life. My brother seemed temporarily lifted from the torment of missing Mom and of hating Dad. To this day, Liz is convinced Buddy knew in advance he was going to die.

A week prior to the accident, he asked Liz, "What would you do if something happened to me?"

I also possess correspondence between Buddy and Liz written fifty-six days prior to Buddy's death that reveals a similar sentiment. There was concern that something might *happen* to Buddy. Unlike most kids, Buddy had never discussed aspirations or career plans with the family. His future was never explored. Perhaps he believed there was no future.

After Buddy's funeral, Dad sold the Mustangs and gave me the keys to a Mercedes.

"By the way, you won," he said.

"What?" I asked.

"You beat Buddy. He died at 16."

After the funeral, I visited Mom at the convalescent home. The place always had an odd stench, the smell of an invalid's last breath. It was as if death was hiding in the ventilation system, ready to snatch patients when the nurses were not looking.

"Missy. Nice to see you. You haven't been here for a few months," a receptionist named Jan greeted me.

"I go to college in Florida now. How's my mom?"

"About the same. We turn her over regularly so she doesn't get bed sores."

"Can I go in now?" I asked.

"Go right ahead," Jan said. "By the way, your father's never been here. Is he still living?"

"Yeah," I said and tiptoed into Mom's room.

I dreaded these visits. I showed up out of a sense of duty. Mom was as thin as kindling. She was frail and slurred her words so badly that I knew there was only a 50/50 chance that I'd be able to understand any particular sentence. It took great effort for her to speak, and I felt like I was torturing her when I made her repeat herself. On the other hand, I knew I was probably her only caller, especially now that Buddy was dead.

"Hi, Mom," I tried to act perky.

She got excited, just as she always did when I visited. "Mi...sss... yyyy."

"Looks like you're doing well," I smiled, but it was fake. She looked horrible.

I rambled on about my classes at the University of Florida and my friends in the dormitory because I figured it was better for her to listen rather than wrestle with the English language.

"Hoooww's Arrr... th... uuuurrr?" she asked.

"Dad?" I said in an upbeat way. "He's doing fine. You know how he's always working. He wishes he could be here with you. But, you know, it's not easy running a big company."

"Buuuuu... ddddyyy?"

"Buddy is doing just great," I lied.

I didn't know whether to tell her the truth. I was afraid that bad news would send her over an emotional cliff, making her vulnerable to the black forces in the air vent.

"Buddy's going to be starting college pretty soon," I continued the charade, even though Buddy would be nowhere near college age if he'd been alive. I figured Mom's mental deterioration would keep her from detecting the ruse. "So he may not be around as much; but he loves you, and he's always thinking about you."

I figured I would tell Mom about Buddy's death during the next visit or the one after that, or maybe the one after that.

I never told her.

I returned to the University of Florida. There were twenty girls on my floor in the dormitory. Some were doubled up in a ten-by-ten space; others had a room to themselves.

Two of these girls attempted suicide during my two-year stay. Although I barely knew her, Donna seemed as complicated and multi-layered as a Russian nesting doll, which conceals smaller and smaller wooden versions of itself. She was obese with a bowl-cut hairstyle and lived at the far end of the hall. She woke one morning, slit her wrists and was hauled off to a psychiatric ward. She never returned to campus. I knew Leeann much better because she stayed in the room next to mine. She was thin and nerdy with that "red-haired" look—freckles and ruddy skin—even though she had curly, dark brown hair that nuzzled the nape of her neck. For Leeann, heavy sighs signaled a bout of acute depression, followed by bizarre food binges. If her depression had not been so serious, her eating escapades, in which she zigzagged all over town from snack bar to sandwich shop, would have been a standup gag.

Hours before she slit her wrists in the bathroom, Leeann sunk into her dorm room bed and related that day's freakish food adventure. Five of us huddled around her.

"I was walking home from class," she was in low spirits. "I went to McDonalds first, had a shake, two burgers and a large fries. Then I kept walking and stopped at the Mexican place. Had three tacos and two enchiladas. Then I kept walking and got a slice of chocolate cake. Then kept walking and got three ice cream bars."

Leeann survived the sliced wrist ordeal and ended up at her parent's home in Ocala. I never saw her again.

Sarah Peck is the only dorm mate with whom I've kept in touch. Her doppelganger would be Diana, Princess of Wales. Sarah was clever with a sarcastic wit and qualified as my favorite person in Gainesville. She remains one of my dearest friends, although I see her about as much as I do the Pope. She is employed by the U.S. government and has worked at embassies around the world. She also helped to establish a new legal system in Afghanistan. If we win the war in the Middle East, it will be because America has a secret weapon called Sarah.

When I was eighteen, cereal was my comfort food. Sarah did not hide boxes from me like some female friends did (because I'd asked them to save me from myself), but we shared a different ritual. It involved Lucky Charms. We would diligently separate the pastel-colored marsh-mallows, which Sarah liked, from the sugary oats, which I preferred. Then we'd have a Gainesville-style "chow down." We were sort of like Jack Sprat and his wife.

I hoped to shed pounds and make Tom my new beau. Like every person with a pulse, Sarah knew of my interest in the singer and informed me that he would be performing at Sunrise Musical Theatre from February 26, 1979 until March 4, 1979. The venue was only a few blocks from her parents' home in Coral Springs, a suburb of Fort Lauderdale. Sarah and I planned to attend the concert together on March 2nd.

I invested in new clothes from Snooty Hooty: a turquoise, silk, spaghetti strap blouse, a black silk skirt, a sheer black jacket and a rhine-stone pair of Charles Jourdan shoes. I also purchased a chiffon and lace handkerchief dress as back-up garb.

The uppity sales clerk eyeballed me when I entered the store, "You're a size eight. Right?"

"No, I wear a size two," I frowned. "I'm not really fat… I just look fat."

Visiting Snooty Hooty was as depressing as being home with my family. There was always an insult barreling my way. But I was pleased with my sexy, new purchases and ready for phase two of my plan. I tele-phoned Sunrise Musical Theatre and spoke to one of the Medlevine brothers who managed the place. I pretended to be my own secretary and concocted an impressive resume for "Missy Laws." It included taking the crown in the Miss Georgia Universe Pageant. A year or two prior, I had participated in both this competition and the Miss National Teenager Pageant; however, I had not finished first in either.

"Missy Laws is the winner of the Miss Georgia Universe pageant," I stated on the phone. "She will be in Florida doing some Maybelline commercials. She would like two ringside seats at the Tom Jones concert and an introduction to Mr. Jones backstage."

"Yes, ma'am," Frenchie Medlevine replied.

Phase three involved reserving a room next to Tom's at the same hotel. I made a separate call to Sunrise Musical Theatre and asked a receptionist for the name of the finest hotel in the area; I figured Tom would stay there. She mentioned "Executive House" at 4300 Rock Island Road in Lauderhill.

"I am with the Tom Jones group," I told an Executive House reservations clerk on the phone. "We want another room. It needs to be located next to Mr. Jones' suite." She took my credit card number.

Shedding pounds was phase four and the most difficult aspect of preparation. When I wanted to lose weight, I sometimes followed the "Do Nothing Diet." It required doing nothing while eating. My attention had to be focused solely on food. I invented this regimen because I was a multitasker. I normally ate while watching television, writing, doing homework or talking on the phone. It was virtually impossible for me to sit at a table and concentrate only on a meal; I'd become anxious and restless. I had type-A personality and hated wasting time. Therefore, when adhering to the "Do Nothing Diet," I tended to abandon the meal after a few bites in favor of something more important and thankfully less caloric.

The other regimen that I followed—which I also invented—was called the "Diet of Distraction." It was based on two premises: forget about food and throw myself into an activity that would propel me away from my gluttonous routine. Vacationing, moving and rehearsing for a school play all qualified as activities that could divert my attention. In order to succeed, I could not weigh my food, mark my calories on a chart, or look up codes in a tiny book.

How many times does a dieter blurt out, "Oh no, I'm not allowed to have any more number threes (miniature puddings) today?" Then, all the person thinks about are miniature puddings. To calorie count or diary-keep is to think about food, and this is a no-no when someone is committed to the diet of distraction. Thinking about food leads to obsessing over food. Obsessing over food leads to temptation. Temptation leads to overeating and never escaping the dreaded see-saw.

I know a lot about see-saws as a former member of See-saws Anonymous. Throughout my teens, I could both lose weight and gain it back before a lemon torte defrosted. Then there were those nights of extreme exercise. I would leave my River North home at 10 p.m. and run to my high school and back in the dark—a 24-mile journey—carrying a rock for protection and hiding behind trees when I saw oncoming vehicles. As Miss Careful, I figured anyone could be a mass murderer. At nine the next morning, I'd hobble up my driveway, convinced I was suddenly skinny.

Another weight loss scheme involved running 200 laps in the house. I'd sprint through the dining area, down five steps to the living room, up two steps to the study (where the television blared), and up three more steps, which landed me back in the dining area. It took me an hour, enough time to complete two half-hour sitcoms. Across the street, the neighbors laughed at my image looping past the front window like a racecar.

Dad didn't appreciate my indoor exercise drill and regularly grumbled, "You're wearing out the rug."

With only two-and-a-half weeks until Tom's show, pounds would have to melt. Starvation would be required. I fasted for seventeen days, and I jogged around the dormitory parking lot each night after class. My energy level plummeted, but oddly enough, my test scores soared. There seemed to be a mental clarity that accompanied fasting. I got great pleasure from watching my dorm mates pig out; and I lived vicariously through their midnight pizzas and bags of Fritos.

Immediately upon arrival in Coral Springs, Sarah got ill and said she could not accompany me to the concert. This was potentially disastrous because I still needed to collect my tickets from the management office, and I figured beauty queens don't attend shows alone. I worried that the crux of my scheme—to get two front row seats—would be derailed. I was already scared that theatre manager, Frenchie Medlevine, would take a gander at me, furrow his brow and blurt out, "You're no pageant winner."

Sarah's parents lived in a stucco home in suburbia and were compassionate souls. They were raising their mentally impaired grandson, who would never mature beyond the age of a toddler. They treated me like a daughter and expressed concern about my plan to get a date with Tom. I was elated, of course, that they actually thought I could succeed since I had spent the past decade ridiculed and pummeled with predictions of failure.

Sarah's father spoke in a serious tone, "You don't know what you're getting yourself into."

"Yes, she does, Dad," Sarah laughed.

At Sunrise Musical Theatre, I retrieved my tickets, and thankfully no one questioned my beauty queen status or lack of bodyguard. My seats were perfect, front and center. I hoped a tenacious, self-starter—frankly, someone like me—would snag Sarah's empty chair to my left because it was embarrassing to be sitting alone. But that never happened.

The house orchestra trotted onto the stage to set up equipment, and I moved into the next phase of my plan: to finagle an invitation backstage. Although Frenchie Medlevine had agreed up front to introduce me to Tom Jones, I knew this would perpetuate the beauty queen charade, and I did not want to be dishonest with Tom. So from my ringside seat, I smiled at a trumpet player. He grinned back. I smiled again, and he edged over to me.

"Hope you'll come backstage and see me after the show."

I nodded that I would and thought to myself, one possible way to get backstage.

Warm-up act Freddie Roman stepped out next, but was ignored by ringsiders. His comedy routine seemed to be a cue for females to touch up their hair and makeup. I half-expected to see a "Cosmetics" sign in the same way a TV show stagehand might hold up "Applause" for a studio audience. Throughout the years, I have witnessed this "fix-up" ritual, regardless of where Tom is performing and who is telling jokes. The ringsider's goal is to ignore the comic. Laughing at jokes is a distraction. At Sunrise Musical Theatre that night, a lady to my right told me that even a mild grin could produce unflattering facial wrinkles and smear lipstick.

"You either want to look perfect or you don't," she said. "Don't be distracted by flotsam."

"Flotsam" was a bizarre word to describe an opening act, but I opted to become her pupil. I extracted a brush from my purse and touched up the ends of my cleavage-length curls.

When Freddie finished his set, there was a fifteen-minute intermission, during which time Tom's band members came onto the stage to ready themselves for the show. Lead guitarist and musical director, Mike Morgan, whom I had briefly met in the hallway at Caesar's Palace in my showgirl costume, was within shouting distance.

"Mike."

He turned. "Missy, nice to see you. Why don't you come backstage after the show?"

"I'd love to," I answered, surprised he remembered my name.

Two possible ways to get backstage.

Five minutes later, Tom burst into the spotlight wearing black pants and a tight white shirt. The audience roared. He was a hunk if there ever was one, and his voice was perfect. Charisma oozed from every pore as he sang "Do Ya Think I'm Sexy". Frankly, he did a much better job than

Rod Stewart. I played with my curls; my heart raced. When Tom saw me, he flashed a flirtatious smile and opened his eyes in a wide, punctuated way as he routinely does to express delight. He clearly remembered me, and showered me with attention throughout the show, just as he had in Vegas. Women around me seemed irritated.

"I'm not helping you anymore," Flotsam lady grumbled.

I felt like Cinderella on the night of the ball. She and I had some things in common. Like me, she had been adopted, surrounded by naysayers and had low self-esteem. Like me, she had been treated as an outcast. Like me, she had donned her finest threads with hope of meeting her prince charming. But, unlike me, she had a fairy godmother and access to magic dust. I knew all too well how Tom's seeming interest could lead to nothing more than a failed attempt to get backstage and another year-and-a-half wait for another concert.

The show ended, and audience members filed from the theatre. I was still at my seat when a man with a sleazy casting couch air about him sashayed onto the stage and squatted down in front of me.

"I'm John. You want to go backstage?"

"Sure," I said.

John directed me to the side-stage portal and past security. I followed. I was thrilled, but also hesitant because I was uncertain of our destination. Was he leading me to a band member or a roadie, or escorting me to his own private quarters? I prayed I was on my way to meet Tom.

It turned out John Moran was an advance man, who arranged publicity and appearance details for Tom. He led me into a room with a velvety couch and wet bar. There were ten Asian school children in uniforms standing next to a chaperone.

"Sit here," John motioned to the couch. "Tom will be out in a minute."

"Okay, I... I will." I stuttered due to my excitement.

The Asian kids seemed relaxed when Tom emerged from the back room. Each child shook his hand; they assembled for a group photo, and then departed. Tom wore a bright blue sweat suit and blue embroidered clogs. I giggled to myself because clogs seemed like such an odd thing for a guy to wear. They looked as though they had been handmade in Bali or on some exotic island.

I was both a nervous wreck and in a state of ecstasy when Tom settled next to me on the couch. We were alone in the room.

"Missy, how are you? Are you still dancing?"

I was amazed he remembered both my name and my avocation.

"Sometimes. I'm in college now."

As we chatted, two theater employees entered and set a table in the corner. Several other men, including "advance man" John, appeared.

"Have you had dinner yet?" Tom asked me.

In reality, I had not had breakfast, lunch or dinner for seventeen days and was hungrier than a post-hibernation hedgehog.

"Well, I don't want to be an imposition," I meekly replied.

"No, come on." Tom signaled me to the table.

March 1979 was prior to my conversion to vegetarianism, so I ate chicken and Tom had steak. Also at the table was "advance man" John, Lloyd Greenfield (Tom's manager who had hung up on me in Las Vegas), and Mark Woodward (Tom's son who was three years older than me). At the time, Mark worked as the show's lighting designer.

Tom told me that his jewelry had been stolen four days earlier from the private section of his dressing room.

"It's not the jewelry that bothers me," he said. "It can be replaced. What bothers me is that it had to be a friend who stole it. I just wonder who it was."

After dinner, the five of us chatted in the dressing room and watched the TV show, *Fantasy Island*. For the second performance of the evening,

Tom situated me on a stool, side-stage, so I had a clear view of him. He smiled at me periodically.

"We are going to a disco tonight if that's okay," he said directly after the second show.

"That sounds like fun," I replied.

I quickly realized that Tom was a chivalrous, old-fashioned Welshman. He had a manly and decisive way about him, but he was also gallant. He asked my opinion before making a decision that involved me. Because I was fairly demure at eighteen—rather than the more assertive woman I am today—I responded with "I leave it up to you." He seemed to be content with that response. I know I was content.

The five of us (Tom, Mark, Lloyd, John and I) rode in a black limousine to the nightclub, Studio 51. I assumed the name was patterned off Studio 54 in New York. Tom rested his hand gently on my knee during the journey. I felt like a princess. It was my first trip in a limo and a far cry from bumping along in a skittish, old Ford Mustang. Inside the discotheque, we found dark gray couches, upbeat music and an Egyptian ambiance. We were escorted through brown vinyl ropes to a VIP section, which was elevated a step above the rest of the room.

"Is that your wife?" an intoxicated man shouted at Tom from outside the VIP ropes.

"No," Tom said.

"Is that your woman?"

"Yes," Tom answered.

Oh my God, I thought. I'm his woman. I had no idea. I tried to act calm, but was inwardly ecstatic. The intoxicated man leaned closer to Tom and prattled on about something, in addition to accidentally dumping half of his drink onto the carpet. I could not make out his words, but I was impressed with the clear effort Tom made to be polite. In my head, I was making a comparison between Tom's maturity and kindness, and the juvenile and shameless actions of some Lovett boys who, for example, beat up and ridiculed younger kids. Lloyd and John eventually hustled the drunken man away from Tom.

The discothèque was dark, but I could faintly see my reflection in a bronze mirror adjacent to the couch. When I saw my face, I suddenly freaked out, but again this was happening inside my body. Tom and his entourage had no idea. My panic had to do with the fact that I would surely have to make a decision that night about whether or not to stay with Tom. I had never had sex and had no idea what I was going to do "when" he propositioned me. It was not a question of "if"; I was certain it was "when."

It was odd being in a state of not knowing because I had always been a person who knew my own mind. I simply was not the wishy-washy type. For better or worse, I was more like a bulldozer: strong-willed and focused. I shook my shoulders, shutting off the "freak out" alarm in my head. I did not want to think about my dilemma, and asked Tom if he wanted to dance.

"I get enough of that during the show," he smiled and held me tighter.

Throughout the evening, Tom either had his arm around me or his hand on my knee. I felt cared for and protected. There were bottles of Dom Perignon on the table before us, and everyone held a champagne glass, including me. I periodically put the drink up to my lips out of politeness and camaraderie. My glass was naturally full by the end of the evening since I didn't drink. Tom did not notice I'd never taken a sip or gotten a refill.

"Are you going to finish your champagne?" he asked. I shook my head, handed it to him, and he downed it.

At four a.m., we left the disco. The limo dropped us off at our final stop: Executive House. As we walked down a corridor, I thought about my hotel reservation and even predicted which room would have been mine. John and Lloyd said goodnight and departed. Mark, Tom, and I entered a suite and came upon a dimly-lit dining room, accented by two equidistant doors; they led to bedrooms. There was also a step-down living room directly ahead and a small kitchen off to the right. The color motif was brown and orange; there were geometrical lines and scattered patterns of beige flowers. The look was perfectly normal for the 1970s, but would appear cheesy today.

Tom and Mark seemed nervous, clearly about me. In an attempt to cover their apprehensiveness, they mumbled about minutia and nibbled on grapes from a fruit bowl. I marched into the pitch-black living room alone and sat on a couch, facing a blank wall. Panic hit me a second time. Oh my God, I thought. What am I going to do? I had absolutely no clue whether I was going to stay or go. Tom was an absolute doll and I adored him, but this was a big step in my life. I glanced at Tom and Mark, who glanced back at me. No one cracked a smile. We were all wrapped in a question mark.

Tom and Mark slowly separated, inching towards their prospective bedroom doors. I rose and walked towards Tom, frantically repeating inside my head, "What am I going to do? What am I going to do?" But the second I reached him, I suddenly knew the answer. It was miraculous, like I had a fairy godmother of my own. It was as if the answer had been there all along. I did not have an ounce of hesitancy, and my timing was perfect.

"Are you going to stay tonight?" Tom asked.

"Yes," I said.

If he had asked me five seconds earlier, I don't know what would have happened. Maybe I would have turned into a pumpkin.

We entered his bedroom, which consisted of chocolate brown, wall-to-wall carpeting and '70s style furniture. There was a queen-sized bed with an orange quilt, and white-and-gold swirl lamps on two brown, marble-looking plastic tables. There was a white love seat, a television, a dresser, glass ashtrays, modern art paintings and a portable humidifier that Tom used to keep his throat moist at night. All in all, it was a pretty typical hotel room. Tom's suitcase was on the floor. It looked like mine back at the dorm. It was a vintage piece, similar to what one might find in a Katharine Hepburn movie.

There was a knock at our door. Tom opened it to find Lloyd, who asked what we wanted for breakfast and requested Tom's jewelry. It was okay that Lloyd did not trust me; after all, I was a newcomer in Tom's life. After Lloyd collected the jewels and got our breakfast order for omelettes, he left.

Tom wrapped his arms around me; and that's when I revealed my sexual inexperience and that he would be my first love. He showed me that he was a sweetheart and always a gentleman.

"Are you sure you want to go through with this?" he asked.

"Yes," I smiled.

S H A R O N   V

A Tennis Court Named Fido

With Sharon, Los Angeles 2014

Sharon and I finished up at the museum and then drove to my island of bliss, my planet of beauty, my home. The purchase of this property eight years prior had been miraculous, beginning with a real estate trade—something almost impossible to achieve—and ending with the sale of multiple properties, including 200 acres of desert land that Charles and I owned. The transaction was so incredibly compli-cated that it seemed as if the universe had intervened; either that, or Charles and I were benefactors of colossal luck. We could never have afforded this mini tennis court estate without the unexpected trail of labyrinthine transactions.

At the time, I made most of my income as a real estate agent, first with a local firm, and later with Re/Max, Prudential, and then Berkshire Hathaway. I had access to new listings and felt compelled to inspect every tennis court property that came on the market, even when it was out of my price range. Most were. The brutal search lasted 20 years. Having a court in my backyard was my one financial dream, and I hoped to make it happen before I was too old to walk.

My gray stone house was country French with a picket fence, hardwood floors, walls of windows, two fireplaces and hotel-like amenities, including a pool, half basketball court, spa, and my beloved tennis court, which was a bona fide member of my family. I named it "Fido."

"Wow, your backyard is a resort," Sharon said.

"I don't need to travel. Living here is like being on vacation every day. And what do you see over there?" I pointed to an area next to the pool.

"A lawn and a hill?" Sharon replied.

"No. That's my grassy knoll."

"Your very own grassy knoll," Sharon laughed. "One of life's basic needs."

I introduced Sharon to my two white terriers and told her my other nine babies were anxious to meet her.

"What other nine babies?" she asked, looking horrified.

"My hens, of course."

We moved to a spacious side yard. The coop where "my girls" slept had been partly constructed from Prudential "Open House" signs after I ran out of wood and building materials. The hens were rescues: eight from the animal shelter and one from Craigslist. Excited to see visitors, they ran to us as fast as their little chicken feet could go. I sat on a brick step, and Mae Poulet, my orange Buff Orpington, climbed into my lap.

"This is Mae," I said. "She's the most famous member of our family. She was a write-in candidate for vice-president in the 2012 election. She was on the ticket with a dog from Tennessee. I felt it was time to put a chick in the White House, but unfortunately some human named Obama won."

"I remember you sent me an article about her," Sharon smiled. "She was in the news a lot."

"Yes. Chickens know how to cross the road—or the aisle—to bring everyone together, and studies show they are far more productive than politicians."

I gently placed Mae on the grass and took Sharon back into the house, where my computer was making a beeping sound. An email had just arrived; it referenced my "Tribs over Trolls" campaign, which aimed to drown out online negativity with positive sentiments. "Tribs" are short for tributes; they are compliments. Trolls are people who harass and stalk victims in cyberspace. The beeping meant a victim was making a plea for help. She needed tribs to come to her rescue. I typed ferociously.

"What you doing?" Sharon asked.

"Posting positive comments. I'm supporting a blogger who is being attacked by trolls. She's getting trashed for supporting women's rights."

"My goodness, why would anyone trash her for that?"

"There are people online—part of a sexist undercurrent—who try to frighten females away from their computers," I explained.

"Your advocacy work seems to be very time-consuming. You're always on call like a doctor or..."

"Realtor," I laughed. "I guess I'm used to being on call."

Sharon peered inside an armoire at my photo albums. She plucked out one and opened to a page with pictures of my brother and mom.

"You've been through a lot with Buddy's death and your adoptive mother's suicide, but you've handled it well."

I perched on the couch, and Sharon sat beside me.

"Maybe we should continue with your life story?" she pulled my memoir from her purse. "I'm dying to know what happened next with Tom."

She resumed the story about my date in Fort Lauderdale in March 1979.

S I X

Murder, Jealousy and a Witch Hunt

T HAD BEEN SEVERAL HOURS since Tom and I left Studio
51, and I felt like a spa tub: warm and tingly on the inside and
all bubbles on the outside. Too happy to get any rest, I kept bubbling in
and out of the bedroom where Tom slept. I kept my effervescence on a
hushed level. I was well-aware he had two shows the next evening, and
I didn't want to wake him. I would peel back the covers ever so slowly
and wiggle into or out of his embrace. Although he was a deep sleeper,
he periodically woke to guzzle water from an oversized container kept
by the bed. Then, he would settle back under the covers and wrap his
athletic arms around me. I devoted half of my time that night to cuddling with Tom, appreciating the perfect evening I had just enjoyed.
The other half was spent in the living room of the suite thinking about
life, my crazy diet, my insecurity about weight, and school.

My food science test was on Wednesday, and the prognosis looked
grim. I had not studied. Dr. Howard Appledorf's class involved breakneck
note-taking. I had a binder the size of *War and Peace* back at the dorm
with confusing scribbles about proteins, enzymes and monosaccharides.
I rejected outright Appledorf's mantra, "Junk food is healthy." It was
given its name for a reason.

Dr. Appledorf was a popular instructor at the University of Florida. His 750-seat class was always "sold out." Known as the "the junk food professor," he frequently appeared on national talk shows where he would peddle his controversial idea that a person can get all necessary nutrients from fast food. I did not subscribe to this view, but thoroughly appreciated his out-of-box thinking. Radical thinkers always got a gold star from me.

Dr. Appledorf was murdered in 1980, only two years after I completed his course.

According to a Gainesville, Florida police captain, Dr. Appledorf endured a slow and excruciatingly painful death by asphyxiation. His apartment looked like a scene from a slasher flick. There were partially-eaten meals positioned next to his corpse and blood-colored writing on the walls. "Murder" was scribbled beside its mirror image, "redrum" a term used in Stanley Kubrick's 1980 movie *The Shining*. Trash and food were strewn about.

Dr. Appledorf had been blindfolded and gagged with a necktie. His ankles had been secured with a belt, his head had been squeezed into a burlap bag, and his body had been wrapped in a sheepskin rug. Bed linens had been used to cut off the supply of air to his lungs. A cigarette had been extinguished on his flesh.

It turned out Dr. Appledorf was gay, and the three men involved with his murder were male prostitutes he had once commissioned for sex. They wanted revenge. Today, two of them sit in prison and the third resides in a mental institution.

I thought about Dr. Appledorf's unusual and flawed philosophy in Tom's suite that day. But I didn't know how flawed it was until many years later when I determined that one of the root causes for my chronic migraine headaches was MSG (monosodium glutamate), which is routinely injected into fast food.

I suffered from migraines before I was old enough to say the word, "eye ache," my childhood name for the excruciating pain that pulverized one side of my face eight days out of every month. While my Lovett school friends enjoyed recess between classes, I'd lie in my usual spot on the cot in the nurse's office.

While my classmates whizzed through standardized tests, I held a cold pack to my forehead and struggled to discern the fuzzy print. While my buddies hoofed it up at the spring dance, I lay in a hatchback of pain in the parking lot in my date's Saab. My life was a struggle until things took a turn for the worse.

I started getting migraines every day, and the one prescription medicine that had occasionally decreased pain no longer worked. I pushed through weeks, months, and years, experimenting with conventional medicines as well as alternative remedies, such as acupuncture, homeopathy, massage and hypnosis. Nothing helped.

I got closer to relief when I learned about MSG. The substance is now as common as blue jeans. It is 15 times more prevalent in food than it was in 1969; and some people, like me, are sensitive to it, despite the fact that the FDA says it is safe at normal levels for most people. Today, I not only avoid junk food, but I try to avoid restaurants and traditional grocers. I eat primarily organic products from health food stores and have been a vegetarian for 30 years. My incidence of migraine has decreased dramatically.

I was still with Tom in Fort Lauderdale, and I could feel a migraine coming; but I was unwilling to let pain ruin one of the best experiences of my life. Tom, Mark, John, comedian Freddie Roman and I were having breakfast in the dining area of the Executive House suite. The light fixtures above us were the shape of clouds, an appropriate image for my fantasy date. It was mid-afternoon. Tom's schedule reflected that of a musician. He normally went to sleep at eight a.m. and woke at four p.m.

for breakfast, although the previous night had been altered slightly due to an earlier than expected closing time at Studio 51.

"You have to fire him," Lloyd barreled into the suite, fuming about a band member.

"Don't talk about someone when he's not here to defend himself," Tom said. "We'll discuss it later."

Having grown up in Atlanta, which I sometimes called the "gossip hub of the South," I was impressed with the way Tom refused to participate in a stealth verbal attack on a comrade.

Tom was at the head of the table in a plush white robe given to him by a fan. It bore his initials. He was eating a grapefruit, and I could see his legs and bare feet from my spot at the table. I wore his thick, navy robe. He was even cuter at this time of day because he looked so natural, less like a star. Part of me wished he was just a guy with a normal job so I wouldn't have to compete with millions of women for his affection. I was certain I would have been attracted had I met him in Wales when he worked as a bricklayer or door-to-door salesman.

After breakfast, Tom and I sat on the living room couch alone and had an introspective conversation. We discussed many topics, including his childhood, during which he suffered a bout with tuberculosis when he was 12. We even talked briefly about his wife, Linda. I have always had warm feelings for her and am glad he has moved closer to her in recent years.

Tom gave me the impression his marriage was "open," or more accurately that he had a "don't ask, don't tell" relationship. In other words, his wife was aware that he was seeing other women and chose not to make an issue of it. This meant that he was technically not cheating because there was no deception. She had given him passive approval. His marriage was unconventional, but beyond this, I had no comment. I knew I would not personally want this type of relationship; but as a postmodern, I didn't condemn those who chose this lifestyle.

I snuggled up to Tom on the couch; and he massaged my neck and shoulders, something he did quite frequently. I knew my chance of marrying him someday was slim, but I was naïve and hopeful. I hated the idea of wasting time with a man who was "taken" since my dream was to be married before age 20, but Tom was someone with whom it was worth making an exception. Plus, walking away was not an option. He took my breath away. I *thought* I was in love with him at age nine, but I *knew* I was in love with him sometime between the backstage dinner and snuggling up beside him at Studio 51.

"Do you think we could get together again tonight?" I asked, afraid I might not get the answer I wanted.

"Sure," Tom replied. "We'll drop you off at your car when we go to the theater. You can go home and change and come back."

Sarah's father gave me a long look of disapproval when I entered his Coral Springs home. Sarah pounced over with glee, begging to hear details. Sarah's mother was somewhere in the middle. The family had been worried when I did not return from Tom's concert. At three a.m., Sarah's mom had driven to Sunrise to find my car was the only one in the parking lot. She thought the image of my lone car was amusing. Frankly, I did, too.

"I have to get ready," I revealed. "I'm going back."

Excited, Sarah and I dashed to her bedroom to pull out my backup dress, which I suddenly realized was more alluring than the first. It was a feminine, handkerchief-style garment, comprised of chiffon and lace. I also grabbed my prescription because the lack of sleep and possibly the MSG-enhanced food had brought on a dreaded migraine. The medicine—which did not always work—killed the headache in no time, and I felt perfect when it was time to become Cinderella again.

"Back so soon?" Tom said in his typically charming way when I entered his dressing room at Sunrise Musical Theatre. He gave me a kiss.

The first show had ended, dinner was wrapping up, and Tom retreated to the back room to prepare for the second performance. The usual members of the entourage were present. Comic Freddie Roman told a story about Tom's opposition to prejudice. It had a stirring effect on me.

"There was a woman in the dressing room," Freddie said. "She asked Tom how he could possibly work with three black women and a Jew. He kicked her out. Just like that."

The three, captivating African American ladies in the story—Cynthia Woodard, Fanita James and Jeannie King—were The Blossoms. They sung backup for Tom, and at one time, for Elvis. They had even recorded with the legendary Phil Spector, who sits behind bars on murder charges. Freddie—the teller of the tale—was the Jewish American. He is currently the Dean of the New York Friars Club. I counted them all as my friends by the second evening. They floated freely in and out of the dressing room as did others in the band. The fact that Tom's friends and acquaintances were hard-working musicians or plain-spoken Welsh or English countrymen, rather than celebrities, was something I found impressive. There were no pretenses with Tom; he was humble and authentic.

The side-stage stool was my perch for the second show. Afterward a drama unfolded. I was not a happy camper when "advance man" John dragged a woman into the dressing room and stuck her next to me on the couch. She was callous and not more than a four on a one-to-ten scale. I admit I was insecure having another woman in the dressing room, but I felt my evaluation of her was purely objective.

She tried to strike up a conversation with me. Across the room, I could see Tom, Lloyd and John huddled together, eyeing us, as if they were conducting a scientific experiment.

"I do hair, honey," the woman said. "And yours looks like a rat's nest. Split end city… I could fix it up if you come to my shop."

I couldn't believe a total stranger would be so rude, so I nodded, and then ignored her. She wore a tight, bumpy, polyester dress. This was before bumpy polyester was fashionable—that is, if it ever was.

Her name fit her absurdity: it was Frosty. I thought, Oh great. I'm sitting next to a snowman.

"I'm Frosty. Tom is soooo old, you know?" she whispered into my ear and flashed a hideous expression, contorting her mouth. "He must be 35. I could be chillaxin' at Pete and Lenny's right now."

Now she was not just insulting me. She was insulting Tom. How callous and unappreciative, especially considering she and I were the only two outsiders permitted in the dressing room that night. I almost wondered if she was "a plant," in other words, put there by John to gauge my reaction or see if I'd jump to Tom's defense. She seemed too outrageous to be real.

"So, don't you think he's kinda old?" Frosty repeated a little louder, and then blew a tiny bubble with her gum.

"Excuse me," I said and walked across the room to sit next to backup singer Cynthia. I was upset, insecure and close to tears.

"What's Frosty doing here?"

"What?' Cynthia asked.

"That woman. What's she doing here? She's not even worthy of being in the dressing room. She doesn't have a nice thing to say."

"There's nothing to worry about," Cynthia tried to comfort me.

"Maybe Tom wants to go out with her instead of me."

I looked up to see that Tom, Lloyd and John had shifted their gaze towards Cynthia and me. They were still in huddle formation.

"He's here with you, isn't he?" She tried to be soothing.

For ten minutes, Cynthia and I had girl talk, although it was really nothing more than Cynthia trying to raise my confidence level which was now flat on the floor.

"Are you ready to go, my love?" I was surprised to find Tom hovering over me with a smile on his face.

"Sure." I felt a little ridiculous for being so jealous over a guy with whom I'd had one date, but the feelings were clearly out of my control.

159

Tom and I got into the limo with the other members of the entourage and headed back to Studio 51. I never saw Frosty again. But, in case I do, my blow dryer will be turned to high, the "melt" setting.

Frosty was not the last woman who would upset me. With respect to boyfriends, jealousy was like a shadow. In certain circumstances, it just emerged. It was a vice that seemed to be embedded in my very being. Perhaps it was supposed to function as protective armor for my heart, but in reality it was a snapshot of uncertainty, fear of loss, and low self-esteem. Although Tom's affection had elevated my confidence considerably, I still did not believe I could capture the heart of a man without an assist from luck and perseverance.

The red-and-white, neon, Studio 51 sign was visible as Tom and I stepped from the limo. Hand in hand, we moved under the disco's awning where we came face to face with a guy dressed in John Travolta white. He looked like he had stepped out of *Saturday Night Fever*.

"Hello there," Travolta flirted with me.

Tom seemed bothered and pulled me close, out of the guy's sightline.

It is heavenly to have a total stranger flirt with you in front of someone you are trying to impress. I have often thought it would make sense to start a service called "Compliments–R-Us." For a fee, someone would appear on your date, praise your beauty in front of your boyfriend and leave. It could be a moneymaker.

Inside the club, I excused myself to go to the restroom and so did "advance man" John, who pulled me aside when we were away from Tom and the rest of the entourage.

"Stop looking at Tom like you're in love with him," John warned. "He knows it and so does everyone else."

John left me standing in the semi-darkness. I got the sense he had taken the initiative without consulting Tom, but I could not be sure. Maybe his reprimand was related to the Frosty incident. The entourage had no knowledge of her churlish remarks and may have deemed me "out of line." I prayed I was not teetering on the edge of "break-up" bluff.

Later, we returned to the suite at Executive House, where Lloyd dropped by for jewelry pickup. Tom said it was not necessary. Before going to sleep, Tom and I lay in bed, talking for hours. I specifically remember hearing about his interactions with Elvis.

"The King" had died a year and a half earlier from an overdose of prescription medicine. Tom was seriously opposed to drugs and had tried to veer him away from this unhealthy—and ultimately deadly—habit.

Tom held me in his arms and recounted fascinating tales about the two of them. At one point he said, "Elvis would keep me up all night into the morning when I had a show the next day. I'd keep saying I had to go, that I needed to rest my voice. But he wouldn't let me leave."

"He clearly admired you and cared about you as a friend," I said. "But it sounds like you were also a rival."

On the following day, Tom and I had breakfast in the suite with the entourage, and by late afternoon, Sarah and I were on our way back to the University of Florida, while Tom was headed to the next city on his U.S. tour. There had been no mention of a future rendezvous. I hoped I would see him again.

I was weeded out as a witch and burned at the stake, figuratively speaking, on the University of Florida campus upon return from my date with Tom. Of course, I was not really a witch, but according to Paige, the sorority president, I was just as heretical.

"Please don't leave," Heidi begged. Sorority mates ran up beside me as I made my final departure from the house.

"We want you to stay," Laura said. "Paige is a religious freak, and I'm gonna get her disbarred or impeached or whatever you call it."

"You need to fight this," Anita pressed. "It's illegal."

"Ya'll are really sweet," I said as I reached my car. "But it's no big deal. I don't want to fight. It's not worth the energy. I'll still see you at the dorm and around campus."

I had been excommunicated from sisterhood, a fitting outcome, I suppose, for a rebel who had rejected the unspoken rule: all members of the sorority had to be Christian and attend church. If I had been aware of this stipulation in the first place, I would never have joined. This sorority had seemed just like the others: a campus social club. But in reality, it had been twisted into "the personal dogma of Paige."

It had started on a Monday. The witch hunt was underway. Paige was looking to sniff out the culprit: namely, me. My crimes were two-fold. The first involved my not being Christian. Paige had made false assumptions about my faith. Although it was against Panhellenic rules to base membership on religious beliefs, she did not care. She had no intention of sharing dinner with a nonbeliever.

My second infraction involved polling girls in the sorority to find out if they were Christian or secretly renegades like me. I learned that a full one-third of the membership did not believe Jesus was the son of God, and thus did not fit the hidden requirement for sisterhood.

"I polled everyone and 34 percent don't believe in Jesus," I proudly produced the statistics.

Paige was enraged. I had burst her sorority bubble, sullied her carefully-crafted Christian zone. She grabbed the paper from my hand and crumpled it in an angry, but controlled way.

"This is a Christian organization. I'm sure you understand." Paige flashed a stern look and pointed at the door.

Although I had almost finished my first year as a pledge in which I endured mild practical jokes and carried out menial tasks for senior members of the sorority, I was not particularly bothered by the idea of severing the tie. I lived in the dorm and spent little time at the house anyway. My identity did not depend on the affiliation. Plus, I was ill-equipped to argue because I hated bickering and personal confrontation. If there were an Olympic gold for "conflict avoidance," it would have surely been mine.

I retreated to the dorm to study for Dr. Appledorf's food science exam and to ponder over the religious fervor that was the craze in those days.

Gainesville in 1979 was a town within a church, and I was the resident heathen.

SHARON VI

I am a Little Ball in a Boat

With Sharon, Los Angeles 2014

"I think Elvis was a little jealous of Tom," Sharon said. "That's what it sounds like to me."

"Elvis was one of the most successful people on earth," I replied. "But maybe successful people need to keep track of their competition. That's how they stay on top."

Sharon and I were still sitting on the couch in my family room. Behind us were bookcases filled to capacity with reading materials, mostly about philosophy. Next to us was a brick fireplace and on the ground were throw pillows, something my husband detested. He claimed they were like little daggers, puncturing his soul. He regularly hid them in closets. I would find them, pull them out and place them back on the floor so my soul could rejoice. Sometimes marriage is a tug-of-war.

"Did you ever feel guilty about going out with Tom since he was married?" Sharon asked.

"No. I wasn't unfaithful to anyone. I didn't have a boyfriend. I had no contract. Relationships are just contracts."

I told her that I felt the decision in "extra-marital" encounters rests not with the "other woman" or "other man," but rather with the person who is "involved." I was not seeing another guy. I'd made no promises and had no obligations. I viewed romantic relationships as contracts, no different from business agreements. For example, if a salesperson wins the new coffee contract with a company, she is not blamed for hurting the person who previously had the contract. There is no concern about distressing the person who faces cancellation.

"It seems illogical to have guilty feelings about hurting a spouse, yet none about hurting another coffee salesperson," I argued.

"You're so romantic," Sharon laughed.

"But some people will still condemn me because I'm female," I continued.

"What do you mean?"

I explained how moral outrage about "cheating" often reflects sexist attitudes. There is a widespread belief that the "other woman" is a homewrecker, while the man is blameless. The guy is generally let off the hook because "having affairs" is perceived as part of his nature.

"Males are seen as impulsive, while females are viewed as temptresses," I said. "By going out with Tom, I figured I'd be the target of this chauvinism… at least with some folks."

"I think you're right," Sharon's cell phone rang, and she announced, "It's Ricky."

I froze, hoping my dogs would stay quiet. Sometimes they reacted to sidewalk passers-by, closing garage doors or other sounds from the neighborhood. Barking would alert Ricky that Sharon was not waiting in the hotel room like an acquiescent wife; and if he became suspicious and inquisitive, I was certain Sharon would confess the whole 26-year truth. The rooster would be out of the hen house, so to speak. She'd do time for our "crime" and so would I because I might never see her again.

"Hi Ricky... Yes... That's good...," she said. "Yes... Sounds interesting... Will I see still you at six?... Okay. Bye."

Sharon hung up; her expression revealed that all was dandy in marriage land. It seems our relationship had once again escaped the nick of the razor blade.

"I know you'd confess if he asked any questions," I said.

"Probably so," Sharon admitted. "I don't know why Ricky gets jealous... You've been plagued by jealousy, too."

"Yes, but jealous moments have also played a positive role in my life," I said.

"How?"

I told her that they have helped me evaluate the free will versus determinism debate, which involves the basic question, "Do people have freedom of the will or are they pawns of the universe?"

"I know you have a doctorate in philosophy, but I don't. What exactly is determinism?" Sharon asked.

I told her it is cause and effect. It is like gravity. What goes up must come down. One thing hits another thing, which hits another thing, ad infinitum. I asked her to imagine the world as a boat on the ocean. It is filled with little balls. The balls roll, bang into each other, bounce, rush to side and then back to the center of the floorboard. These balls, which lack free will, are propelled by the forces of the boat (or of the world). Their roundness and composition also affect their movement. In a "determined" world, everything—people, animals, plants and inanimate objects—are just like these balls. They are propelled by cause and effect, by heredity and environment, by internal and outside factors.

"On the basis of *logic and science,* I knew I was on the side of determinism," I said. "But I figured I should also examine the issue on the basis of *experience*. Ordinary actions would give me no insight. I needed instances of extreme emotion."

I told Sharon that to test my feelings about my access to, or lack of, free will, I would try to put myself in the *exact* same mindset that I had during pivotal emotional moments, such as when I was jealous. I would quickly realize I took the *only* course possible at the time. I was wholly "determined" to do that which I did. I had no free will. I was a pawn of the universe.

I was a little ball in a boat.

I added, "This means that if an impartial observer had been furnished with complete information about me prior to the Frosty incident, she could have accurately predicted my detailed reaction, including the exact words I would utter to backup singer Cynthia."

"Most people believe in free will," Sharon said.

I agreed and told her that it is drummed into Americans as soon as they are old enough to be blamed. Free will is the basis for finding fault with others. It is the arguably most venerated component of western culture, western law and western values; and it is the foundation for Christianity, for Judaism, and for Islam.

"It is a destructive fiction," I said. "Plus, freewillists believe humans are unique in that they can make unhampered choices and resist the 'determined' forces of the universe. They are turned into mini-gods. Plants and most other living beings are not normally granted this omnipotence or aptitude for self-causation. Mere animals, it is often argued, are determined; and when they appear to act freely, it's just 'instinct.'"

"But it feels like people are free," she said.

"This 'grappling' with 'options' is illusion," I explained. "The internal tug-of-war is a verbalization or clarification of some of the causes bearing upon a person, some of which might be viewed as responsibilities, and others of which might be described as pleasures. There are scientific tests which prove people make so-called moral decisions before they are even conscious of the 'choices.'"

"I've never really thought about any of this," Sharon admitted.

"Determinism is my favorite subject," I said. "I have some philosophy texts on it. Would you like to take one with you?"

"Sure," she said.

I handed her a book from the shelf. "I guess I should get you back to the hotel."

"Let's continue the car ritual," she said.

"What car ritual?" I asked.

"I read your manuscript out loud while you drive."

Sharon and I headed to her hotel, while she read about my experiences as a student at the University of Florida.

The Resident Heathen

W HERE WAS EVERYONE? Something seemed "off." My University of Florida dorm appeared to be deserted. It reminded me of those science fiction movies which portray lifelessness after an atomic bomb or a radiation leak. I stopped, removed my noisy high heels, and tiptoed down the rest of the hall. Why take a chance, I thought. Perhaps there was a gunman around the next bend. As I neared the common room, I heard a cacophony of muffled sounds and whispers. I opened the door to find the room pitch black, except for suspicious shadows. I moved my hand along the wall until I found the switch, and I flipped on the lights.

"What are you doing?" Rena said in a hushed, but freaked out voice.

"Turn off the lights. Hurry," Dottie panicked.

Many of my dorm mates were present. Why were they sitting in the dark? Who were they hiding from? My gunman theory was starting to congeal. I quickly switched the lights back off.

"What's going on?" I whispered.

"We're hiding from the door-knockers. They'll be here any minute," a voice replied.

"Who are the door-knockers?" I asked, thinking this must be a violent gang like the Crips or Aryan Brotherhood.

169

"They're born-again Christians," Rena replied.

"You're hiding from Christians?" I was confused.

"Yes," she said. "Otherwise they won't leave us alone."

At the University of Florida, Christianity was as common as spiral notebooks. Proselytizing was all the rage. To this day, I don't know whether the frenzy was limited to Gainesville in the late 1970s, or whether there was a broader movement in the nation.

Door-knockers descended on my dorm once a week: Tuesday night at seven. They were "conversion experts" or zealots out to nab the spiritually indecisive. They loved getting their hooks into impressionable freshmen. They wanted disciples for their church. They made a quick pass down the hall—clamoring on every door—and if they found no one home, they left. Religion was their food. This hunger could be satisfied by drawing one student into a heated, biblical debate. Once they nabbed their Tuesday night victim, they left everyone else alone; at least, until the following week.

"I'll be the decoy. I don't mind," I said. "I like to debate religion."

"You'd do that for us?" Dottie was surprised.

"Sure," I replied. "It might be fun."

Thereafter, I became the sacrificial lamb, the debate monger, the go-to gal for controversy. I learned how to cut the door-knockers off at the pass and lead them to my dorm room, where I would embark upon Socratic Method. I got a thrill out of trapping them in inconsistencies. I knew the Bible inside and out; I had studied it extensively at Lovett.

Back in high school, Dr. Jim Curtis—the school's minister and religion instructor—even let me teach class during his half-hour absence one day, although he was familiar with my unapologetic unorthodoxy. I was the only student who got to "play teacher." I think he liked my outspokenness and passion for the subject.

Lovett had a mandatory chapel service, which I loathed because it was formal, conformist and Scripture-based. But the school also offered a weekly voluntary communion service, which was refreshingly casual and ethics-centered. Of the hundreds of people at the school, I was one of the ten or twenty people who regularly attended.

For a small subset of school peers, my lack of "faith" was a perpetual grievance. One of these girls physically assaulted me.

I left math class that day, carrying a tall stack of books. I was heading to the lunchroom. I veered past the water fountain and down a flight of steps, where two Bible-thumper bullies lie in wait. They stood on the staircase landing like spiders hoping to trap a moth. They were intimidating, and there was no one else in sight.

"She's descending into hell," one heckled me. "That's where Jesus-haters go."

Each time I took a step downward, she called out, "The first step of hell, the second step of hell…" and so forth. Then the two of them laughed.

When I reached the landing, the second girl mouthed, "You're evil", and kicked my ankle with her saddle shoe.

"Ouch," I said in shock. The pain, which was sharp, quickly turned into a throbbing sensation. I said nothing, figuring retaliation would make things worse.

The girls flashed smug scowls, and then stepped aside to let me pass. I continued on my way, checking periodically to make sure they were not in pursuit.

I was never again physically assaulted by Christians at school, but there was plenty of verbal backlash. The phrase I heard most often was "You're going to hell." These words sometimes came at me in the hallway outside my locker, sometimes on the bridge in front of the campus and sometimes at a schoolmate's home on the weekend. The devout girls at Lovett believed that my failure to accept Jesus as savior was a fatal flaw that doomed my soul to damnation, and they enjoyed mentioning it to me again and again like nagging windup dolls.

But the sanctimonious attitude displayed by a few Lovett students was nothing compared with that which I encountered at University of Florida. Not only did I face persistent door-knockers and random proselytizers on the college campus, but I was also paired with three different born-again Christian roommates during my two-year stay at the university. None were from the same sect; in other words, their beliefs differed greatly. The other girls in my dorm thought my bad luck was hilarious and quipped that either the school was playing a cruel joke or God was getting revenge on me for being the gadfly of Gainesville. Despite our religious differences, I got along with my roommates and used my close proximity to them as an opportunity to fine-tune my argument skills prior to debating outsiders.

My University of Florida dorm was not home base. I never felt completely at ease in the four-story, brick building with white, concrete-block walls and tile floors. Upon my arrival in Florida, I decided it was important to designate a location or anchor point where I could feel at home. I needed this spot because I was feeling alone and scared.

"Aren't you coming to Florida with me? To help me get settled into college?" I'd asked Dad in Atlanta a week prior to my move to Gainesville. I was 18 years old.

"Nope. You can do it yourself," he replied.

"I don't know. Maybe you should come with me. Just for a day or so."

"Nope. I'm not coming." He was stern and left the room.

Dad was into self-sufficiency. I was normally in agreement with him about "independence," but at that exact moment, I was full of anxiety and hesitancy. I was fearful about moving to another state where I didn't know a soul. Since Dad was not a person who changed his mind, I knew

I had to suck it up. Looking back, I'm glad he forced me to go it alone. It helped me to become an adult.

When I arrived at the University, my first order of business was to pinpoint this anchor point or what you might call "substitute parent." I needed a place where I could feel safe and comfortable, where I could exhale. The local Holiday Inn won this distinction. I had always liked hotels, and it was low-key compared with the Gainesville Hilton. In addition, I found the rooftop pool area aesthetically appealing with its perfectly situated round tables and uniform row of lounge chairs. It looked like a canvas of modern art.

From the wee age of eight, I treated hotels like theme parks. No sooner did my parents check us in, than I found my way to the secret passages and hallways that were reserved for staff. I felt compelled to inspect every door, room, and cupboard. By the time I was 17 and trying to get to Tom's backstage dressing room at Caesars Palace, I was a wizard at exploring off-limits areas.

I always hated real amusement parks with their hordes of people, commercialism, revolting junk food and never-ending concrete. When I was dragged there by my parents or peers, I would search out a square of grass, and ask to sit there quietly with the bugs until everyone was ready to leave. Hotels, on the other hand, provided a stream of never-ending escapades. I would raid the hotel kitchen in the middle of the night, just as I did at summer camp. Even when I was not hungry, it was fun creating an edible concoction in the semi-darkness while trying not to get caught.

Hotel conference rooms were a featured attraction, especially when they included a stage. I would sing and dance, imagining the white tablecloths and empty seats as adoring fans. When catering employees rambled into the room, as they sometimes did, they would chuckle and depart. No one ever scolded me.

As I got older, conference rooms served a wholly different purpose: they provided perfectly adequate sleeping quarters. I traversed the country quite a bit during my high school and college years, but often lacked funds to pay for accommodations along the route. Sometimes I would stop in a hotel parking lot late at night, curl up in the backseat and catch a cat nap, but more often I would drag my blanket and pillow past the front desk to a dark conference room where I would crawl under one of the long banquet tables and sleep. The tablecloths usually touched the ground, so entering employees did not detect my presence.

One time, I helped a penniless French guy snag free "conference room" accommodations at my "anchor point," the Holiday Inn.

I filed out of a University of Florida Theatre class one evening and heard, *"Je ne parle pas anglais. Ou puis-je le sommeil? Je n'ai pas d'argent."*

I turned to find a quirky, young man who resembled the Jack in the Box fast-food character. He had pale, rounded cheeks, blue eyes and a plastered smile on his face. His black cap was severely crumpled. It looked like it needed immediate medical attention.

I had studied French from first grade through high school, and understood that "Jack" spoke no English, needed a place to stay that night, and had no money. Helping him seemed like an exciting challenge because for the first time in my life, I had the opportunity to put those hundreds of French classes to work. Naturally, I led him to my home base: the Holiday Inn.

We found the banquet room in use by an insurance firm, so I took "Jack" to backup sleeping quarters: a broom closet on the second floor. I told him that he could stay there until the conference room was clear. As I headed down the hall towards my dorm, I turned for one last look:

"Jack" was grinning and waving appreciatively from among the cleaning products. It was a funny sight indeed.

Sleeping under banquet room tables or finagling past security to meet Tom is much like being a philosopher. All three require imagination and finding exceptions to rules or situations. In philosophy, a theory is presented, and a philosopher's job is to test it. If an exception can be found, the theory fails. A person who crashes a party or finagles herself into prohibited areas must also find that loophole or exception to the "tough security" rule. If one can be found, then security is not so tough after all. To this day, I am unsure about the chicken or egg relationship. I do not know whether philosophizing or sneaking through the back corridors of hotels came to me first. Both are arguably manifestations of the same skill.

Although the Gainesville Hilton failed to become my anchor point, it served another important purpose: it was my entertainment center. While my friends were boozing it up at campus parties, I was fine-dining at the Hilton.

I had, of course, been kicked out of my college sorority for irreligiosity, and unlike dorm friends, did not aspire to be a fraternity "little sister." I found the popular pastime of "partying hard" at frat houses unappealing. It had nothing to do with snobbery, but was about a preference for quietude. I did not drink or smoke pot; plus loud music, banal chit-chat, and crowded rooms were no fun, a recipe for a migraine and a waste of time.

The only university party I attended during my college years began with an "immaturity alert." This is like a Google alert, but for childish conduct. Four rowdy, fraternity boys urinated on the front lawn of the

Kappa Alpha (KA) house. They were pledges from a neighboring house on fraternity row and were completing a hazing ritual. "Brothers" watched from afar and laughed. I tried to ignore their dangling man parts as I stepped onto the front porch of KA with my dorm mate, Terri.

Inside, Confederate flags hung on the living room walls. The earliest documented use of a KA Confederate flag was at a University of Florida "Old South" event in 1942. In 1998 or 1999, the KA order banned the use of the flags nationwide, and in 2010 it outlawed the use of Confederate uniforms, which had been popular at formal events. To the dismay of a number of my southern friends, I had always aligned myself with "The North."

"Beer, girls?" A guy wearing a T-shirt and tie motioned to a keg.

"No, thanks," I said, but Terri accepted.

Although the scene was less raucous than the recently released *Animal House*, the "brothers" seemed determined to pattern themselves after the flick.

I felt like I was standing inside a Bose speaker. I didn't care whether it was live or whether it was Memorex, it was darned unbearable. Terri and I had to scream at each other just to communicate. I thought about how much I enjoyed having a quiet dinner with Tom and how he was light years more mature than these bozos. Suddenly, a guy accidentally sloshed beer onto my blouse.

"Want to go to my room?" he shouted in my ear.

I stared at him like he had a gargantuan mole on his face.

"No thanks, Sonny," I said with the flair of a feisty grandma.

I tended to treat most guys my own age like they were too young for me.

"I'll go," Terri clamored.

I looked at her as if she had a gargantuan mole on her face.

"I want to be a little sister, and this is probably the easiest way," she screamed as she headed off to a seedy room with "Sonny."

I left the party. Terri became a "little sister" the following year.

After the fraternity party, I went back to my dorm. A student handed me a phone message. It said, "Mark Woodward called. He'll call back tomorrow at six."

"Tom's son called?" I was enthusiastic, but nervous.

I had left a message for Mark about seeing Tom again, although it had only been three weeks since our first date in Fort Lauderdale. Was it too soon? Did John Moran's cautionary words mean I had crossed the line? Maybe Tom was no longer interested. I was unsure and insecure.

At six p.m. the next day, the telephone area in the common room looked like a scene from *Legally Blonde* when Elle Woods got accepted to Harvard. Dorm mates held their breaths and huddled around me for moral support. When Mark confirmed that I could see Tom in Atlanta a month later for my birthday, there was a loud squeal of "girl joy." My nineteenth birthday was sure to be an affair to remember.

The Gainesville Hilton was nothing like a fraternity party. It meant a suit and tie for males and evening finery for gals. It was classical music and candlelight. When I was bored with the dorm, I would sometimes venture to the Hilton to meet businessmen for platonic dinners. The conversation was better than most of what I could find in Gainesville. I was on a student budget, and it meant free gourmet food. It could lead to professional connections and more solid friendships than the ones forged while screaming over a deafening PA system.

I would linger at the bar until someone invited me to dine in the adjacent restaurant. It always happened. I never left hungry. This is how I met Tito Bacardi (one of the executives with Bacardi rum) and David Toma (an ex-police officer, who was the subject of the two 1970s TV shows: *Toma* and *Baretta*). I also met director Arthur Hiller and mentalist The Amazing Kreskin. This is how I came to dine with U.S. Ambassador Andrew Young and his friends, and how I came to meet singers Frank Zappa and Helen Reddy. I soon learned the Hilton was where visiting celebrities resided. I hung out with the Eagles off and on for two days, Jimmy Buffett and his pals for one, and actor Vincent Price for an hour when he was in town performing *Oscar Wilde.* These experiences were never sexual or romantic. They were an interesting diversion for a bored college girl who hated partying, college football games and school events. I was meeting accomplished people who might be good contacts. I was also exploring the secret to success, which I have since learned is perseverance.

I met Bob Hope and his manager, Mark Anthony, at the Gainesville Hilton one evening in 1979 and rescued them from a tense predicament on the following day. Bob was to perform at the Florida Stadium for the Gator Growl in front of tens of thousands of people as part of his nationwide college tour, but the car that was supposed to take him from the hotel to the venue did not arrive. I was there because the plan was for me to accompany them to the show and watch Bob's performance from side stage. (I'd gotten to know Bob and Mark Anthony on the prior day; and they'd invited me to hang out with them). It was only minutes prior to call time, and although Bob was calm, several members of his entourage were in panic mode about their lack of transportation.

"Where's your car?" Mark Anthony asked me.

At the time, I was driving my dad's Mazda RX7 because the Mercedes was in the shop. I knew I could only fit one person, plus a possible contortionist in the rear hatchback area.

"It's in the parking lot," I answered. "But it's small."

"Go get it. You're driving us."

Bob climbed into the passenger seat, and his conductor got into the hatchback area where he scrunched himself up like a slinky. At the stadium, I watched the show. Many of Bob's jokes confirmed the university's "party school" status.

Bob said to the crowd, "I love your graduation ceremonies. Instead of mortar boards, party hats, I met a student who's majoring in Mixed Drinks… This is the only school in America whose diplomas say RSVP."

The jokes made many in the crowd puff up with pride, but made me feel like I should pack up my stick-in-the-mud and transfer elsewhere. A year later, I would do just that. I'd begin study at the University of Nevada, Las Vegas.

S H A R O N   V I I

Is God a Mobster?

With Sharon, Los Angeles 2014

Sharon and I were on the 405 freeway, heading toward her hotel.

"You have some very strong opinions on Christianity," Sharon said.

"I had bad experiences with it in Atlanta and Florida," I replied. "I saw first-hand the damage it can do. When you are told every day that you are going to hell, you start to wonder about the source of the belief. Plus it was the most religious people who attacked me for supporting the Civil Rights Movement."

"It doesn't sound like they were really very Christian," Sharon said. "How did you feel about the requirement to study the subject in school?"

"I enjoyed it," I said. "But the more I read, the more I saw huge problems, the damage it had done, the damage it was doing to society. Because the Bible is held in high esteem, it is capable of huge destruction. It can produce a great deal of hatred and prejudice."

179

"What do you specifically see as the problem?"

I mentioned the Inquisition, as well as other tortures and killings that have been perpetrated in the name of religion. Then, I cited specific biblical passages, such as the Genesis passage in which God applauds Abel for giving him the gift of dead animals, but looks down on Cain's gift of vegetables.

"How could anyone have respect for a God like this?" I said. "He seems to prefer violence over nonviolence."

Then I mentioned the Abraham and Isaac story in which God orders Abraham to kill his own son.

"This turns God into the Godfather or a hit man," I said. "I think religion should inspire people to help others and to respect and value all life forms. The Bible promotes slavery and the notion that women and animals are inferior to male Homo sapiens. It also relies on moral absolutes; this perpetuates hatred, the judgment of others, and the notion of evil. Moral absolutes create an 'I'm okay, you're not okay' attitude."

"Plus, who came up with the ridiculous idea that God is male?" I added. "Give me a break. This reinforces male superiority in society."

"I've always found it interesting that you and I followed the same religious path," Sharon said. "Before we even met."

"I know," I replied. "It's really weird."

Sharon had been raised Christian, just like me. We both rejected the religion. Then she went to a Unitarian church for a time, as did I. Then she converted to Reform Judaism, again like me. But I was a cultural Jew rather than a scriptural Jew because obviously I had problems with the Torah.

"But we're not exactly the same any more, Sharon. Now, I'm a Jewish Jain. I've added the eastern religion of Jainism. It's centered around the notion of ahimsa."

"Ahimsa?"

"Yes, nonviolence to all living beings," I said.

180

"I have done a lot of reading and I think reincarnation may be real," Sharon said. "I also think there may be angels—people who have passed on—who can guide you."

"Really?" I said. "I rely a lot on hard evidence when formulating my views. But I believe things happen that humans cannot perceive. Science is not all-knowing or infallible. Our senses and technology will never be strong enough to access the whole truth of the universe."

"Have you run into anyone really religious who has nude pictures on the Internet?" Sharon asked.

"Of course," I said. "There was an 18-year-old, born-again Christian from a small town in Oklahoma. Her father was a preacher, and her mother taught Sunday school. She called me from the bus station in tears. She had been disowned by her family and driven out of town."

"Driven out of town?"

"Not physically, but emotionally. She had little money and wanted to know if there were any halfway houses for girls like her. I connected her with a nonprofit."

"Wow, that's a depressing story," Sharon said. "I think I'd rather hear about romance and your birthday date with Tom Jones."

She returned to my manuscript.

Jonesing and the Warthogs

HE PEACHTREE PLAZA HOTEL looked like a resplendent rocket bursting from the earth. It was Atlanta's tallest building until 1987. Inside this glass-clad, phallic symbol were sophisticated furnishings and affluent clientele; and at midnight on my nineteenth birthday in 1979, Tom and his entourage were in a suite waiting for me.

"You look like you're ready to get married," Tom quipped as I entered.

He gave me a kiss, and I dropped my bulky suitcase, which fell to the floor with a thud. His marriage comment referred to my white lace handkerchief dress, which I had purchased directly out of *Cosmopolitan* magazine. It was the only time I bought blindly without having an inkling as to fit. To my astonishment, it was perfect upon arrival.

"Do you think you packed enough? I'm only here for one night." Tom flashed a boyish smile and eyed my oversized bag which could have held three small children.

"I thought it was a night and a day," I joked back. "You mean I didn't need to pack those eighteen pairs of jeans?"

Freddie, Lloyd and Mark were present. An alluring chocolate cake and some plates were on a catering cart in the corner.

"We're celebrating your birthday and Lloyd's birthday," Tom said as he disappeared into his bedroom with my bag.

He reemerged five minutes later and snuggled up close to me on the couch. "My manager, Gordon Mills, is in town. He'll be dropping by tonight."

"Really? I've always wanted to meet him," I said.

"Why do you want to meet him?" Tom seemed bothered. "Are you interested in him instead of me?"

"Of course not." I looked at Tom as if *he* had packed eighteen pairs of jeans. "I'm only interested in meeting him *because* of you."

Tom was humble and often expressed bewilderment as to why women were attracted to him. "I cannot understand it" were his usual words. I was bewildered as to how he could be bewildered, and told him so.

The comment about Gordon was not my first glimpse of this side of Tom. At Sunrise Musical Theatre on our first date, Tom had been worried that I might be more attracted to Mark (since he was closer to my age) or to one of the band members. Had Tom known about my ten-year desire to date him and my shenanigans in Vegas—including confrontations with Alma, the security guard—he might have felt comforted. I thought it was a little too soon to reveal the hurdle-infested course I had maneuvered to meet him.

Tom's periodic jealous moments were endearing. They showed a vulnerability that seemed incongruent with his handsome looks, strength of character, confidence in his vocal abilities and adoration by millions. He didn't act like a sex symbol. He acted like the sweet guy next door.

Gordon Mills—who hung out with us in the suite for an hour that night and in the dressing room the next day—is often credited with discovering Tom, and had co-written the hit song, "It's Not Unusual." I only remember him as tall, thin and energetic. After this trip, I would never see him again. He would die from cancer six years later.

The evening's entertainment included a British comedy album. This was my first realization that British English is wholly different from U.S. English. The comic sounded like an overwrought chipmunk; it was a turntable of gibberish to my American ears. No matter how hard I tried, I could not understand a word, so I excused myself to go to the restroom, which was only accessible through Tom's bedroom.

Once in Tom's bedroom, I froze at the sight of my suitcase. It was empty. Tom had hung everything in the closet, including things that would normally go in a drawer. It was embarrassing because I didn't really have eighteen pairs of jeans. Instead I had a few outfits and a vast assortment of provocative lingerie. I was not sure whether the unpacking was a gentlemanly gesture or whether it was a self-defense measure—for example, confirmation that I didn't have illegal drugs or a paparazzi camera. If protecting himself was the reason, it was understandable since we had only met two months earlier, and this was the first time I had appeared with luggage.

"You look like an angel," he whispered when I returned to the couch.

"I see you unpacked my suitcase and hung *everything* in the closet," I smiled.

"You have some very nice things," he flirted. "I especially like that purple one."

"The corset? It's from Frederick's."

He nodded in a suggestive way. I buried my face in my hands.

Moments later, I was jolted from my embarrassment by a heavy rap at the door. In walked the person I least expected: my nemesis, Alma Davis. She did not wear her tight, brown, Caesars Palace security uniform, but instead a Sunday school type frock and black patent leather heels. She looked slightly less like an Amazon warrior, but still bore a halo of intimidation. I went through my own four stages of grief. I was shocked, confused, depressed, and revved up in full tattletale mode.

"*She's* the one who wanted your pants to rip," I told Tom, pointing my finger at the "I'm innocent" expression on her triangular face.

"It's okay," Tom whispered, letting me know he did not care what she had said.

What was she doing in Georgia? She didn't travel on the road. She only handled security for Tom in Las Vegas. Was she going to spill the beans about my backstage antics and how she caught me red-handed? I figured this was no picnic for Alma, either, because the last time she saw me I was a pesky outsider, and now Tom had his arm around me on the couch.

"I'm in town visiting friends and thought I'd drop by," Alma said and took a seat across from me.

Lloyd turned off the chipmunk. I remained quiet during her entire half-hour visit and was relieved when she said nothing to me or about me.

It was hours later. Tom and I were sitting on the bed in his room watching a National Geographic program. The chipmunk was finally hibernating, the birthday cake had been half-eaten, Alma had departed, and the entourage had retreated to their rooms.

"Don't you miss going outside?" I asked Tom.

"No," he said.

"I guess you don't need to go outside with shows like this," I quipped, motioning to a cheetah on television. He laughed.

All of the sudden, there was a knock at the door. It was Mark requesting champagne. Tom refused, but after a brief altercation, he relented, handing him a bottle from a cardboard box on the floor. I felt bad. It was no doubt difficult being a firm parent in my presence. It brought back memories of asking my mom and dad for something in front of guests, knowing "yes" was much more promising.

Mark turned his sneaky strategy on me, asking me in front of Tom if he could drive my car on the following day. He knew I had a white 450 SL Mercedes in the hotel parking garage. I agreed, passing him the key ring which bore a capital "A."

"Thanks, Albert," Mark said.

"It stands for Anne, my middle name," I said in an attempt to counter his smart aleck remark.

Mark strutted out of the room like William the Conqueror.

"Actually, it's my dad's car. His name is Arthur... but don't tell Mark," I confided in Tom.

Although it did not technically qualify as "outside," on the following afternoon, Tom and I strolled around the Omni International's enclosed mall checking out restaurants, arcades and the theatre. The entourage accompanied us. It was pleasant being somewhere other than the hotel, performance arena or Studio 51 discotheque. I have always considered it important to test how a "boyfriend" behaves in different situations and locales and around different types of people.

The Omni International, which is now called the CNN Center, had been purchased by Atlanta media mogul Ted Turner, who was a close friend of some of my Lovett friends. Hand in hand, we strolled: Tom in his button-down shirt, blue jeans and boots and me in my Calvin Klein denims and a long sleeve, purple gauze blouse with a draping neckline. Tom was always affectionate in public and seemed indifferent as to whether a tabloid photographer might be waiting behind the next door. He told me he was rarely noticed because people are not *looking* for him.

We stopped for lunch at a sidewalk café, where tables jutted into the pedestrian areas of the mall. Tom reacted in his usual way in an attempt to save me from myself. He whisked away the bread plate, positioning it outside my reach. He had come to accept it was his duty to fend off my doughy foe, the saboteur of my girlish waistline. He knew I wanted to lose weight and that I had a serious weakness for rolls. To this day, plain bread—without butter, jelly or garnish—remains on my top ten food list. My body may be 55 percent water (like other humans), but the rest surely consists of French baguettes and bagels.

After lunch, Tom and I headed over to the Omni Coliseum where Tom was performing that night. I watched Tom's performance from a portal near the dressing room, along with members of the entourage and promoter Cecil Corbett. When Tom mentioned "Frederick's" to the crowd as part of his repartee between songs, I knew it was because of my purple corset. It was not part of his normal act. It felt nice knowing I had made a contribution to his show, albeit an insignificant one.

Watching one's "boyfriend" perform is utterly electrifying. Plus, it makes a girl feel special knowing she will see him after the show. Each and every time I saw Tom on stage, I emitted "happiness molecules." These are conspicuous atoms of bliss that even a cyborg could detect. I was also an expert at spotting them and would sometimes play my own version of "Where's Waldo?" at concerts. I found that I could spot a performer's "Waldo" (spouse or date) with an astonishingly high success rate.

To the applause and cheers of 15,000, Tom burst off the stage at the end of his show and immediately locked his sexy self—sweat, adrenaline, drenched shirt and all—in a tight, little bathroom with me. It was romantic, sensual, exciting and perfect. My purple corset and I were in high spirits. We got lots of one-on-one attention.

Half an hour later, Tom and I emerged from the bathroom to find an Omni employee putting a tape recorder on a table. It held a cassette of a tune that a songwriter was trying to get to Tom.

"Great show," the employee said, slipping out of the dressing room.

"Thanks." Tom looked curious and pushed "play" on the recorder.

The sound of music filled the room. A minute later, the entourage, including Gordon Mills, entered.

"This is pretty good," Tom was pleased with the song.

Gordon abruptly pushed "stop," snatched the tape out of the recorder and tossed it into the trash.

"I already told this guy no." He was incensed.

Tom flashed an "oh well" shrug. Gordon clearly made the final decision about which tunes would be recorded.

I imagined a struggling songwriter in a battered Chevy in the Coliseum parking lot, hoping for his first break. Should he have gone directly to Tom (bypassing the proper channels) or would that have agitated Gordon more? Did he bribe the Omni employee to deliver the tape or was the employee a friend of his? Maybe the employee *was* the songwriter. Would he eventually "make it" and publicly tell his tale about trying to get this tune to Tom? These thoughts darted through my head as I watched Lloyd set up a television and VCR in front of the couch.

"A fan gave this to us. Come watch," Lloyd announced.

We looked at old footage from the *This is Tom Jones* show. It brought back memories of kissing the TV set as a child and being teased by Buddy.

"I was heavy back then," Tom said, looking at the screen, but the entourage affirmed how great he looked.

"I'm going to be performing in Macon, Georgia in two weeks," Tom held me close. "Would you like to get together again?"

"Sure," I smiled, realizing the trip would probably seal the fate of my Food Science exam.

Grades were not a priority at the University of Florida. Tom was.

I was at the Macon Hilton, and there was no sign of Tom. He was supposed to arrive at midnight, but his private plane was late.

Earlier, two women in crimson pantsuits, sporting stiff bleached white hair, entered the hotel lobby. One approached me.

"I'm Mrs. Warhaftig. What are you doing here? You're not supposed to be here," she confronted me.

"What do you mean I'm not supposed to be here?" I asked. "Do you work for the Hilton, Miss Warthog?"

"It's Warhaftig," she was annoyed. "I'm with the Tom Jones Fan Club. I'm going to ask you again. What are you doing here?"

She knew good and well we were both waiting for Tom. I was not sure why she was looking to pick a fight.

"I'm waiting for a friend,… Excuse me," I didn't like her demanding tone, so I moved towards a bellhop, who was the only other person in the lobby.

She rejoined her gal pal on the couch. They glared at me. I figured they were hoping for face time with Tom, and resented me because I was potentially a distraction.

Because the warthogs were unfriendly, I spent the next four hours talking to the bellhop who, at 75 years old, could not really hop anymore. He still worked because his Social Security check did not cover his monthly expenses. He was a congenial guy, but could in no way be called physically attractive.

Finally, at 3:55 a.m., a black limousine pulled up. Tom and his entourage climbed out and headed towards us. The warthogs eagerly greeted the singer, who said "hello," but did not stop to talk. He motioned for me to join the group. The warthogs scowled at me as the elevator doors snapped shut behind us.

Lloyd unlocked Tom's suite and to everyone's amazement, there were two more warthogs sitting on the living room couch. They looked like they had visited the same pantsuit emporium and hair spray academy as their friends downstairs.

"How would you like it if you came home, and I was sitting in your living room?" Lloyd barked. "We're on the road all the time, so this is our home. Get out."

He pointed at the door, and they lumbered away, speechless. In the midst of Lloyd's angry words, Tom had led me into the bedroom to escape the confrontation.

He kissed me, "You look thinner than I remember."

Oh no, I thought. He remembers me as fat.

"And you have bedroom eyes," he whispered and gave me another kiss.

That's better, I said to myself. I'm glad I don't have laundry room eyes or creepy basement eyes.

A few minutes later, Tom and I joined the entourage in the living room for refreshments and conversation.

"Hey, what car do you have this time?" Mark queried, as if he mostly liked me for my transportation.

"Red Mercedes 350 SL," I said. The vehicle naturally belonged to Dad.

"Can I borrow it tomorrow?" Mark was enthusiastic.

"I suppose so, but no wisecracks about the key chain."

When Tom's regular bedtime—eight a.m.—rolled around, the gang said "good night" and headed for their rooms. But, oddly, Freddie seemed to linger at Mark's bedroom door, which was on the other side of the living room.

"Is Freddie staying in Mark's room?" I asked Tom, confused.

"Why do you want to know?" Tom said. "Are you interested in Freddie? Would you rather be with him?"

"Of course not... Are you insane?... I think you're insane."

"Mark has to show him something, that's all," Tom smiled.

The next morning after breakfast, we headed downstairs to the limo, which was prepped to take us to the Macon Coliseum for the show.

"Good-bye, Missy, and have a nice time," said the 75-year-old bell-hop, who hobbled from his post to open the lobby door for us.

"I will. Bye, bye," I replied as I climbed into the limo.

Tom was bothered as he settled next to me in the backseat, "Who is that guy? Why is he talking to you? How do you know him?"

"I met him last night when I was waiting for you… for *four* hours."

Tom still seemed upset, so I shook my head in disbelief. "The man is 75 years old. He can barely walk."

Tom did not appear convinced. He somehow seemed to think I found the bellhop appealing.

"I love it when you're jealous," I said.

"I hate it when I'm jealous," he pouted playfully, and then placed his hand on my knee in his usual affectionate way.

Tom's security guard, Alma, loved belts.

She begged, "If you die first, you have to leave me all your belts."

Admittedly, I had a pretty spectacular collection. I agreed, but told her if she died first, she had to leave me her two Tom Jones road jackets. They had been made exclusively for the band and entourage.

Ironically, it was only two months after the Macon date. Alma had turned from adversary into one of my dearest friends. The friendship began when we ran into each other at Caesars Palace and laughed about our past skirmishes.

"I haven't had an enemy since high school… other than you," I said.

"I've never been your enemy. By the way, I love that belt," she replied.

Anyone who loves my belt can't be all bad, I thought to myself. Chitchat led to lunch at her suburban Las Vegas home, which led to a comedy-filled dinner in her dining room. There were only five of us, but two of the guests were comics George Wallace and Bobby Kelton, who made it a memorable night. George was in working mode; he would invent jokes, and then rapidly scribble them on a scrap of paper. The first course included salad and three puns. Dessert course included pumpkin pie, a tummy chuckle and a wisecrack.

Alma could be summed up in one word: encouragement. She had a supportive attitude about life; she was a "you can do it" girl. When other people told me to give up on a goal, Alma said, "Nah, you can do it." She was "all moral support, all the time."

Confronting put-downs and naysayers was old hat for me; I had learned how to turn negatives into a positive. "I'll show you and succeed" was my unspoken, standard response. This moved me forward, turning pessimistic comments from a friend, relative or stranger into a springboard for a new venture. But, I never had to "show" Alma; she was on my team. She was my ally.

One of Alma's best qualities—independence—led to her downfall.

In the early 1990s, a black blotch appeared on her left breast. It enlarged, but being a strong-willed and feisty woman, she believed she could handle it on her own. A doctor was not necessary. She did not tell me about the blemish until it was too late; she died of skin cancer in her fifties. I miss that triangular face and spunky spirit.

Her Tom Jones road jackets hang in my closet.

I was finishing up my tenure at the University of Florida and preparing for a move to Las Vegas. It was "sautéed mushrooms" Sunday. This was my treat, my gift to the other girls on my floor. I had gone to an all-you-can-eat salad bar near the university for lunch and asked the manager if I could take a grocery bag of white mushrooms back to the dorm. To my surprise, he gave me the green light. In the dormitory's common room, I cooked them in batches, spooned them onto a dozen plates and yelled, "Who wants fungus?"

Hallmates appeared, baffled. One ran down the corridor, bellowing, "Everybody, follow me to the 'shroom room."

A bunch of us were eating when the phone rang. It was for me.

"Hi, It's John," John Moran said. "Did you hear about the plane crash?"

"What?" I panicked. "What are you talking about? Is Tom all right?"

"He's fine. A plane went down somewhere near you… in the South. I just thought you might know about it."

"Why do you start a conversation like this? Are you trying to freak me out?"

"Small planes are dangerous," John said. "I worry about Tom. He's always flying."

"Great," I said sarcastically. "Now you've got me worried, too. As if I don't have enough problems with my 'fatty acids' test tomorrow."

"Are you still taking Food Science?" he did not wait for an answer. "I just called to tell you that next Friday is okay."

"So you called with good news and bad news," I replied. "I get to see Tom next Friday, but at some point, he will die in a fiery plane crash."

"Yep, that's about it," John laughed and hung up.

I concocted a surprise for that Friday night date: whipped cream. I instructed a hotel bellman to buy Reddi-Wip and bring it to the suite in a brown paper bag. He was told to be covert and discreet. I cracked open the living room door at the designated time to find this man in the hallway with a gritty expression.

"I've got it. And, rest assured, no one saw me," the bellman whispered.

"Thanks," I slipped him some cash.

He handed me the nondescript bag. I hid it behind my back and wandered into the bedroom to find Tom folding down the bedspread.

Without saying a word, I ambushed him with the can of cream, laughing. "Don't worry. There are only 15 calories per serving…"

Tom snatched the container from me and launched his own attack, pushing me onto the bed. He squirted the substance into my mouth.

Spending time with Tom was always a blast. Looking back, my life at the University of Florida was one date, followed by a wait of a few months for another date, followed by a wait of a few more months for another date; and so forth. I lived for these special moments. My heart was full. My soul was a velvet quilt. The in-between time or other aspects of my college experience—such as classes, Hilton dinners and hanging in the dorm with gal pals—felt like filler or disposable bubble wrap.

S H A R O N   V I I I

There's Conflict and There's Conflict

With Sharon, Los Angeles 2014

I dropped Sharon off at her hotel a full hour before Ricky was scheduled to return from the convention. I was relieved that we were early. We had escaped another spousal checkpoint, another hubby roadblock. The interstate called our relationship was thankfully still intact. We'd encountered no accidents or breakdowns in 26 years. At least not yet.

On the following morning, I picked up Sharon up for our "healthy day." The plan was to buy veggies at the local farmer's market, create gigantic salads, and take a hike in the hills.

During the drive to the farmer's market, Sharon asked me to expound on an issue that confused her.

"You launched a bold crusade against Hunter Moore," she said. "People call you a troll slayer, and you were voted one of the fiercest women in the world. Yet, you say that you shy away from conflict."

"True," I said. "I suppose there's conflict and there's *conflict*."

I explained that I will leave the room rather than engage in a battle of personal attacks or bickering. On the other hand, I love debates and will fight for ideas or change. Plus, I enjoy helping victims, especially when there's something important at stake.

"You seem to have focused on three victim groups in your life," Sharon said. "African Americans, animals, and women—especially when they are affected by online harassment."

"True," I replied.

"So I want to know what happened after you left Florida." Sharon plucked my memoir from her oversized bag. "Do you mind?"

"No, I don't mind."

Sharon resumed the story, delving into my bizarre and hilarious experiences in Nevada in 1980.

From Sex to Saks

MOVED TO LAS VEGAS, and I was still an ideological outlaw.
It did not seem to matter where I lived, my views were never
in sync with the majority. In Atlanta, I was a "radical liberal" and when
visiting Los Angeles, I was called a "radical conservative." Of course, my
views had not changed, only the geography had. In Las Vegas, I seemed
to fluctuate between being tagged a "stick in the mud" and a "goody-
goody." But, I didn't care because my value system was designed for me.
It did not exist to please others. I felt comfortable bucking the norm. In
Vegas, the norm was flagrant promiscuity.

"Hey, Miss Goody-Goody, hurry up," Lynn yelled.

I was parking the Mercedes, which Dad had been letting me drive off
and on since Buddy's death, on a residential Las Vegas street in front of a
nondescript, chocolate brown house. Lynn had already exited her Honda
and was tapping her foot on the pavement like an antsy schoolmarm.

"I don't know why I let you talk me into this," I yelled through my
open window.

"You don't want me to end up dead, do you?" she said. "You're getting paid so stop complaining."

"Why are you in a job where you could end up dead?" I slammed the car door.

Lynn was a "darn good hooker and a bit of a looker" in her words. She resembled actress Jamie Lee Curtis, except her hair was shoulder-length and as kinky as she was. If it could talk, the tabloids would be combing it for titillating tangles and steamy split ends. R. Couri Hay, a *National Enquirer* columnist who I had once met at a party, phoned me periodically hoping I'd be loose-lipped about some of my celebrity escapades, but I was never willing to sink ships. I figured Lynn's mouth-watering adventures were probably even more newsworthy.

Lynn lived downstairs at my apartment complex on East Rochelle Drive in Las Vegas, but I barely knew her. Actually, I didn't *barely* know her, but I *would* soon. She was my first prostitute acquaintance. I had moved into the complex two weeks earlier from Gainesville, Florida. I'd planned only to stay for the summer of 1980 until fall semester classes began at Loyola Marymount in Los Angeles. But, the Loyola roommate situation got discombobulated, so I applied to the University of Nevada (UNLV) instead.

When I first arrived in Vegas, I talked on the phone with a Caesars Palace executive who promised me public-relations-related employment; but when I got to his office, I learned he just wanted me to roll in the hay with high rollers. That was his idea of PR. I turned down the offer; and now I was earning fifty bucks so Lynn could roll in the hay. I was her bodyguard, although no doubt less fierce than anyone else in this specialized field. Lynn normally worked through casino bellhops, who provided a measure of safety. They were witness to her presence in a room. This situation was more precarious because Lynn was going to a strange house. That is why she needed me.

As an aficionado of the amoral universe, I had no judgments about Lynn's highly unusual occupation. If she wanted to do it, fine. But, for me, it would not be right. It did not comport with my value system, which meant sex had to be linked with love. Girlfriends—from Georgia, Florida, and now Nevada—considered me stodgy and old-fashioned, but I had always appreciated antiques. Some things, even ideas, were made better in the olden days.

We rang the doorbell and a bathrobe-clad man answered. He was decent-looking and could have snagged a date on his own. I figured he found the no-nonsense, all-business "relationship" with a call girl appealing.

"I'm Lynn."

"I'm Arnie. Who's this?" He pointed to me.

"She's a friend," Lynn replied. "She's just here to watch."

Flabbergasted, I furrowed my brow. "Watching" was not supposed to be part of the job description.

"This isn't *The Dating Game*," Bathrobe Arnie said. "I don't need a chaperone."

"I'll just sit here in the living room and read a magazine," I said.

"She's in training, huh." He winked. "Okay. Both of you come with me."

The master bedroom furnishings were decidedly discount, and the sangria-colored curtains were drawn. Bed sheets and blankets were in a chaotic swirl as if a speedboat had run over them. Already in the room were two naked specimens: a guy who looked like Norman Bates in *Psycho* and a woman who looked like Bette Davis in *Whatever Happened to Baby Jane*, except thinner. It turned out they had also been hired for their services.

"Hello, nice to meet you both," I stammered, feeling like I had dropped into a kooky nightmare. "I'd shake hands, but I have Howard Hughes Syndrome."

"Is that contagious?" Norman Bates asked, as if he'd been sequestered in a creepy roadside motel all his life.

I shook my head and made myself comfortable on a love seat near the door. I stacked up pillows on either side so no one else could sit.

"Want some popcorn, mom?" Bathrobe Arnie joked.

"No, I'm doing just fine," I replied as if I was an elderly matriarch.

Arnie removed his bathrobe, and Lynne undressed; and to my surprise, bisexual activity ensued. I tried to look at it as an educational experience. Few get to see *Debbie Does Dallas* in 3-D. Lynn never looked at me. I think she was embarrassed.

"You doing okay, mom?" Arnie shouted periodically.

I waved as if I was on a parade float. It was not only a sex session: the four of them were drinking alcohol, and snorting cocaine and Amyl Nitrate. Amyl Nitrate is designed to heighten sexual pleasure. This was the first time I had seen illegal drugs; and I prayed the police would not barge into the room and arrest me.

I thought about how this would be the last time I would help Lynn. I thought about how disgusting mechanical sex was between strangers. I thought about how prostitution could become legal if a camera was switched on, and everyone was paid as a porn actor. I even thought about the furniture I needed for my new apartment and what classes I wanted to take at UNLV. I thought about a lot of things during that strange hour and a half.

Finally it was over. Lynn and I headed for our cars.

"Wait till you've been in Vegas a whole month," Lynn said. "You'll change."

"I've already changed," I replied. "I'm not riding shotgun with you again."

Las Vegas in the 1980s was all about high rollers, call girls, complimentary food and shows, 1950s décor, being laid back and knowing everyone who worked on the strip. It was a small town in big city clothes.

"Come on, let's go to my room," a guy grabbed my arm at the Desert Inn three months after Bathrobe Arnie's orgy.

"I'm not a hooker," I politely said and reclaimed my bicep. Then I continued walking through the casino.

My real thoughts were not so polite: How dare you touch me and who do you think you are, Scumbag?

It incensed me every time I entered a casino because people immediately assumed I was a prostitute. I could see it on their faces, and I could occasionally hear it in their snide remarks. It was not just an assault on me. All young women seemed to evoke sexist stares and demeaning propositions. A week earlier, a man had offered me $15,000 to sleep with him. He had started at two hundred dollars and bid upward from there.

"For $15,000, I will get you a couple of girls much more beautiful than me," I finally countered.

"Nope," he replied.

"How about three?" I said.

He shook his head. I was willing to play pimp, but for no sum would I become a prostitute. That ended our negotiations.

Las Vegas was both vinegar and oil. The acerbic, vinegary side involved this negative perception of women. The assumption was that all females had a price; and they had no value beyond their bedroom skills. The oily side of Vegas, however, meant handsomely greased palms and the ability to slide into snazzy parties. Any remotely attractive female could glide through town like a princess, getting rich and enjoying VIP treatment. I had learned to brave bitter remarks and stares in order to hobnob with celebrities and CEOs backstage and at exclusive events. I was making potentially powerful connections and having fun. I felt like a mighty puppeteer. I had Las Vegas at the end of my string and could bring it to life on a whim.

I was still moving through the Desert Inn casino when a security officer stopped me.

"Could I see your ID?"

This was the first time this had happened. I rummaged through my purse and pulled out my Georgia driver's license, which I still used, despite having left the state two years prior. I knew I was underage and would get ousted.

"You're only 20. You have to be 21 to be here." The security officer led me to a non-gambling section of the hotel.

A week later I would get a fake ID, as Lynn had suggested. It would list me as 25 years old, but it would rest in my purse untouched. Never again would security question my age. Vegas was lax about these sorts of things in the 1980s.

Being booted was no big deal because I had only used the casino as a short cut to reach the front desk where I was meeting Dad. He had stopped in Vegas for a couple of days prior to a Salt Lake City business meeting. Dad always stayed at the Desert Inn when in town.

"Hi, Dad." He was reading a brochure at the front desk.

"Hi, Missy." He held out a piece of paper. "I thought I'd buy some furniture today for your apartment."

"Sure," I smiled, seeing the address for a nearby store.

Dad had always been generous with our family, and he liked assuming the role of big spender. Uncle Tween was critical, saying he tried to control people with his money. I partly agreed, but felt Tween was placing a negative spin on a decidedly positive trait. It is true Dad sometimes cared more about buying what *he* wanted rather than *I* wanted, such as when he gave me the motorcycle rather than the Tom Jones album for Christmas, but I appreciated that he was no Scrooge.

We left the Desert Inn and drove to a discount furniture outlet.

Dad pointed to cheap fiberboard pieces. "We'll take this table... And this dresser."

The sales lady eagerly jotted down every word. The experience was reminiscent of the televised Martin Bashir interview "Living with

Michael Jackson" in which Jackson reportedly spent over a million dollars in an exclusive store. Like Jackson, Dad was sashaying up and down aisles saying, "I'll take this and that." Unlike Jackson, Dad was selecting the pieces with the lowest price tags. I didn't care about cost, but I did care about the ugliness factor. Ugly was simply not going to work for me.

"I don't really think these things are very nice," I told Dad.

"They'll be fine."

"But, if I don't like them, then it is a waste of money," I said.

He ignored me.

"I like this table and chair set over here," I pointed to the furniture. "But, there is nothing else in the store I like."

"That set is $1,150," Dad said with alarm. "We're getting this set over here for $160."

"I don't want to waste money," I said. "I'd rather not get anything."

"What does all that come to?" Dad asked the sales clerk to tally the cost of the items he had selected.

"$1,135 plus tax," she said.

"We'll take it," he announced and went to the counter to pay.

I pulled the sales lady aside. "I don't want any of this stuff. I just want the table and chair set. Okay?"

"Okay, as long as you pay the extra fifteen dollars," she said. I agreed.

I was unsure whether she would, in the end, take instruction from me or my dad; but a few days later, I was delighted when my $1,150 table and chair set arrived. It remained a cherished part of my furniture family for 27 years, which brought the cost to a reasonable $42 per year or ten cents a day, a pretty good value for Dad's dollar.

Our afternoon furniture adventure was followed by a gourmet meal at the Delmonico Room, located on the south side of the Riviera Hotel. In those days, the Riviera was my favorite hangout. I knew most of the staff as well as the showroom entertainers.

"What's the price for the chicken radicchio salad without the chicken?" I asked the waiter.

"The price does not matter. Just order what you want, Missy," my dad chuckled.

This was our usual ritual. I would be handed a menu without prices, and I would ask the cost of various entries. Then, I would complain that the amounts were too high. Dad would claim to hate my thriftiness, although his actual reaction was laughter rather than anger or reprimand.

"It's fourteen dollars, ma'am," the waiter said.

"What is it *with* the chicken?" I was playing comparison shopper.

"Fourteen dollars," he replied.

"It's the same price with or without the chicken?" I was horrified.

"Yes, ma'am."

"That's ridiculous. I'll just have the green salad."

The waiter departed.

"I understand you're dating Tom Jones," Dad announced.

"How do you know that?"

"Ike told me," he replied.

"Ike?" I asked.

"He's the private investigator I hired. He's been watching you, Missy. I don't approve of Tom Jones. I've had him checked out, too."

"What?" I panicked. "What are you talking about?"

"I'm not at liberty to discuss it," he said. "It's mainly a precaution. Someone might kidnap you to get to me."

"Why would they do that?" I asked. "You think I'm the Lindbergh baby?"

The waiter arrived with the bread plate.

"Drop it, Missy," Dad offered me the basket. "Want a roll?"

It was clear he wouldn't offer further details. Once he put down his foot on a subject, he was intractable.

I figured his disclosure was calculated. It was meant to put me on edge, to control my behavior from afar. He wanted me under his thumb even when his thumb was 2,000 miles away.

Dad had packed some of my college registration materials that had been erroneously mailed to his Atlanta home. He suggested I accompany him to his hotel room after dinner to retrieve them from his suitcase.

"Excuse me, are you staying here?" a Desert Inn security guard blocked me from the guest elevator.

"No," I said. "I am just going to my father's room for a couple of minutes."

"Sorry. We don't allow that sort of thing here," he said, convinced I was selling sex.

"This is my dad."

"Yep, she's my daughter," Dad confirmed.

The guard reluctantly allowed us to pass, but clearly pegged us liars. Despite the delicious dinner, I now had a bitter aftertaste in my mouth. We had collided with the vinegary side of Vegas, and it had roundly embarrassed me in front of Dad.

The Frontier Hotel was built in 1942 and has the distinction of being the second resort to open on the Las Vegas Strip. Although it had been owned by an assortment of seedy characters and gangsters, Howard Hughes held the reins in 1980. Dealers wore black and white uniforms with bolo ties, and the place was never short on old geezers in bandanas and boots gambling away their pensions. The cowboy motif gave the place a primitive and dusty feel. The slot machines were ready for retirement, the carpet was geriatric, and the creaky, electronic, front doors had a John Wayne swagger. But, I did not mind. I preferred the relaxed vibe at less-upgraded resorts.

Elvis' first Las Vegas performance was at the hotel in 1956. Other entertainers included: Siegfried & Roy, Mel Tillis, Mickey Gilley, Johnny Lee and Wayne Newton. Many of the celebrity parties at the Frontier fit the Wild West theme. They were indeed wild.

It was two a.m. and a few weeks after the furniture-buying spree with Dad. I wore my red-fringe cowgirl shirt and Stetson hat as I crept through the "employee only" hallways and backstage areas at the Frontier. Tom's dressing room at Caesars Palace had not been the only target of my curiosity. I was like eyewitness news: I did behind-the-scenes investigations at virtually every hotel on The Strip. It was partly for fun, partly as a first step toward getting to know the showroom entertainers and partly to learn how Las Vegas operated. The layouts provided a wealth of data, which, in turn, gave me confidence and know-how that few visitors had.

A casino employee headed in my direction, but I dashed around a corner out of sight. I had never been ejected during these furtive missions. When seen, the trick was to avoid eye contact and to act like I knew what I was doing. However, it was preferable to avoid detection in the first place.

After the employee disappeared, I heard voices coming from a door emblazoned with a gold star, which I assumed to be singer Wayne Newton's dressing room since he was the headliner at the Frontier that week. I tentatively knocked. A black man nicknamed Bear cracked open the door and spoke in an almost hostile tone.

"What do you want?" He towered over me like an old oak.

I conjured up my most innocent-sounding Southern drawl, hoping he wouldn't pelt me with his acorns, "I just heard some voices and wondered what y'all are doing. May I join y'all?"

"We'll take a vote," he smirked and slammed the door in my face.

Bear was all bark and no bite. His legal name was Michael Forch. He looked like a linebacker and worked as Wayne's right-hand man and bodyguard. Like Lloyd Greenfield, he came off as harsh initially; but also like Lloyd, he was harmless. Bear had a smile like an incandescent light bulb. It could warm a room. He was a sweet man.

"Okay, you can come in," Bear opened the door.

Wayne Newton and a few of his friends and entourage members were huddled around the bar drinking wine. Wayne wore black slacks and a navy, velvet smoking jacket which bore his name. I was introduced to Larry Wright (nicknamed Emo), Joe Schenk, Slick, Peaches and Alan Campbell. I chatted with them for ten minutes.

"Why don't you go on up to my suite? There's already a party in progress," Wayne suggested. "I'll meet you there later."

I entered Wayne's suite to find two sofas full of snarling women. The room was as competitive as a Miss America pageant and as stressful as a search-and-rescue operation. I sat in an arm chair, envisioning steam emanating from the females like the dry ice used during Wayne's concert. I tried to strike up conversations, but the living mannequins had no interest in winning Miss Congeniality. As reality show contestants often say, they were "not there to make friends." They had only one goal: to win Wayne's attention for the evening.

Wayne had been estranged from his wife, Elaine, for some time and would divorce her in 1985. In a Sally Jesse Raphael interview a few years later, the entertainer would publicly admit he had been a womanizer.

The females in the suite were gorgeous, and I had empathy for their jealous and possessive feelings. But, they were mistaken about me. I was not a Frosty. I was not their rival. I was only there for the adventure. Although I thought Wayne was a handsome guy, he was not for me. Plus, I was dating Tom at the time.

"You look familiar," I said to a woman in a tube top.

"Yeah," Miss Tube Top said. "I saw you in Tom Jones' dressing room last week. I was with one of the bandmembers."

"Oh, that's right," my cerebral synapses kicked into gear. We struck up a conversation and exchanged phone numbers.

Wayne, Bear, and other members of the entourage breezed through the door.

The women grinned like pageant finalists, while Wayne walked around the room planting smooches on their lips. When he got to me, I turned my head, forcing him to kiss me on the cheek. I wanted him to know I was not vying for the sash and crown. Wayne was obviously an attractive, charismatic guy with a bunch of pretty admirers, but I was merely in the suite to schmooze and make friends.

Wayne retreated to the bar to talk to Bear. Moments later, I was invited to go to the back room to hang out with Wayne, probably because I was the only woman to reject the lip lock. I was certainly not more attractive than the others. In fact, I felt rather unpolished in my cowgirl attire. I declined, and another woman was selected for the all-important one-on-one.

Suddenly, Miss Tube Top walked up to Bear and whispered in his ear. They glared at me.

"I understand you were in Tom Jones' dressing room last week," Bear said. "If you're going to go see him, then don't bother to come see us."

Without missing a beat, I rose, "Fine. Goodbye."

I marched out the door. It barreled shut with a loud thud. Bear probably expected me to promise never to visit Tom again. He was also probably not serious about the ultimatum, but I had just met him and was unfamiliar with his sense of humor. Two days later, I received a phone call.

"Wayne wants you to come back," Bear said.

"Okay. I'll drop by tonight."

The social scene was much the same.

"You are always welcome in my dressing room," Wayne said warmly.

I hugged him and Bear. All was forgiven.

Wayne and his friends kindly allowed me to hang with them whenever I wished. The after-show get-togethers were typically star-studded. They gave me an amazing opportunity to hobnob with famous athletes, entertainers, CEOs, politicians and even royalty. I was able to gain a private audience with otherwise inaccessible people and ask them questions, such as "What is the secret to success?", and "What is the most important lesson you have learned in life?", and "What was your biggest mistake?" Wayne provided me with a fascinating opportunity that few young people get. Many of my former Atlanta and Florida friends confided that they were getting drunk, smoking pot or hanging out at noisy bars. They were doing the expected. I was doing the unexpected; and it thoroughly pleased my rebel nature.

I was also lucky because Wayne was in high demand and usually performing somewhere on The Strip: from the Frontier to the Sands, Desert Inn, Aladdin, Stardust or Tropicana. While living in Vegas, I probably spent one evening per week in his dressing room. I treasured Wayne's friendship and even became friends with a few of the persistent "crown seekers."

I needed money to survive in Las Vegas, plus my one-bedroom apartment was empty, except for the $1,150 table and chair set and a rented double bed. Since I was no longer escorting the escort Lynn, I applied to be a sales clerk at Saks. They were opening a new store in town. I knew nine-to-five jobs and I didn't mesh. There was no harmony. But I figured the position would not be so bad because I had requested very part-time status, and I had a stimulating life apart from work, attending classes, seeing Tom and hanging out with Wayne and other celebrities on The Strip.

Selling worthless rocks had been my only sales job prior to working at Saks Fifth Avenue. I remember it well. I was eight years old.

With my brick red Crayola, I colored a one-inch rock thoroughly on the back, front and sides, making it look like a ruby. My "Lake Burton" friend, Anne, created an "emerald" with a green-tinted crayon. Pretend gold was made with some paint from a kitchen cabinet, which Mom had bought to repair a chipped figurine Buddy had dropped.

Anne and I would sell our "precious jewels" door-to-door in the neighborhood surrounding my house in Atlanta. It cost five cents for a ruby, emerald, amethyst, or blue sapphire, and ten cents for a piece of gold. Most neighbors were receptive. We were enterprising third graders out peddling our wares. Sometimes we could make a full two dollars in an afternoon.

Now I was working at Saks. And I suddenly realized there was a major difference between selling clothing and peddling worthless rocks: I was never tempted to buy the rocks. I was spending my entire Saks paycheck on the store's merchandise. The more time I spent around garments, the more I would become fond of individual pieces. I would find myself sneaking a blouse to the wrong section of the store to hide it among dissimilar blouses, so no one would purchase it before I could. I clearly had a shopping disorder. Clothes were irresistible, and I knew I could not work in their presence. I quit the job after a few months.

I needed money to survive in Las Vegas. So, shortly thereafter, I invented a controversial, new profession and called it "chip chatting."

S H A R O N I X

The East vs. West on Emotion and Anger

With Sharon, Los Angeles 2014

"You had so many adventures in Vegas," Sharon said as we pulled into Calabasas.

The area was sun-soaked gardens, newer construction and smartly dressed pedestrians. I parked in a dirt lot down the street from the farmer's market.

"I almost forgot," Sharon added, reaching into her purse. "I bought you a book on vitamins. I have a copy myself at home and refer to it constantly."

"Thanks," I smiled, placing the book on the seat.

Sharon panicked. "Turn it over. Someone might steal it."

"You think someone will steal a book based on its title?" I laughed, but I obeyed her request, flipping it over, front cover down. I locked the car.

We moved down the sidewalk, observing the trees and roses in the center section of the roadway, horses in a barn off to the left and a cluster of businesses on the right: a wine gallery, an interior design shop and a Mexican restaurant. A politician in a business suit stood near a florist.

"I'm running for the local water board," he said, offering a flyer about his campaign.

"Sorry. I don't live in Calabasas," I said. He smiled and withdrew the paper.

At the market, Sharon and I wandered past fruit and vegetable stands, buying and sampling the goods. Also, for sale were plants, dried figs, free range eggs, cashews and other nuts, root vegetable chips, vegan desserts, pumpkin butter, balsamics, bamboo pillows, sugar-free jams, raw juice, fresh bread, cheeses, organic cotton clothing and popcorn.

"Is it me or does popcorn seem a little out of place?" I asked Sharon.

"That seems out of place, too," Sharon pointed to two women screaming at each other in the distance. They were in search of a scapegoat.

"It's your fault," one shouted.

The other yelled, "You're the one who told me to park there."

They were playing the blame game over a parking ticket, turning an otherwise peaceful marketplace into a place of turbulence.

"Has anyone ever called you unemotional?" I asked Sharon.

"Unemotional?"

"Yeah. You're such a practical person. I can't even imagine you crying," I said.

"Past boyfriends called me private," she replied. "I don't like my information out there. I don't do the Internet or Facebook."

"I'm not talking about privacy. I'm talking about emotions," I said.

"I remember crying over a breakup 40 years ago, before I was married," she said.

"The Hebrews lived in the Sinai desert for 40 years. Both you and the Hebrews have endured some serious drought," I laughed. "Did you ever see the movie, *Seven Psychopaths?*"

"No," Sharon replied.

I told her that there was a scene in which Myra is murdered and her husband Hans—played by Christopher Walken—just shrugs and says something to the effect of "oh well." Although he has showered her with attention and adored her every second of the movie, after he learns of her death, he does not get angry, cry or depict any emotion at all. I assume the screenwriter wanted to reinforce the "psychopath" label with this lack of affect.

"Yet, when I saw that scene, I realized that some people might call Hans enlightened."

I explained how this got me thinking about Eastern religion and culture as opposed to that which is "Western." Most people in the West would criticize a person if he didn't cry or get upset over a lost loved one. If he went to a funeral smiling, people might judge him to be a nutcase; or at best, insensitive. His response would not be deemed admirable or appropriate.

"That's true," Sharon replied.

"Yet in the Eastern world, there is a goal of detachment, overcoming desires in relation to people and things, escaping emotional suffering and anger," I said. "Within the Eastern framework, Hans might be called enlightened, a man who has reached nirvana, a person who has internalized the idea of acceptance. He cannot change her death so he immediately accepts it like a saint or a wandering ascetic might."

"This topic goes full circle back to your diatribe against western psychiatrists and their all-too-common diagnosis of mental illness," Sharon said.

"True," I laughed.

Sharon and I sat on a bench with our bags full of goodies, and we people-watched.

"I don't think I can wait any longer," she said.

"What do you mean?"

"I want to hear about chip chatting. It sounds so intriguing," she said. "Do you think I could continue?'

Sharon went back to reading about my over-the-top life in Las Vegas in my early twenties.

T E N

Chip Chatting

INVENTED CHIP CHATTING.

In my first year in Vegas, I made $100,000 in this strange field working two to three evenings per week for about five hours at a time. This sum would translate into a $290,000 salary in 2014, a hefty sum for a 20 year old, especially for forty to sixty hours of work per month. It was a heck of a lot more profitable than clerking at Saks and less hazardous than protecting Lynn from casino Casanovas.

I was surely not the only chip chatter in town; although, I have never met anyone else in this "industry." My methods did not require lying, stealing or sex. In fact, I was never alone with a stranger. I remained in the public areas of Vegas resorts at all times—the casino, bar, restaurant and showroom—which are crawling with cameras and security and are probably the safest places in the world. Although controversial, chip chatting was not illegal, and it did not conflict with my value system. It did, however, clash with Dad's and Tom's value systems. Both expressed distaste for my new "profession." But, I was impervious to their negativity. I felt self-sufficient for the first time in my life.

Fred Flintstone, who had given me $7,700 at Caesars Palace when I was 17, was the inspiration for this new profession. Vegas was the place to get rich. It was the place to be if I wanted to fill my empty apartment with fine furnishings. It was the place to be if I wanted to satisfy my clothing habit. It was the place to be if I wanted to be independent rather than rely upon Dad's almighty dollar.

My friend, Darla, wanted to get rich off Sin City, too; although her plan did not involve chip chatting. I met her at the Las Vegas Hilton where she worked. She had relocated from a small town near Dallas because she figured some things could never be bigger in Texas, namely her bank account. She had devised a detailed business plan, which included working as a craps dealer for three years, then moving back to the Lone Star State to open a business. Like so many young females in town, she saw Vegas as a vehicle to wealth rather than as a station wagon to family and kids. Darla wanted to get in and get out fast. It was a stopover, not a place to stay and grow old.

Darla's apartment building, which was a block from downtown Vegas, was as dreggy and unkempt as a landfill; but it was cheap. Two evenings worth of tips generally covered the rent. I hated visiting her because seedy places brought out the fugitive in me. I'd become overwhelmed with angst and get a craving to cut and run.

Darla and I also differed on the food front. She liked the all-you-can-eat buffets that were popular in the 1980s. The low cost helped her stash cash fast. I disliked them because the food tended to be unhealthful and there was too much of it, which provided a temptation to overeat. I preferred quiet, candlelit cafes with mouse-sized portions. Afterwards, I didn't feel like the circus fat lady. We had just finished eating at a buffet I called "Pork Out Palace" and were heading down the sidewalk towards Darla's landfill. Suddenly, we were stopped.

"Come inside, girls," Darla and I were motioned into a store-front where tourists sat facing a stage designed like a *Price Is Right* showcase. There were gifts and prizes from a shiny motorcycle and a state-of-the-art television set to placards describing fancy European vacations.

We agreed to watch the free show. A fast-talking con man performed amateur magic tricks, asking audience members for money with the promise of valuable prizes for the right guess. Person after person fell victim.

"It's easy to win," Con Man scammed a blonde tourist who handed him forty dollars.

He pulled out playing cards, "Now take a look and tell me where the face card is. You will win this diamond necklace."

He shuffled the deck in such a way as to make her think she knew the answer, and she pointed to a card.

"Sorry, you lose," he revealed a five of spades, pocketed her money and moved on to the next sucker, who happened to be me.

"Gimme twenty bucks each," Con Man confronted Darla and me. "Come on, come on. Don't be a drip. Have some fun. You can win."

It was utterly out of character for me to go along with a scheme like this, but I succumbed to the pressure and followed Darla's lead as she plucked cash from her jeans pocket. I handed over a twenty.

"You just have to watch the ball and tell me which cup it's under. Then you will each get a thousand dollar gift certificate."

Con Man quickly rearranged the balls and cups, "Okay, now guess. Where is that little ball?"

"It's under the right cup," Darla pointed.

"Nope, it's in the middle," he revealed it and pocketed our forty dollars faster than a cashier at a crowded Wal-Mart. Then, he moved on to the next patsy.

The show ended with no winners other than Con Man himself. The audience filed out of the room.

"I want my money back," I told Darla.

"Forget it," she headed for the door, as a fresh crop of tourists were being ushered into the store-front for the next "show."

I broke into tears and approached Con Man, "Please give me my twenty dollars back."

"Nope. You lost," he said callously and pivoted away from me.

I continued to cry. Patrons seated for the second show stared. Con Man quickly realized I could hurt profits.

"You have to leave now," he said forcefully.

"I want my twenty bucks back," I blubbered.

"What's the matter with her?" a nearby audience member questioned.

Thoroughly irritated, Con Man took a twenty dollar bill from his pocket and shoved it towards me like he was throwing a punch, "Now, get out of here, and don't come back."

"Thank you," I said. I found Darla waiting for me on the sidewalk.

Although my tears were authentic, looking back I have to wonder if part of me knew that by creating a spectacle, I could con Con Man. I was not trying to be sneaky, but maybe "getting around the rules" was so entrenched in my essence that I was like a plane on autopilot.

It felt good to have my money back, partly because I am a thrifty person; and partly because doing something so outwardly stupid is not okay with me. I already had an inferiority complex about intelligence and certainly didn't need be ridiculed by a two-bit hustler. Deep inside, I could hear Dad bragging, "First, my daughter outsmarted Magic Marvin, and then she outswindled a professional con man." In Dad's world, I had won. I would have another visit from Lady Luck an hour later when I would officially become a chip chatter.

According to Chinese superstition, the number four is cursed; it is nearly identical with the word "death." But that night, it represented a birth for me. I stumbled into my newfound career at the Four Queens. The casino signage looked like a gold-and-brown-striped beehive. I was at the bar alone because Darla had to pick up her sister from McCarren airport. She wanted me to wait at one of the casinos near her apartment so we could meet up later for a movie.

As I sipped orange juice, I noticed a preppy man in an argyle sweater, peering at me while pretending he wasn't. I was immediately suspicious.

After all, the argyle is not Nevada's state bird, and conservative clothes are not exactly sanctioned in Vegas. I sashayed up to this man, feeling sure he was Dad's detective pal.

"Ike. How are you?" I was overly gregarious and gushy. "You're looking awfully dapper today."

Ike's face turned the color of oatmeal, and his lips curled into a knot.

"Uh… How…did… did you know my name?" Ike's southern drawl tripped over itself.

"Dad told me to be on the lookout for you. To make sure you're behaving yourself."

"He did?" Ike had wide eyes.

"I'll be watching you, Ike."

I returned to my seat, leaving him ruffled and probably unsure whether to report the incident to my father who would take him off the case since his cover was blown. It would be his decision. I did not plan to leave Ike and his argyle without a job.

Moments later, a heavy-set man approached from the opposite direction and slid onto the stool next to me.

"Hi. My name is Ralph."

"I'm not a hooker," I whipped out the words.

This was my standard reply in an effort to dodge demeaning propositions, and it would remain part of my script as a chip chatter.

"I'm glad to hear that," he said, just as every man did; but I didn't believe him.   .

My cynical brain figured most men simply hoped to get me up to their room *for free*. They probably thought they could win my affection with a little charm and conversation. Of course, this was delusional thinking. First, I was a single-minded gal who was in love with Tom. Secondly, I was so utterly picky about men that even if I had not been dating anyone, the chance that I'd be interested was as slim as winning Con Man's *Price Is Right* showcase.

"Do you want to gamble?" Ralph asked.

I noticed Argyle Ike was gone.

"Sure," I shrugged and accompanied him into the casino.

Ralph bought $600 worth of green $25 chips, gave me half and sat next to me at a blackjack table. It pained me each time I lost a hand because I viewed it as money that could have gone to pay rent or buy a desperately needed couch. Of course, Ralph and I sometimes won, but our losses were far greater. When I got low on chips, Ralph simply replenished my stock.

A cocktail waitress brought Ralph a Bloody Mary, and he tipped her $100. He clearly had money to lose.

Then it happened. I secretly slipped a chip from the stack Ralph had given me into my purse, which was situated in my lap. No one noticed. A little later, I did it again. There were no cop cars or complaining pit bosses. Nothing happened. I had been sitting with Ralph for ten minutes and had $50. I was excited. This was the same amount I had earned in that revolting hour and a half with Bathrobe Arnie and Lynn. This was the same amount I had made after an exhausting afternoon on my feet at Saks. I excused myself from the table and left a message for Darla saying the movie was off.

Ralph turned out to be a pleasant enough fellow, and by the end of the gaming escapade I had secretly slid 19 of the chips that Ralph had gifted me into my purse for a grand total of $475. I never told Ralph that I was keeping some of my chips because I knew it would hurt his feelings. He'd know I cared more about cash than chatting with him.

"Well, I'd better be going. It's getting late," I announced.

"Want to go to my room?" Ralph asked.

"I told you I wasn't a hooker," I replied. "I have a very strict value system."

"That's right. I remember." He continued, "You want to meet me here tomorrow at four to gamble some more? I don't know anyone in Las Vegas. It's kind of lonely."

I agreed. In effect, Ralph had paid for my company. I was part entertainment; I had provided conversation. I was part therapist; I had listened to personal problems regarding his estranged son. And I was part ego boost because Ralph was not physically attractive, and I had provided him with a 20-year-old female to flaunt on his arm. It was a win for Ralph, who clearly had money to squander. It was a win for me, who needed the cash. And it was a win for the casino because they, like Con Man, got most of the loot.

Ralph was my first customer, but there would be many after him. As a chip chatter, I would plant myself in a casino bar. One night I might head to the Tropicana, Sahara, Circus Circus or Hilton. On another, I might hit a smaller resort, such as the Flamingo, Barbary Coast or Maxim. On rare occasions, I would venture downtown to the Golden Nugget or Union Plaza. It took no more than five minutes for a man to approach me; then I would deliver my famous first line, "I'm not a hooker." Surprisingly, no one ever bailed after this revelation.

Sometimes the man and I would have dinner in the hotel or go to a show. Usually we would gamble, but not always. I never asked for chips, but I always accepted if offered. There were a few evenings when I went home with nothing because the guy was only interested in food, shows and conversation. On many evenings, I went home with a thousand dollars. On rare occasions, my take was considerably lower or startlingly higher. There was no way to predict generosity and a man's predisposition towards gambling. Chip chatting was a game of chance.

Men usually invited me to their hotel room at the end of the night, and I would deliver my standard final line, "I told you I wasn't a hooker. I have a strict value system."

"That's good" and "I remember" were common responses. No one ever got angry. But, I had no fear because I had been honest up front and casinos were as safe as police departments. A scream would bring a posse of security guards within seconds.

"Why didn't you get any chips?" Darla whispered to me two months later in the restroom at the Riviera Hotel.

I opened my purse, and it looked like a Brink's money bag. It was chip heaven.

"Wow, you got all those?" she was astounded. "I didn't see you take even one, and I was watching closely."

Darla had been curious about my new career, so she had come to observe me in action as I gambled with a lad from Canada. I was relieved to learn that even with upfront knowledge, she could detect nothing. I had been paranoid all along, assuming dealers and casino managers were suspicious and ready to oust me. I didn't even want to think about the "eye in the sky" employees who lurked on the other side of one-way mirrors in the ceiling and who documented every move at the tables. Surely they were on to me. But, I would get caught only once during my chip chatting career: it would happen a year later at the Hilton in what would be a frightening and embarrassing experience.

The Las Vegas MGM looked like a baroque movie palace. I glanced at the emblem of the burgundy and gold lion on the wall and thought about the sociability and vulnerability of the species, which was in decline due to loss of habitat and conflict with humans. Like this great cat, I was in a social mood. I was meeting a friend for dinner, and then would spontaneously agree to dine with a bunch of strangers.

I was adjacent to the front desk when two, chic Middle Eastern males, who seemed highly Americanized, introduced themselves. I asked the tall one named Abdul what he did for a living.

"Uh. Well. I don't really work," he seemed secretive. "Now, tell me about yourself."

"I'm waiting for a dinner date," I said.

"That's too bad," Abdul confessed. "I was hoping you'd join us and some friends for dinner at Café Gigi. If you get through early, join us for dessert. We'll be in the gourmet dining room. Drop by at 10:30 if you can."

I didn't see this as a chip chatting or romance-related adventure. I simply thought these well-spoken fellows might be amusing. In my twenties, I was as outgoing as a tour guide. I was delighted to meet new people and always up for a wacky adventure.

"I wish life was as fun as a sitcom. It's so boring," a friend said to me years later.

Her words were jarring. Her spirit was obviously in disrepair. I explained how life should be much fuller than an episode of *Seinfeld* or *Friends*.

"The key involves having unusual experiences, taking chances, meeting interesting people, doing the unexpected and not yet imagined, experiencing different cultures and doing things for others, animals included."

I was proud of the fact that several gal pals called me "Lucille Ball with a mission." This meant I did zany things which provided for memorable moments, but I also had a deeper goal to improve the world somehow. Looking outside oneself in this way is vital for personal happiness.

"But, it's so scary," she added. "You crash celebrity events, for example. But, I don't want to get in trouble."

"It's not about gate-crashing. It's about life-crashing," I told my friend. "I look for the bold zones in life. I sometimes do outlandish things that are controversial or adventurous, but that could not really land me in trouble or put me in danger."

At 10:30 p.m., I entered a bold zone to find Abdul and his ten elegant friends at a table at the MGM Grand's Café Gigi. There were six men and five women. Like me, they were young baby boomers. The women were lookers and dressed in Parisian designs while the men wore tailored suits. Most were French nationals on vacation. I felt gawky in my off-the-rack department store frock, and assumed I'd been invited to round out a perfect dozen and balance the male-female ratio at the table.

"I'm glad you could make it," Abdul said. "Would you like some champagne?"

I said "yes," out of politeness, just as I always did with Tom; although I would not take a sip. My new, well-to-do friends were clearly stuck on gambling; and they enjoyed announcing their wins. Although I was a chip chatter, I never bet with my own money because this was not a bold zone; it was a danger zone. Gambling always led to victory for the casino.

"I just lost 175 before dinner," Abdul whispered to me. "It only took me 15 minutes."

"That's too bad," I figured 175 dollars was not too devastating, considering the guy was paying for a party of twelve at a pricey joint.

The after-dinner plan involved seeing Wayne Newton's midnight show.

"The limos are waiting," Abdul announced, so we headed out of the restaurant and through the hotel exit. Everyone but Abdul and me got sidetracked by blackjack.

"I'll have to go back in and drag everyone out here. You wait here," he said when he realized the others had been lost to attrition.

Abdul reentered the MGM, and the limo driver popped out of the vehicle. I had befriended this man a year earlier. His name was Beryl. He drove for various celebrities. I had a tendency to get to know chauffeurs because they had confidential information about upcoming VIP events, and they would give me details.

"What are you doing here, Beryl?" I gave him a hug.

"So you're dating the prince now?" he looked impressed.

"What are you talking about?"

"The man you're with. That's Prince Faisal of Saudi Arabia."

"What?" My jaw dropped. It was then that Abdul and his friends came out of the MGM and joined me at the car.

"I just lost 75 more," Abdul said.

"That's a shame," I replied even more nonchalantly than before because I figured a prince could afford to lose seventy-five dollars.

After Wayne's show, Abdul said to me, "We will be going out again tomorrow night. If you can join us, we'd be glad to have you."

The next evening was much the same, except I dressed more stylishly; and we dined at Chateau Vegas and attended Bill Cosby's show.

"I lost another 750 this afternoon," Abdul announced as we sipped on drinks in the showroom, waiting for the comedy to begin.

I was confused why a billionaire would be mentioning such trivial sums. One of Abdul's friends leaned in my direction and whispered.

"He's talking about 750 *thousand* dollars. You know that, right?"

"No, I didn't. I guess I don't need to feel guilty about ordering a second orange juice."

Dumping three-quarter-million dollars in an afternoon was not something even an "old money" Atlanta gal like me could comprehend. It was also not something my "new money" show biz friends could do without consequence. Abdul was in a different financial league. His family was like the MGM lion; they were king of the jungle.

Abdul never revealed his royal link. I was glad he did not try to impress me with his title or wealth. Plus, he and his friends treated me with respect. There were no sexual advances or propositions. After Bill Cosby's show, Abdul gave me his phone number in Houston, and we said goodbye. I never called or saw him again.

My time with the Prince was much better than a sitcom.

I found myself chip chatting at a Las Vegas Hilton blackjack table with 65-year-old Ohio businessman, Douglas. Darla was not working at the craps tables on that rainy evening.

"You got 21. Good job," I praised Douglas' perfect hand.

Three hours earlier, I'd met him at Benihana, which was tucked away in the southwest corner of the hotel. I was finishing my salad when Douglas approached me.

"I was born 65 years ago today," Douglas said. "Let me buy you a salad."

"I already have a salad."

"Let me pay for it, along with a main course," he replied. "Then we could do some gambling."

The chip chatting bell went off in my head. I had not intended to work that night; but like sleepy traders at the four a.m. session of the New York Stock Exchange, deal-making was deal-making. Financial opportunities could not always be lassoed to fit within my schedule. I wished I'd chip chatted with Prince Faisal a year earlier, and I didn't want to lose out on another potential windfall.

Salad led to vegetable tempura, which led to an after dinner-smoothie, which eventually led to the all-important blackjack table where I was dropping chips into my purse faster than the pelting rain. I had brought the wrong pocketbook. It was unfortunately not conducive to stealth behavior. There was no way to slip the loot inside the main pouch quietly and secretly, so everything had to be stuffed into an open exterior pocket for all to see. Plus, there was a thud every time I dropped a chip. It sounded like a collision of wooden hockey sticks.

Douglas may not have been a high roller or a whale, as they call people like Prince Faisal who wager a hundred thousand dollars or more per hour; but he was also not a guppy or goldfish. He was a good-sized trout, throwing down chips faster than a fish gobbles up zooplankton. I could barely keep up with him. The moment my pile got low, Douglas gifted me another enormous stack of black hundred dollar chips. Because my purse hung from my left shoulder, Douglas, who sat on my right, was probably the only person without a clear view of my newly acquired riches.

Then it happened. The dealer whispered to the pit boss, who whispered to the floor manager. They stared at me as if I was a pesky bottom-dweller, stockpiling chips that the casino could have instead been scooping into their coffers. I realized that I was in competition with them for Douglas' money, even though it was really my own money at that point. My loot was visible to them, as well as to the "eyes in the sky." I knew I had been caught. Would they reel me in? Would Hilton security haul me outside and ban me from the premises? Would I be arrested and go to jail?

I didn't think chip chatting could be illegal. First of all, Douglas had given me the chips, and a person has a right to do whatever she wants with a present. If he had given me candy, I could let friends eat it or even re-gift it. It would be my choice. I figured the same rules should apply to chip chatting. I remembered the numerous times my parents gave me lunch money, and I opted to starve so I could put the funds in a piggy bank.

Secondly, I knew chip chatting could not be illegal because it was something I had invented. There was no legal precedent. Even if anti-chip chatting legislation was someday passed, it would not apply to me. The U.S. Constitution does not permit retroactive law. Actions that were legal at the time cannot later be declared to have been criminal. Lastly, I figured chip chatting was an insignificant blip on a casino's radar. They had more important matters to deal with, such as card counters, hookers, embezzlers and thieves.

Despite these convincing arguments, I was scared. The casino floor manager moved in my direction, and I panicked.

"I need to go to the restroom," I blurted out much too loudly.

"Ok," Douglas said. "I'll be here."

I scampered away as fast as I could without drawing attention or spilling my stash. Periodically, I glanced back to confirm I was not being tailed. I locked myself in a ladies room stall and repositioned the chips in the main zipped portion of my purse. Although I did not make a tally, I knew this was one of the biggest wins of my career. I had two choices: I could desert Douglas and flee the Hilton as quickly as possible; or I could return to the blackjack table and take my chances. I didn't want to abandon my new friend without explanation because I thought he might feel rejected. Also, I believed I was within my legal rights to chip chat, so I sheepishly crept back to the table.

It was clear Douglas had been informed of my small fortune because he ignored me. Although he had gifted me the chips, he obviously did not like that I had kept some, rather than lose them all to the casino.

"I'm back," I said to the side of Douglas' face.

"He's not interested in gambling with you anymore," the dealer's eyes looked like harpoons. "You need to leave."

The pit boss stared at me from his wooden stand. I tried to compensate for my embarrassment and hopefully avoid punishment by becoming a charming adolescent.

"Ok, I understand. It was really nice meeting you." I said to Douglas in a little girl voice.

He did not respond, so I hurried away from the table toward the exit, hoping security would not throw a net over me. Normally, I would cash in my chips at the end of an evening, but not tonight.

The weather had also turned on its little girl charm. The pounding rain had lightened to a delightful sprinkle, and I sprinted to my car. Relieved, I drove towards my apartment, but relief became terror again when I turned onto Flamingo Avenue and heard the sound of a police siren. There was a flashing light in my rear view mirror. I had not been speeding, so assumed the worst as I pulled to the side of the road. Suddenly, a second squad car swerved in front of my vehicle, almost hitting it. I climbed out of my car in disbelief, wondering why the Hilton didn't just arrest me on the premises. The swerving cop seemed to be high on caffeine. He jumped from his black and white and pointed a gun at me. I slowly raised my arms. I was scared and confused.

"What did she do?" Caffeine inquired of the other officer.

"I was just wondering why she had a Georgia license plate," the other officer replied.

"Stupid rookie," Caffeine was furious, and for a moment I thought he was going to shoot his fellow cop.

Instead, he crammed his gun back into its holster like a cowboy, jumped in his car, and screeched away as if to make a statement. The sound was probably detectable all the way back at the Hilton. Caffeine surely acted against police department policy. It cannot be permissible to point a weapon at someone without provocation and without even knowing whether she had committed a crime.

"Well, have a nice evening," Rookie said. He seemed too flustered to resume the license plate inquiry.

I drove home and sorted my chips into thousand dollar piles on the living room carpet. They came to a hefty $7,100. For safety's sake, I planned to wait a week before cashing them in. I was wearing my gorgeous, $600, sapphire blue lounging gown from my favorite high-end boutique, Suzy Creamcheese. A knock at the door jolted me from Richie Rich land and back into "Hilton is after me" paranoia.

"Who is it?" I shouted, looking through the peephole.

I caught a glimpse of Lynn's right eyebrow and realized it was preposterous to think a hotel casino would follow me home.

"How's Bathrobe Arnie doing?" I joked, opening the door.

"How would I know?" Lynn wandered into my living room. "I just wondered if the landlord raised your rent. He raised mine."

"No," I replied.

"Wow, this place was empty last time I saw it," Lynn said. "How'd you buy all this fancy junk?"

"I'm doing pretty well in my new profession," I motioned to the thousand dollar piles on the carpet.

I explained the basics of chip chatting, but Lynn seemed irked. I got the impression prostitution was less profitable, despite far greater investment.

"This carved desk is fab," she ran her fingers over the grooves.

"If you want one, I can tell you where I got it."

"Nah," Lynn pointed to her nostrils. "My savings account's here. I've got a nose for money."

"You do drugs?" I asked.

"I'm Coke. You're Pepsi. I'm the real thing. You're an imitation. Chip chatting is bullshit," she flashed a self-important smile and left. I never saw her again.

A few days after the hairy ordeal at the Hilton, I saw Tom at Caesars Palace.

"You haven't grown at all," Tom joked, as I entered his dressing room.

Although Tom was always a riot, Jay Leno was the professional comedian at Caesars Palace that week. Jay was Tom's warm-up act, but he had not yet experienced the lift off of fame. He was just one of the unknown faces that graced the Vegas strip and hole-in-the-wall comedy clubs in New York. I met Jay for the first time during this trip and was convinced he would become a star.

While dating Tom, I had always observed the show from side stage or from his private booth or from the rear of the concert hall. But that night—before going backstage—my pal Angelo, still the Caesars Palace maitre d', thankfully stuck me in an empty front row seat.

230

"Which color do you like?" a freckled brunette asked for my opinion as Jay started his act onstage.

She revealed a nail file and two bottles of nail polish: magenta and a true red.

"You're doing your nails *now*?"

She nodded, and I chose magenta to match her scarf.

My nails looked like they'd been gnawed off by an angry bat. Although I never chewed on them, they were uneven with craggy edges. Since I would see Tom after the show, I figured an emergency manicure was in order.

"Can I use the red?" I whispered to Ms. Freckles and pointed to my hopeless claws.

She passed me the nail file and polish. Filing was easy, but when I got around to brushing on the red, it took great concentration not to spill the bottle, which was balancing on my knee. I tried to tune out Jay's jokes and had successfully completed my left hand and my right pinky when I just could not contain myself any longer. Jay was just too funny. He was performing a bit about a Hugh Hefner Playboy bunny and talking in a high-pitched voice. I *had* to laugh and knocked the bottle over onto my dress, making a bright red dot an inch above my knee.

A little later, when Tom bolted onto the stage, another goofy thing happened: his heel broke off. No one seemed to notice, except Tom and me. We chuckled to each other while he picked up the heel, still singing, and set it aside on the drum platform. It felt like our own private joke, and it reminded me how preferable it was to sit ringside.

After the show, I found Alma guarding the backstage.

"Hey, did you cut yourself?" Alma zeroed in on the bright, red dot on my dress.

"No, I was doing my nails during the show… Don't ask," I shook my head and headed into the dressing room.

The next morning when Tom was asleep, I ventured down to the Caesars Palace pool, found Lloyd reclining in a lounge chair and joined him. A group of fans were congregated at a nearby table; they had beach towels, cups and T-shirts bearing Tom's picture and name.

Jay Leno emerged from the hotel in swim trunks and slowly climbed into the pool. He scanned the area as if to say, "I'm here, everybody." No one noticed. He was just another anonymous hotel guest. He peered at Tom's fans, and his expression told me he would persevere, that he would push forward, perhaps until the masses had beach towels stamped with the image of his remarkable chin. He seemed downright pleased when I crouched down next to the pool.

"I enjoyed the show last night."

"Thanks," he beamed from waist-high water.

"I laughed so hard, I spilled my nail polish."

He looked baffled.

"You're going to be a huge star," I said and walked away.

I ran into Jay many years later when he was the host of *The Tonight Show*. My car had stalled in the parking lot at Whole Foods in Sherman Oaks, California. I was stranded, but Jay came to the rescue. He did not recognize me, and I did not mention that we had met years earlier. He had just finished shopping and gave me a lift back to my house, reinforcing his widely publicized reputation for helping strangers in need.

I saw Tom periodically for three years in various locations throughout the country: from Los Angeles to Massachusetts, from Indiana to North Carolina. To his credit, he was always honest with me about our relationship. He never said he loved me or made me think there would be commitment at the end of the trail. He may have known I was in love with him from day one, but he surely knew by the second night in Fort Lauderdale when John Moran gave me the stern warning to temper my affection. I never followed John's advice because I couldn't.

Although Tom did not fully reciprocate, I never stopped wanting the relationship to become something serious and permanent. I was young, naïve and hopeful. I was sexually faithful to him, despite the fact that I knew I was one of many. It pained me to know, but I knew.

"What would you do if you got pregnant?" John asked me backstage one night at Caesars Palace.

"I wouldn't have an abortion. I don't believe in it for me," I said. He was silent.

On the following day, my heart was completely broken when John told me that Tom could not see me anymore. The bad news was delivered near the Caesars Palace registration desk where I coincidentally ran into John.

"Oh, Missy. I need to talk to you," John pulled me aside. "About our conversation last night… Tom can't see you anymore. Sorry."

"What?" I was in disbelief.

"Tom can't see you anymore."

"What are you talking about? I need to speak to him," I said.

"You can't," John said. "I can't allow that."

"What do you mean? I need to speak to him."

"I can't allow you backstage and don't try calling the suite. Sorry," John walked coldly toward the guest elevators.

"Does Tom know you're having this conversation with me?" I yelled. He did not answer, and I broke into tears.

I had to assume John was not acting unilaterally, but I also knew the people in Tom's inner circle had a great deal of power. Maybe Tom was no longer interested or maybe he felt I was too much of a risk. I ducked into a vacant conference room to suffer in private. Feeling unsettled and distraught, I did something that utterly horrified me: I broke a bunch of drinking glasses that had been resting on a cart. Seeing objects destroyed had always distressed me, so it was all the more shocking to find *myself* hurling cheap glasses against the wall. I must have smashed ten of them.

However, the upset provided an insightful moment. It again confirmed my lack of free will. I tried to imagine doing things differently with Tom, but realized I had acted the only way I could. When I put myself in the same frame of mind, it was obvious I had no access to choice. I *had to* tell John that abortion was not right for me. I *had to* fling the glasses against the wall. I was a churning barrel of emotions, a product of cause and effect. It was comforting to know I was only reacting to stimuli, and at one with the tossing, tumbling forces of the universe.

It was also comforting to realize that *now* is not necessarily *next week*. Tomorrow is not necessarily next year. "Tom can't see you anymore" isn't an immutable truth about life. It is not like gravity or geometry; there is often wiggle room in a heart. Minds can change. Passion can reenter a room. Men named John can even get fired.

I knew romantic reunion was a long shot. But, then again, long shots and I were old and illustrious pals.

S H A R O N   X

Politics and the Peeping Tom in Prison

With Sharon, Los Angeles 2014

Sharon and I left the farmer's market with bags full of fruits and vegetables. We headed for my car.

"You were only 20-years-old when you invented chip chatting," Sharon said. "Lots of people at that age party night and day. But, you were creative and enterprising."

"Some people criticize me. They think it was wrong to accept chips from strangers in return for conversation."

234

"You didn't steal anything. Those were *your* piles of chips. Plus, your conversation is top-notch."

"Top-notch?" I laughed. "Are you saying that you're willing to pay me for our talks?"

"Well, I don't know about that," she grinned. "But you're kind of a philosophy guru."

I shook my head, even though I liked the compliment.

"Some people think they're the morality police," I said. "Attacking me probably makes them feel superior."

"You endured Hunter Moore, death threats and door-knockers. Who cares about a few sanctimonious nobodies?" she said.

We reached the car, and I spoke in an overly dramatic way, "Look. It's a miracle."

"What?" Sharon gasped.

"The vitamin book… It wasn't stolen. I guess you were right about turning it over." Sharon laughed. We drove to my house.

"Could you grab the mail?" I hollered, while unlocking the front door.

Sharon took a bundle of letters from the box, and then flipped through them with a vexed look on her face.

"Why do you have a letter from prison?" she seemed tense. "You're communicating with felons?"

"Let me see," I opened the envelope and read the contents to Sharon. An inmate named Jesse wanted my help. He had sneaked into the ceiling crawlspace at a Pennsylvania tanning salon and secretly videotaped 73 female customers in the nude; some of them were underage. Then he uploaded the videos to the Internet. Fifty porn sites—mostly outside of the United States—still featured the images. Jesse was serving up to 20 years in prison for the crime. One of the customers, a 17-year-old, was further victimized when her embarrassing images were passed around her high school.

"He wants me to try to get the videos off the Internet," I said to Sharon. "He says he regrets the pain and humiliation he caused."

"You don't believe him, do you? You're not going to help this criminal!"

"I'll be helping the victims," I said, placing the letter on the dining room table. "Let's make lunch.

Sharon and I prepared two salads with the ingredients we'd bought at the farmer's market. Then we sat under the gazebo in my backyard and ate from oversized bowls, using utensils as well as our hands. We probably looked like barbarians from the Paleolithic era.

"A lady at my Democratic club told me things taste better when you eat with your fingers," Sharon said.

"What does a person do at a Democratic club?"

"Democratic things," Sharon said. "Are you a Democrat or a Republican?"

"Neither. I'm independent. According to polls, forty percent of the public identify as independents. Yet the Democrats and Republicans try to frighten us away from voting third party. It's all about instilling fear and manipulating the masses."

"You must lean one way or the other," she said.

"Nope. I'm not a leaner. I vote the issue."'

"Okay. Let's take one. How do you feel about stem cell research? For or against?" Sharon asked. "I am in favor. We can achieve medical miracles. Plus, the rest of the world will be doing it. If we don't, we'll be left out in the cold."

"There's an assumption that issues only have two sides: the Democratic position and the Republican one," I said. "But that's false. In this case, I ask a different question: how will stem cell research affect animals? They are tortured and killed in the vivisection lab. That's not a question either political party asks."

"Okay," Sharon said. "Let's take another issue. What do you think about gun control? For or against?"

"I am in favor of permitting weapons for self-defense," I said. "But I am against hunting rifles because they are weapons of murder. Naturally, neither Democrats nor Republicans agree with me."

"I'm not sure we are going to agree on many political issues," Sharon laughed. "So maybe we should continue with your Vegas story. It's fascinating, like a world all its own."

"It was a truly unusual place in the 1980s."

Sharon went back to reading my memoir. The chapter, which began at the Sahara Hotel, described my first encounter with singer Frank Sinatra.

What Happens in Vegas Ends Up in a Book

 THOUGHT FRANK SINATRA was being chip chatted at the Sahara Hotel.

The Sahara, nicknamed "The Jewel of the Desert," was the sixth resort to open on the Las Vegas strip. It was where Abbot and Costello made their last appearance and home of the Jerry Lewis Labor Day Telethon in the 1970s. It was where I had breakfast with George Carlin and had dinner with Jim Stafford and where I hung out with Buddy Hackett and Don Rickles. Getting to know these entertainers took no particular skill or special connection. It was just a matter of being gregarious, introducing myself and seizing the moment or practicing "carpe diem" as it is expressed in Latin. The Sahara was also where I first met Frank Sinatra, his son and Flip Wilson.

The hotel had a rich Moroccan flavor like an appetizing bowl of vegetable couscous. The casino's color palette included reds, oranges, black and brass. Huge, plastic statues of semi-smiling camels were perched in several corners as if to observe the gaming action. The House of Lords, Don the Beachcomber and the coffee shop were popular eating escapes inside the hotel, and the Casbah Lounge, which was adjacent to the craps tables, was a trendy spot for drinks and conversation.

Flip Wilson was the Congo Room headliner that night, and Frank Sinatra's son was the opening act. I ventured backstage after the show to meet the entertainers as I often did when looking to put chocolate syrup and sprinkles on what was starting to feel like a plain vanilla life. Gorging myself with sundaes, figuratively speaking, seemed appropriate in Vegas, the city of exaggeration and overembellishment.

Backstage security was generally lax in the early 1980s. Tom—who had Alma—was one of the few performers with a bodyguard. Flip Wilson's dressing room, which was up the steps and to the right, was open access; guests were inside sipping drinks and chatting. I blended into the crowd, got introduced to everyone, including the entertainers and musical arranger Don Costa who was close with the Sinatra family.

"Some of us are meeting downstairs for a drink," Don said to me. "Would you like to join us in the bar?"

"Sure," I replied, always eager for excitement.

"I have to make a phone call," he continued. "I'll meet you there."

Like Casablanca, the capital of Morocco, the slightly elevated bar had suddenly became the focal point of the hotel because Frank Sinatra and his wife, Barbara, were sitting in a large, roped-off area. Guests and entourage members ordered drinks in this special section. I noticed some of my new acquaintances from backstage: Jilly Rizzo (Frank's best friend), Larry "Nifty" Victorson (Frank's personal assistant), Flip Wilson, and Dan McIntyre (guitarist for Frank's son), among others. Don Costa, who had extended the invitation to me, was not yet present, so I was reluctant to join the group. I eyed two prime spots that were not yet taken: one was next to Frank Sinatra, and the other was next to that seat.

During my moment of hesitation, a woman jumped into the chair next to Frank. I quietly reprimanded myself for being a slowpoke and nabbed the remaining one. I made causal conversation, pretending like I belonged; and even eavesdropped on the conversation between Frank and the young woman on my left.

"I want to go gamble," she said. "May I please have 500 dollars?"

The singer handed her cash.

"I'm going to put it all on roulette. On black," she announced and trotted into the casino.

I was shocked. Was this woman a chip chatter? Did Mr. Sinatra just hand out money to strangers? Maybe I should ask for a thousand. Or two thousand. I wondered if my strategy to accept chips *only* when offered had been all wrong. I thought about the countless self-help books that suggest being direct with one's needs, rather than waiting like a wallflower at the school dance. My spontaneous right brain urged me to go for it with Frank, while my logic-oriented left brain begged me to refrain. I glanced at a life-size, plastic camel, hoping for advice. His serene expression told me to be content with my journey rather than risk unnecessary humps. I was becoming friends with some interesting people; it was not wise to wager it all on green.

"I won." The woman returned to her seat and offered the money back to Mr. Sinatra. "Here's your five hundred dollars."

He refused the cash.

"Thanks, Daddy," she said.

I suddenly realized my blunder. The young woman was not a chip chatter; she was Tina Sinatra. I was thankful for the camel's sound advice.

"Let's head over to Caesars for some dinner," Frank suggested to everyone in the VIP area.

Because I was in the right place at the right time, I was included in the invitation. It was a memorable evening or a hot fudge sundae with the works.

After supper at Caesars with Frank and his entourage, I drove to the Hilton to give Darla a birthday gift. As usual, she was working the profitable eight p.m. to four a.m. shift at the craps tables. In those days, tips were shared only by the dealers who worked at a particular table on a certain shift. Working late meant significantly better money.

I marveled over Darla's wizardry with the dice stick and her break-neck chip counting. Ten minutes later when she was off-duty, I handed her *Sylvia Porter's Money Book*. It seemed an appropriate gift since finances occupied both the left and right sides of her brain. She tore off the silver wrapping paper, read my sappy Hallmark card, and gave me a hug.

After fulfilling my duty as Darla's birthday fairy, it was time to head home; however, upon leaving, I noticed a problem. There was a ridiculously long line of tourists waiting for cabs. Many seemed annoyed. The late show at the Hilton had just ended, and showgoers wanted to get back to their hotels. Cabs were the only viable option for car-deprived visitors in the 1980s. The monorails had not yet been built, and the bus system was not yet synchronized. Bus waits could top forty-five minutes, so this mode of transportation was not ideal for tourists. In fact, Vegas had the tiniest bus system nationwide for a major U.S. city. Walking was only possible when the weather was temperate and when the destination was near. The Hilton was in an isolated area off The Strip, thus inconvenient to all locales with the exception of the Landmark.

Being an entrepreneur meant seeing a need and satisfying it. I was prepared to do just this. There were too many customers and too few cabs. Although chip chatting was lucrative, I made an on-the-spot decision to launch a part-time business. I approached several frustrated souls at the end of the line.

"I've got room for three people in my car," I announced. "I will take you to any hotel on The Strip right now for ten bucks per person."

Hands flew into the air like doves lifting off from a beach, and I motioned for three individuals to follow me. It was a tight squeeze into Dad's Mercedes, which he was still letting me borrow, but my passengers were grateful for cutting thirty to forty-five minutes from their wait time. After drop-offs at the Silverbird and Holiday Inn, I circled back for a second load. There was virtually no traffic on The Strip in those days.

This was my first stint as a bandit cab driver; I did not realize it was illegal until some twenty-five years later when I saw a special on TV. A license is apparently required to cart others around for money. In fact, according to Internet articles, even transporting someone from one city to another—as advertised on Craigslist—is illegal when profit is involved.

Government statistics reveal that the median income for taxi drivers and chauffeurs in 2008, including tips, came to $21,550. This meager sum comports with my experience in 1980. Cabbie compensation was paltry as compared with chip chatting profits, and I never got tipped beyond my per person fee. The job, however, afforded me a few extra belts for Alma to admire and a few more pair of Charles Jourdan shoes; plus, I remember it fondly as an integral part of my exotic experience in the City of Lights.

It seems I was not the only bandit cab driver. The "problem" has been around for decades; and in some cities, such as Los Angeles, half the cabs are unlicensed, and the number is on the rise. When caught, cabbie scofflaws can be fined $1,000, lose their vehicles to impound for 30 days and go to prison. Besides these risks, the homicide rate for cab drivers is the highest among U.S. occupations. It is four times greater than the rate for police officers.

I had no knowledge of these hazards, but was discriminating about passenger selection, readily consulting intuition and common sense. I dropped off female passengers at the last stop, whenever possible, rather than allow myself to be alone with a male. Since my customers had sat through a Vegas show, they seemed unlikely to be criminals. It was hard to imagine Jesse James, Charles Manson or David Berkowitz paying to see a performance by Joan Rivers, Steve Martin or Siegfried and Roy; and then waiting patiently in a lengthy line for a cab to take them back to their rooms at the Circus Circus.

The Circus Circus was pink and white and shaped like a Big Top; trapeze artists entertained high above the gaming floor. The resort provided the backdrop for scenes in a number of films, such as *Diamonds Are Forever*, *Austin Powers: International Man of Mystery* and *Honey, I Blew Up the Kid*. At least one episode of the show *Starsky and Hutch* was filmed in the casino; and Robert Urich would often steer his Ford Thunderbird past the front door on the TV show *Vegas*. In September 1996, rapper Tupac Shakur was shot in his car on Las Vegas Boulevard just outside the hotel.

Circus Circus was publicized as the place for families, even in the 1980s when the focus of Vegas was high rollers and convention-goers. It was also the location of the most life-altering moment of my life, a moment more personally revealing than spotting that sequined dress at the mall, and more inspirational than sitting with Amy on that hill in Atlanta and feeling like I should undertake a mission to make the world better.

It was Saturday morning. Grazing at another pig-out palace seemed outright unappealing, but I had agreed to meet Darla at the $1.99 Circus Circus breakfast buffet as thanks for giving me a lift from the airport two weeks prior. Darla had a sense of time much like a broken watch, so I always had a book jammed into my purse for those "where the heck is she" moments.

Leaning against a white wall at the entrance to the resort, I noticed the establishment's Coney Island-style, merry-go-round sign, which would be replaced a year later with a billboard shaped like a quirky clown. Both reflected the silliness and childish delights that were the Circus Circus in the 1980s. The parking lot and fountain to my left seemed to peer over my shoulder as I plucked a book from my purse, one that I had spontaneously purchased on the previous day without reading the jacket cover. It was titled *Animal Liberation*, written by philosopher Peter Singer. I began chapter one. The next half hour would change my life.

It was 30 minutes later. I was a churning kettle of horror, surprise, shame, newfound awareness and even sorrow for the hundreds, if not thousands, of animals I had unknowingly oppressed and killed.

I was a hypocrite. I had eaten animals, worn them, and never given thought to their suffering and death. I also knew that when I stopped, I would never escape from my embarrassing predicament. I would remain a member of the group I now saw as oppressors.

The words in the book sliced through me like a vivisector's blade. Although my emotions were on the job, it was the logic that most touched me. The author was discussing "speciesism" or "prejudice against non-humans." A speciesist thinks animals have less value than humans and are worthy of less consideration, a prejudice that stems from western ideology (culture, tradition, religion and philosophy), from arrogance and from a desire that some humans have to feel superior to others.

I had always prided myself on being anti-prejudice, but now I knew my life had been one big, fat inconsistency; and inconsistency is a fatal flaw for a philosopher. It was illogical to be against "isms"—racism, sexism and anti-Semitism—while eating meat and willingly contributing to the suffering of animals.

Based on sheer numbers, I realized that helping animals was the most productive way to spend my time and that speciesism was the most pervasive and harmful form of bigotry. One hundred and thirty million nonhumans are killed for sport annually. Sixty billion animals are killed for food in the world each year, and just a one percent drop in U.S. meat consumption would save over 100 million animal lives. "Hundreds of millions" and "billions" are not quantities used when tallying human suffering and death. Animals are truly the voiceless and forgotten.

The book had become the cause or trigger that would produce a miraculous effect. I was "determined" to change my behavior. I could no longer be a hypocrite. I could no longer claim to hate prejudice while oppressing animals. I could no longer support violence when I had always sided with the victim. It was simply not in accordance with my value system.

I would change my behavior right there at the Circus Circus. Ironically, this was the same resort where a baby elephant had roamed the gambling floor in 1968 at the casino's grand opening. I had seen a photo of him seated at a blackjack table, a situation I now saw as objectionable. But when the elephant went to the bathroom on the casino carpet, the original idea of letting exotic creatures roam inside the structure was seen as a mistake, and animals were banned from the premises.

"There you are. Always reading a book," Darla hovered over me. "Ready to eat?"

I tried to shake the heaviness of *Animal Liberation* from my body like a dog removing water after a bath. I wanted to temporarily slide back into Vegas superficiality, if only to be lighthearted during the meal with Darla. But, I had changed. My new burden was there to stay.

All I remember about the breakfast buffet were pink plastic dinner plates, mirrored walls, rambunctious children, lumpy Cream of Wheat and that my meal was wholly vegetarian. The platters of sausage and bacon were no longer slabs of meat. They were dead animals. They were former living beings who'd had needs, desires and interests.

I never ate meat again.

Not long after breakfast at the Circus Circus, I was at McCarren airport en route to Washington, D.C. I was going to Ronald Reagan's inaugural festivities; he was the president-elect. The terminal was congested. Passengers stood single-file at the gate in a long and winding line, which snaked in front of the ticket desk, behind rows of occupied seats and past tourists in matching T-shirts. Then, it extended into the main walkway of the building. I knew what this meant. It was bad news. My flight would be full and virtually unbearable. It would be like traveling in a closed egg carton. Plus, my chance of obtaining an empty row on the plane was unpromising at best.

When flying, I almost always snagged a full row. I was an expert at keeping an eagle eye while everyone boarded, cognizant of each and every vacant seat. Then when passengers were no longer dribbling in, I would scurry to an empty row and make myself comfortable. I could not remember a time when I had failed to seize that all-important extra space. Since I was petite, I could raise the arm rests, and comfortably stretch out on three seats and sleep.

This was crucial not just for comfort, but for health reasons. Traveling meant "migraine alert." It was rare for me to disembark from a long flight without a headache. A long flight was anything greater than two and a half hours. Sleeping on a full row at least gave me a fighting chance. If I came down with a migraine during a flight, I knew I would probably be ill for three to four days. This would make the trip an experience of interminable suffering and a waste of time.

I handed my boarding pass to the gate agent. "Are all of these people going to Washington?"

"Yes," she said with a smile. "We're overbooked. We need volunteers to take a later flight."

I stared at her. I had no idea what this meant.

"If you're willing, we could put you on the next available plane to Dulles," she added. "It's in less than two hours."

I hemmed and hawed, weighing the odds for getting a less jam-packed flight with the alternative of a protracted wait at the airport.

"We would compensate you, of course," she added.

"Really?" I shot back, all perky. "How much are we talking about?"

"I can offer you $400," she said.

"If you can do $500, you have a deal," I countered, figuring this would pay for my entire Washington D.C. hotel bill.

She checked her computer. "We could do that."

I had been bumped. I was officially a bumpee. I used my airport "wait time" to figure out details of what I considered a promising new employment opportunity. It seemed innovative and intriguing. I'd never heard of it. I wondered if it was workable. Although I had no plans to quit chip chatting, I loved shifting into creative mode and applying investigative thinking, venturing into the bold zone of ideas.

With a pen and pad, I sat in the terminal, jotting down thoughts.

"Hi," a passenger with a briefcase said. "What are you writing, young lady?" He tilted his head and tried to read my notes.

"I'm working out a business plan."

"Really? What kind of business?" Briefcase asked.

"Professional bumpee."

"What?" He looked confused.

"When a flight is overbooked, airlines need to cut some passengers. They pay for that. I am trying to figure out if someone could make a living getting bumped from flights."

I showed Briefcase my executive summary. Then I explained the market strategy and how one might take full advantage of all present and future "professional bumpee" opportunities.

"The competitive analysis section of the business plan is irrelevant," I said, "because there doesn't seem to be competition in the field."

"That sounds about right." He laughed.

I told Briefcase that the most important aspect involved operations. I was trying to draft an outline on how the business would function.

"How *would* it function?" he asked.

"Fully refundable tickets are necessary," I said. "The bumpee would volunteer up front to be taken off any flight, for the right price, of course. But she'd also need to be able to cancel at the last second if a flight wasn't overbooked."

"But if she didn't get bumped, she'd end up with nothing," he said.

"She'd need tickets for at least three or four flights," I replied. "I anticipate a 25 to 35 percent success rate or an income of approximately $500 per day."

"It sounds boring. Nobody wants to hang out at the airport," he said.

"That's not true. The airport's a great place to meet men. Much better than bars. People are friendly and have tons of time to talk. You can make great contacts here."

Briefcase laughed. "Are you here to meet men?"

"Nope. Not me," I smiled, tucked away my notes and stood. "My plane is leaving soon. It was nice meeting you."

"You, too, young lady. Good luck with your new business venture."

I arrived in Washington D.C. This was one of those "I-know-so-and-so" deals, which is only a slight improvement over a "let's do lunch" handshake. I was an acquaintance of Ashley Hall, who was an aide to Nevada Senator Paul Laxalt, who was close friends with Ronald Reagan, who had just been elected president. Actually, I'd worked on Reagan's 1980 campaign. I had been given tickets to the inaugural festivities and viewed them as gratitude for the thirty or forty volunteer hours I'd donated to the campaign. I was 20 years old and excited about hobnobbing with elected officials and other political types.

The first night was the All-Star Inaugural Gala. It was January 19, 1981. Frank Sinatra, who had donated four million dollars to Reagan's election war chest, was producing the televised show, and I was supposed to sit in section 110, seat S, row 10. I assumed it was a cheap seat in the auditorium which accommodated 20,000, but never bothered to look. I always felt restless as an audience member, unless sitting ringside at Tom's show. I wanted to be backstage where I could hobnob with the rich and famous. Like the obligatory fruit platter and plush couch, I always wanted to be a green room fixture, regardless of venue.

It was 7:30 p.m., and the event began at 8:30. In my ruffled, black dress, I scoped out the stage entrance at the Capital Centre in Landover, Maryland, where I noticed three security officers. I took a deep breath and marched towards them, feigning confidence.

"Is this the way to the backstage area?" I questioned.

"Yes, straight ahead."

The guards assumed I was a member of the orchestra due to my black frock, and let me pass. I slid past another security officer, who was stationed outside the green room, but who was involved in a conversation with another guard.

Johnny Carson and Bob Hope were in the show, among other headliners. I noticed Donny and Marie Osmond, Dean Martin, Debby Boone and Ben Vereen in the green room with me. They were also scheduled to entertain the crowd. This was a controversial night for Ben; his act was a tribute to the popular vaudeville comedian Bert Williams who had died in 1922. Ben wore blackface with white lips and an oversized hat. This would upset many African Americans, according to newspaper articles, after the fact. But I was oblivious to Ben's unusual get-up because I was happy to see someone I knew.

"Ben," I opened my arms.

He gave me a big hug. I had originally been introduced to him in his dressing room at the Riviera hotel by a bellman. Ben and I had become friends and had even dined together with his band in the Delmonico Room, the same restaurant where I quibbled over price and gobbled up a salad with Dad.

The Inaugural Gala stage was bright blue with white stars, but from where I stood with Ben, I had no view of it. Leaving the area, however, even for a quick peep, was risky. The guard made it clear I was in jeopardy of expulsion.

"Where's the restroom?" I asked.

"If you leave the green room, I'm not letting you back inside," he said with full knowledge that I had crashed.

I appreciated that he was not kicking me out and figured I should stay put until my bladder exploded.

"Are you going to Frank Sinatra's private party?" Ben asked me.

"I don't know," I said. "When is it? Where is it? And how do I get there?"

He told me it was at the Madison Hotel and gave me what details he could remember. I headed over to the party after the Gala.

The Madison Hotel had opened in 1963 and was the summit of luxury. It had been praised by former presidents and was a short jaunt from the White House. I stepped out of a cab at the entrance, pushed forward the revolving door and stood in the empty lobby as if it was a jigsaw puzzle. I had no idea how to fit the pieces together. Ben had not known exactly where the party was being held, although he remembered something about a meeting room. I was unclear about my destination, but figured big shots and bouncers could be watching. As two hotel employees peered at me, I took baby steps, while trying to act self-assured and hoping for a miracle. I knew if I floundered, it would be obvious I was not an invitee.

Suddenly, I heard a sound behind me. It was country singer Charlie Pride and his wife. I assumed they were attending the bash. I jumped behind them and followed closely like a huntress. When the singer ascended a staircase, I noticed security officers in the distance and assumed they were guarding the VIP event. They could see us, but they were too far away to hear. Since I could think of nothing to say to

Charlie Pride, I jumped next to him and *pretended* to speak. No sound came out. Charlie looked at me as if I was nutty. I put on a convincing show for the security officers, laughing in an overly dramatic way and moving my lips as if I was on good terms with the star. The guards smiled at me, convinced I was a member of his entourage.

"I'm Charlie Pride," the singer said to a woman at the top of the staircase.

She crossed his name off the list, while I stared straight ahead, hoping no one would question my presence.

"You can go right in," she said to Mr. Pride.

I moved along with the singer into the event, and then ducked inside the restroom where I met a friendly woman named Victoria. She insisted on escorting me back into the party and introducing me to her husband.

"This is my husband, Ed," she said.

I shook the hand of *The Tonight Show* sidekick, Ed McMahon. I suddenly realized the party was not just A list; it was A-plus. I recognized Charlton Heston, Henry Kissinger, Jimmy Stewart, Pat Boone, Ethel Merman, Mel Tillis, Maureen Reagan and Frank Sinatra, among others. I hobnobbed with the famous guests. Joanna Carson stood a good ten feet from her late night television host husband, who wore a white bow tie and white vest with his tuxedo.

"Your wife is beautiful," I said to Johnny Carson, who beamed, as if I had said exactly the right thing.

"Yes, she is. Isn't she?" he replied, gazing at her across the room.

Moments later, a bespeckled man tapped me on the shoulder.

"You're Missy Laws. Aren't you?'

I whirled around, wondering if I was getting booted from the affair. Out of the corner of my eye, I could see Frank Sinatra and some of his friends, and wondered if maybe they'd sent this stranger over to me. I had been purposely avoiding them because I was not sure how they would react to my party-crashing. Maybe it would be an open-armed

"Great to see you." On the other hand, maybe it would be an admonishing "What are you doing here? You weren't invited." I did not want to take a chance. I was one of the few non-celebrities in attendance and probably looked out of place.

"How do you know my name?" I asked the bespeckled man.

"Somebody told me," he teased.

"What's your name?" I asked.

"Fred de Cordova," he answered, and my "never let them see you sweat" demeanor turned into perspiration station.

I squealed like a pathetic fan, "You're kidding! I've always wanted to meet you!"

Fred was the producer of *The Tonight Show*; and as a child, I had always said, "Someday I want to meet Fred de Cordova." There was no particular reason, other than I thought he seemed like a neat person. Now I was face-to-face with him and acting like a pinhead. I had been calm and classy during conversations with Johnny Carson, Ed McMahon, Henry Kissinger and some of the biggest stars in the world, but I was acting like twit in front of Fred.

"I think I'll get some hors d'oeuvres," Fred was clearly freaked out by my excitement and headed for the food table. I quietly reprimanded myself.

I hobnobbed with the rest of the guests and eventually had an engaging conversation with Frank Sinatra, but I waited until things were winding down for fear of getting ousted. In the end, he seemed pleased to see me. Ben even showed up briefly with his wife. This was one of my many "bold zone" adventures during Inaugural week in D.C.

It was the evening after Frank's party, and I was wearing my "gaudy, gaudy, gaudy" dress and loving it. This was the silver sequined gown I had seen at the mall with my friends in Atlanta and had tiptoed back to buy the next day. My wardrobe was comprised of lots of outfits like this: some were "one gaudy;" others were "two gaudy." But this was a full "three" on the gaudiness scale.

Although I was captivated by my gown, I was not captivated by the cramped situation; thousands of guests were jammed into a ballroom that would normally accommodate a few hundred. Think rock concert in front of the stage. Think riots after a soccer game. Think cabin fever.

Ronald Reagan had been sworn in as President that day before a crowd of 20,000 in freezing weather. One hundred thousand people had been invited to Washington, D.C. for the inaugural festivities and were spending a reported $11 million on food, hotels and other amenities. A majority of them seemed to be crammed into the John F. Kennedy Center for the Performing Arts with me, but in reality, this was only one of the Inaugural Balls around town.

I was trapped in a sea of well-dressed people, and there was no escape. I felt like a sinking ship. It could take a full half-hour to get from one side of the room to the other. I was moving slower than a spyware-infested computer with dial-up access. People were in my face, bumping into my arms, stepping on my hem, knocking my body, kicking my feet, colliding into my purse, and pushing and shoving with their hands. It was unbearable. I inched toward what looked like a peninsula of relief on the horizon. It was the $1,000 per person VIP area, guarded by fierce-looking security officers and a less fierce-looking, red, velvet rope. You probably know what happened next: I started crying.

My claustrophobia had peaked: it was too much for me. I did not even realize I had a fear of small spaces until that evening; studies indicate that seven percent of the world population has severe claustrophobia, although most people never seek treatment.

"I can't stand it. It's too crowded in here," I sobbed hysterically to a security officer, who was guarding the relatively empty, celebrity-filled area.

"Well, you can't go into this section."

"I can't go anywhere else," I cried. "I can't even move."

Cause and effect were whipping me to death; I felt anxious and freaked out, like I could not breathe. I did not feel like my tears were a ploy to finagle myself into the celebrity area, but part of me has to wonder if my unconscious mind had a "mind of its own." Exasperated, the guard opened the rope for me, just as Con Man had returned my twenty dollars.

"Come sit down," he said. "We'll get you something to drink."

Three security guards escorted me to a sofa in the roped-off section and brought me a drink before returning to their post. I sat there for ten minutes before getting up to mingle. I conversed with folks I already knew, such as Ed and Victoria McMahon, Jimmy Stewart, Fred Travalena and Lou Rawls. And I introduced myself to Rich Little and President Ronald Reagan, among others. On the following day, I returned to Las Vegas with a new revelation: the conversations with celebrities—including the President—had been interesting, but they had not been as exciting as getting into the VIP area in the first place.

It was conclusive: the main thrill of party-crashing was not the "party." It was the "crash."

S H A R O N   X I

Party-Crashing for the Animals

With Sharon, Los Angeles 2014

After "big salad" lunch, Sharon and I headed over to the Santa Monica Mountains for a hike on my favorite trail, which coiled in a circle. In other words, it would eventually take us back to my car. The area was usually devoid of people; this day was no different.

The landscape was desert, but mountainous with large rocks, gravel and dry weeds. The trees in the valleys looked diminutive, like clumps of moss. Sharon and I noticed an indecisive breeze, lizards, succulent plants, the smell of smoke, footprints in the dry dirt, crows moving across the cloudless sky, and a sweeping view of the San Fernando Valley. After an hour of random chit chat, Sharon drew the conversation back to my life story.

"I've heard they do horrible things to animals in research labs," Sharon said. "Animal activists need to get secret video of what goes on inside… sort of like that Peeping Tom from the tanning salon. If the public knew what was happening to animals, they wouldn't stand for it."

"When it comes to research labs, party-crashing is a serious felony," I said. "In fact, it's officially a terrorist act."

"What do you mean?" she asked.

I explained that a 2006 law called the Animal Enterprise Terrorism Act severely punishes those who interfere with the operation of any animal enterprise. According to the statute, a person can be indicted as a domestic terrorist if she causes an animal-related business to lose money, regardless of how trivial the so-called crime might be: graffiti, illegally blocking a sidewalk, intimidation, rescuing a puppy from a research lab. The bottom line is the government doesn't want anyone interfering with a corporation's ability to kill and torture animals.

"That's ridiculous," Sharon looked stunned.

"Only one member of Congress even raised an objection: Dennis Kucinich," I replied. "I guess I'm a terrorist sympathizer… that is, until they abolish this law."

"Our democracy has some real problems," Sharon shook her head.

"Actually, democracy is part of the problem," I said.

"What do you mean?"

"The word 'demos' means people," I explained. "Democracy is a totalitarian regime in which humans—who have *all* the power—use, abuse, murder and manipulate nonhumans for their own perceived gain."

Sharon and I watched our shadows on the ground, keeping perfect pace with us. The sun baked our skin. Our tennis shoes kicked at the dirt, causing it to ascend like flour dust.

"Any political system that ignores the interests of other beings is, in my view, incomplete, arbitrary, biased, and therefore lousy," I said. "Every present and past political system qualifies. All are (or have been) of, by, and for a person (dictator), a few people (oligarchy) or all people (democracy or democratic republic). Animals are not even a footnote."

I explained how nonhumans have been banished from the concert hall and have no funds for Ticketmaster. Money is needed to buy access to lawmakers and legislative protections. Nonhumans have no standing in court, thus no refuge within the judicial system. The executive branch has also ignored them. Every U.S. president reveres democracy and subscribes to the view that the interests of people always trump the interests of animals.

"Nonhumans are truly the voiceless, the powerless, the marginalized and the forgotten," I said. "Even the most underprivileged Americans are privileged: they have legal rights, benefits and assurances. With the exception of a few lucky 'pets,' nonhumans are viewed as a mere means to a human end."

"What would you propose we adopt in its place?' Sharon asked as we arrived at my car.

"Omniocracy or a government with representation for all living beings."

"That's an interesting idea. Did you make that up?"

"Yep," I nodded. "A long time ago."

"Maybe we should head back to your hotel," I glanced at the clock and settled into the driver's seat. "Ricky will be back from the convention soon."

"Car ritual time," Sharon eagerly rubbed her palms together. "We have time for a few more stories. I want to know if you and Tom got back together."

"You can also read about my husband Johnny... back when I was 21 years old," I laughed.

"What?" Sharon looked stunned. "I didn't know you were married to someone before Charles."

Sharon continued reading about my zany life in 1981.

T W E L V E

Dragons and Other Strangers

WAS WEARING A FRUMPY, flannel nightgown, and I had major marriage troubles. I felt neglected. I was not getting enough attention from my husband, Johnny.

Comedic actor Jerry Lewis, star of *The Geisha Boy* and *The King of Comedy*, was in the room, watching us in bed. I figured he was staring at the pink, sponge curlers in my hair and saying to himself, "Of course, you have marriage troubles with butt-ugly curlers like those."

But, I dared not look in his direction because I was trying to concentrate on Johnny and our suffering relationship. I peeped out from under a blanket.

"Are you going to make love to me or not?" I asked Johnny.

"Huh? Wha? Come on. I was just falling asleep," he said. "Turn the light off."

The conversation continued in this vein for ten minutes, and then peaked when I stood on the bed, hurling pillows at Johnny.

There was laughter and then applause from the 30 people in the room. This was a scene from a play. I had been playing the part of Wilma who is married to Johnny in *Lovers and Other Strangers*. Anne Meara had assumed this role in the 1970 comedy, which was nominated for three Academy Awards. I trotted off the stage while the set was being revamped for the next actors.

"Take advantage of what you know is effective," Jerry Lewis said to me as I brushed past him on the way to my seat.

"I will," I nodded, unsure what the heck he was saying.

Was I good or was I bad? Was I funny or not? His message was cryptic, but I was afraid to ask for clarification because the room was so quiet. All eyes were on this famous actor, who had graciously popped into our Las Vegas acting school to lecture and watch our work.

This was the Joe Bernard Acting Studio in the early 1980s. I attended for two years. Most of the attendees were University of Nevada students, dealers, waitresses or some other brand of hotel employee. I believe it was the first time Joe and his wife, Bina—who ran the school with him—had met Jerry. They would become close friends with the actor. Joe would periodically help Jerry prep for movie and television roles.

Other notables would also visit our school; however, producer and director Matt Cimber was the next acting class guest. He visited us one afternoon during "scene study" to tell us he would be directing an upcoming Pia Zadora movie called *Fake-Out*. It would be filmed in Las Vegas and had not yet been cast. He said he'd consider resume submissions from students.

Matt had been the last husband of sex symbol Jayne Mansfield. They had divorced in 1966, a year before she died tragically at the age of 34 in a gory automobile crash that some say resulted in decapitation. However, it may have been more like a scalping or severe head trauma. Whatever the case, the car was mangled and the adults in the vehicle—and at least one of her four little dogs—died. There is the long-held rumor that she had links to Satanism, and was the object of a black magic curse that led to her demise, but it is unlikely this tale is true. All I knew is that Matt had never been a Satanist and never discussed his former wife.

"Got it right here," I proudly produced my headshot and resume. I'd dashed out to my car and retrieved it from a box in my trunk.

"You're awfully prepared," Matt replied. "That's the way to make a good impression."

Then, he turned to the rest of the students. "This movie is SAG. So if you're not in the union, this is your chance to join."

A week later, I received an audition call time.

"You're up for a role as a prison inmate," Matt's assistant told me on the phone.

"Hmm. I never really saw myself that way," I said, figuring I had *not* made such a good impression after all.

"But, I'll be there," I added and hung up the phone, wondering what I should wear.

Side-to-side stripes would not do because they would make me look fat. It was bad enough being a jailbird. I certainly did not want to be a fat one. I needed up-and-down stripes. I searched every closet in my apartment. I eventually found the black and white top I had worn when I worked at Farrell's in Atlanta. I would wear it with solid black pants.

The big day came. I stood in the hallway with other actors for about twenty-five minutes until a member of the crew pulled me aside.

"We are two hours behind schedule," he said. "We don't have time to audition you after all."

I was disappointed. I figured Matt didn't really see me as a prisoner. It was worse. He saw me as an out-of-work actor.

"Maybe there is a dead body I could play?" I said, trying to make light of the situation.

"No, you don't understand," the man replied. "Matt is giving you the part."

I was excited. This was my first real movie role. The Tim Conway flick did not really count because I had crashed the set and was only an extra.

This convict part paid over $1,000 per week. That seemed like a lot of license plates. And there was more good news: it would cost me only $50 to join the Screen Actors Guild (SAG) because I lived in Nevada. Had I resided in California, I would have had to pay a whopping $300. Of course, today, the SAG initiation fee is an even more whopping $2,300, in addition to yearly dues, regardless of state residency.

Only one other student from Joe Bernard's landed a role in the flick. She was more talented than me and obviously more uninhibited. The first day of filming came, and following an exercise class bit, Matt and another crew member approached the actresses.

"Time for the nude shower scene, ladies," the crew member announced. "Follow me."

This was the first time I had heard anything about being naked. I had studied the script from opening dialogue to closing lines and had seen nothing about showing skin. There was no way I would do nudity; and, in fact, I thought that sort of thing had to be spelled out in one's contract. The other girls had indifferent shrugs on their faces and dutifully followed the crew member. I approached Matt.

"No one ever mentioned being naked."

"You don't have to do it if you don't want," he said in a detached way.

"I'm not going to do it."

"Okay, then you are done for the day," he smiled. "See you tomorrow."

And that was it. The other actresses were shot in a prison rape shower scene with Pia Zadora, while I visited one of my favorite Vegas antique shops to find a birthday present for Dad.

I found a heavenly black, white and peach desert plate collection. It was bumpy to the touch because it had raised porcelain dragons. It came with matching teapot, cups and saucers, and charming containers for cream and sugar. To this day, it is the prettiest china I've ever seen. It is wholly in accordance with my essence. As far as I can tell, nothing has ever been in accordance with Dad's essence. I don't think Mom, Buddy or me ever presented him with a gift he liked. Everything always ended up in that same old cobweb-infested closet in the basement.

When I left the antique shop with the dragon china, I was stopped by Elvis. Actually, it wasn't really him. It was an Elvis impersonator named Freddie wearing the usual white, sequined, "three gaudy" jumpsuit.

"Hey, do you sing?" he inquired.

"Well, not really," I replied. "I had opera lessons when I was a child, but…."

"You've got the right look," Freddie interrupted. "I'm auditioning backup singers Tuesday night if you are interested. Seven p.m. No pay, but it'll be fun."

He handed me a business card with the address scribbled on back.

Always up for a silly new adventure, I showed up at the run-down theatre, where Freddie was holding try-outs. Including me, there were only three hopefuls, although I wasn't all that hopeful. I knew my voice was only slightly better than a rusty door hinge. I had a 66 percent chance of being selected because Freddie was picking two of us for six shows he had scheduled at clubs on the outskirts of town.

"Hey, you're here," he handed me the lyrics for *Suspicious Minds*. "Get on the stage with Catherine. Let's give it a go."

The music started; and I did my best to figure out the beat, sing into the microphone and stay on tune.

"Not too bad" was his comment afterwards. I took it as confirmation that I was dreadful. Then he asked Mia to join Catherine onstage for the same song. The sound was decidedly better, and I could tell he was going to give me the old heave-ho. Instead, he called Mia a "hoe."

"I can't do this for free," Mia admitted to Freddie. "I would be giving up real cash. I work at the Chicken Ranch."

Prostitution was legal at the Chicken Ranch. It was a brothel near Pahrump, which is 60 miles northwest of Las Vegas. It opened in 1976, but had been burned to the ground two years later by arsonists. Now the girls were working out of trailers on the fire-scorched property.

"Sorry, I have a 'no sin' policy. What you do is immoral," Freddie preached.

I figured he really had a "no payment" policy and her demand for cash was the real problem.

Freddie faced me, "You got the job."

We performed the six shows at dives around town to relatively small audiences. After our short-lived tour, I never spoke to Freddie again nor saw his name in lights.

Although my relationship with Tom had ended a year earlier, I still hoped to get back together with him. I concocted an outrageous scheme; I knew that if it failed, I would look as nutty as a cheese log and as moronic as a half-baked bowl of tipsy pudding. Plus, my embarrassment would not be a private event. It would happen in full view of Tom and his entourage.

My idea for the "Fake Burt Reynolds Brother Ploy" sprang from a trip I took to Miami in 1979. Wendy Weeks, a fellow student from the University of Florida, and I were driving to a Dolphin football game, something I did many times in those days. I enjoyed hanging out on the field and watching the game at ground level. I had no ticket or VIP connection, but always managed to finagle myself and a friend onto a grassy section ten feet from the players' bench. At the end of the game, my friend and I would stand outside the locker room door and schmooze with Miami Dolphin coaching staff and players. I had no ulterior motive, such as getting a date with a jock. I simply found crashing past security and lingering on the field to be an adventure.

En route back to Gainesville, Wendy and I stopped for gas.

"They are filming a Burt Reynolds movie up the road," the station's attendant said.

"Where, exactly?"

He gave me directions. Itching for another daring exploit, I convinced Wendy to stay the night at a nearby motel so we could maneuver ourselves onto the movie set the following day.

It was on the set that I met the cast and crew, including Burt Reynolds and his brother, Jim Hooks Reynolds. We all had drinks at a bar which I remember as the Greenhouse in Riviera Beach. They were filming *Smokey and the Bandit II*.

When they were twelve, Jim Hooks and Burt Reynolds had been boyhood pals. Jim told Burt that he came from a physically abusive home, and Burt immediately asked his parents to raise Jim as their son. They agreed on the spot. Jim was legally adopted as a "Reynolds" some years later and followed the career path of his famous brother, working as an actor and stuntman in a number of films from 1981 through 1997.

Wendy and I spent the entire afternoon talking one-on-one with Jim—who had no role in the movie—while the others were busy on the set. By the end of the day, I felt I knew him quite well.

Flash forward to Las Vegas, and my desire to reunite with Tom. I'd made periodic calls to his entourage requesting a date; I'd been rebuffed. I was in tears a lot during that time.

But, I knew Tom could be vulnerable. His cool and equanimous disposition could be penetrated by jealousy. I had witnessed this many times. Maybe I could once again access this possessiveness, which could in turn ignite his passion. To do so, I would need to magically appear in his presence with a handsome date. But magic was not an option; my fairy godmother had vanished. Perhaps she was fulfilling other little girls' fantasies. I would have to hatch a plan all by myself.

Getting to Tom was a big challenge because security was tight. Sitting ringside at his show seemed to be the only way to catch his eye.

On the phone, a Caesars Palace ticket agent told me obtaining front row seats was now a complicated matter. My friend Angelo was not the current maitre d'; and a generous tip could no longer guarantee success. The agent rattled on about a silly hoop-jumping process which included joining Tom's fan club, which *might* tell me when tickets went on sale, which *might* help me beat others to the punch, which *might* land me the all-important ringside seats.

"Plus, you may need to buy your tickets a year in advance," she added.

"A year in advance?" I exclaimed. "I don't have that kind of time. I'm not *that* obsessed."

On second thought, maybe I was. After all, I was to prepare a preposterous plan that would rival any *Saturday Night Live* skit. If my ploy failed, I knew I'd be majorly embarrassed.

Older ladies edged out everyone else for ringside seats at Tom's shows, a situation that still exists today. On almost any night in almost any town, the same twenty or thirty female fans can be found sitting at the stage. How these particular individuals win these spots, time after time, is baffling.

"What if a celebrity comes to the show?" I asked the Caesars Palace ticket girl. "Would he or she be able to sit ringside?"

"Of course," she responded. "That would be a different situation."

I hung up the phone. I needed a celebrity date, but had no one. Perhaps I could hire someone to *pretend* to be a celebrity. He could assume the role of an accomplished author, whose face was unidentifiable to the masses; or he could be the relative of a famous person. That's when Jim Reynolds came to mind.

Jim was, of course, the brother of a famous guy; plus, he had stayed out of the limelight, and I knew a lot about him due to our afternoon-long conversation a few years prior. I was also certain Tom did not socialize with Burt or members of the Reynolds family.

I also knew who could "play" Jim. There was a handsome, leading man at my acting school named Al. He was considered a hunk. I often wondered if he was being paid to attend classes because he increased female attendance.

"Sounds like a fun time," Al said, when I proposed the bizarre plan. "I can pull it off."

I briefed him on his role, and then made a call.

"Actor Burt Reynolds' brother, Jim Reynolds, will be attending the Tom Jones show," I told a Caesars Palace ticket clerk on the phone. "He'll bring one guest and will need ringside seats."

"No problem," she said. "I will make the arrangements."

On the special night, I dolled up, thrilled that I would be sitting at the stage; and headed to Caesars Palace with my dapper, fake celebrity date.

"This is where you will be sitting, Mr. Reynolds" a woman escorted us to a booth in the middle of the theatre.

I recognized it as Tom's personal booth, where his friends sat to watch the show. It was far from the stage. Tom would not be able to see us.

"No, no," I panicked. "We're supposed to sit up front."

"This is where Tom wants you to sit," the woman said. "He is taking care of your bill, ma'am."

"No, no," I pleaded. "I don't want him to take care of the bill. We're paying, and we're supposed to sit ringside. Please put us up front."

"You have to sit here," she said. "These are the best seats in the house."

"That's not the way it was arranged..." I complained.

"These seats are much better," Al slid into the booth.

I could tell he just wanted to see the show. He didn't really care about helping me to reconcile with Tom. Defeated, I joined him. The fuse had been lit, and there was an ominous ticking in my head. I knew it was a matter of time before the bomb exploded, exposing me as a fool and a fraud. Someone from Tom's entourage was sure to venture out, uncover the "Fake Burt Reynolds Brother Ploy" and tell Tom. "Telling Tom" would be the worst part of all.

Al blissfully downed a couple of drinks, oblivious to my misery. I gulped down water, hoping to outright drown.

"Missy, what are you doing here?" John Moran suddenly appeared at the booth.

"Hi, John," I tried to act perky. "This is Jim."

John seemed suspicious. "You're Burt Reynolds' brother?"

"Yes," Al replied, jumping into character.

John bombarded him with tricky questions, and although Al put forth convincing answers, I could tell John was not persuaded.

When Al was distracted, John whispered to me, "Are you sure he's really Burt Reynolds' brother?" I assured him that I had no doubt.

John disappeared during the show, but reemerged after it ended. He asked "Jim" if he wanted to go backstage to meet Tom.

"Sure," he enthusiastically replied.

I got up to join them, but John informed me that I was not invited. At that moment, I knew he knew, and I knew Tom knew. Al was oddly quiet when he returned from backstage; I was sure he had confessed.

Months later, John casually said to me, "Don't bring any more fake Burt Reynolds brothers to see the show. Okay?"

The dreaded kaboom went off in my head.

"I'd like to have my lawyer present," I tried to make a joke.

John didn't laugh, but mercifully changed the subject. The incident was never mentioned again.

Several years passed, and in 1985 when I had a new boyfriend, I ran into Tom when he was touring in the Midwest. He asked me out again, but it was too late.

I would do it all over again.

Tom gave me tremendous confidence when I was insecure. He made me feel beautiful, like Cinderella, after a childhood of rejection, pain and criticism. He helped me spring from a twig into a blossom and become the strong woman I am today. He provided amazing experiences and introductions to new friends, lifting me away from a stifling Atlanta lifestyle of conformity and of judging others. From my relationship with him, I discovered that with love, pure intentions, a strong will and enough effort, a person can often succeed.

I learned persistence is a treasure greater than gold.

I was 22 and had been living in Las Vegas for two years. I flew back to Atlanta to visit Dad.

"Where's the dragon china I sent you?" I asked.

You'd think there was a perpetual tornado barreling towards the state because he was always glued to his favorite station: the Weather Channel.

"I don't know," he said with his eyes fixed on the TV. "It's around here somewhere."

I knew what that meant: it was in the basement. The nonchalant way he threw out the comment reminded me of the time he told me Amy was buried in the backyard. I headed downstairs to what I affectionately called his "discards" closet. It was there that I found my china, still in its box, carefully rolled in bubble wrap. Plus, I found sacks of department store clothes with receipts and tags still attached. Dad could not be bothered making returns. Some of the sales slips were almost a year old. I lugged everything upstairs and dumped it on the dining room table.

"I'm taking the china back with me," I said.

"That's fine," Dad stared at the television.

"I'm also returning all of these clothes and keeping the money," I added.

Dad said nothing. I knew he didn't care. He was rich. A few hundred dollars here or there was nothing to him. But it was a lot to me.

I was disappointed in myself because I had spent my entire chip chatting fortune. I had only $500 remaining in my bank account. I had not placed bets; but I had splurged on magnificent furniture and designer clothes. The rationale at the time was that I needed exquisite outfits to look perfect for those moments when I was living the lifestyle of the rich and famous. Now it looked like I would be living the lifestyle of the poor and obscure.

"I'm sick of Vegas and really sick of chip chatting," I announced. "I'm moving to Los Angeles in a month."

This comment was weighty enough to get his attention, and he turned away from the set.

"That's where the fruits and the nuts live." He loved delivering his standard line about California. He always punctuated it with a chuckle.

Then he made me an offer he thought I could not refuse.

"If you move to Atlanta, I'll give you $500,000. I'll buy you a townhouse, give you a Mercedes and support you. If you move to L.A., I'll give you a Volkswagen to drive, and that's it. You get nothing."

"You want to give me a half a million dollars, a place to live and a new car? Plus, you want to support me indefinitely?"

"Or you can fail in Los Angeles," he laughed and gazed back at the TV.

Tween was right about Dad. He wanted to control me with his money. He hoped to transform me into that obedient socialite that he'd always dreamt I'd be. He longed to situate me in that "old money" world, a world that I saw as flawed, as aberrant, as stifling; but that he perceived as the only respectable place for his daughter. Dad aimed to make me dependent on him and to convert me into a fan of fur coats, country clubs and "most ladylike" titles. Perhaps he wanted me to be another Mom, only emotionally stronger.

But I was not Mom. I would never be Mom. Atlanta had been my coffin for 18 years, and I had finally escaped from the darkness of its belly. Nothing could tempt me back, not even gluttonous riches.

I thought about Dad's generous offer—and it was generous—for exactly as long as it takes me to get bored watching the Weather Channel: namely, ten seconds.

I moved to California with only $500 to my name.

Anchors Aweigh

With Sharon, Los Angeles 2014

"So much happened during the first 22 years of your life," Sharon said. "I hope you'll continue writing."

I pulled to the curb at Sharon's hotel, far from the front door so as not to obstruct traffic or impede guests who needed to get by. These were my final "Sharon moments" for January 2014. She and Ricky were flying back to Washington, D.C. the next morning.

Sharon and I continued to chat in the car while bellhops collected baggage, maneuvering it onto their gold luggage stands. A family of six jumped into an idling van. Three bridesmaids exited the hotel lobby in matching yellow dresses.

"Do you still stay in touch with Tom?" she asked.

"Yeah, I see him every five years."

"What about Kayla? Has she ever met him?"

"Twice," I said and related the second experience.

"It was 2004, and Kayla was 17 years old. She and I were on a two-day mother-daughter trip. We visited Tom, who was performing at the MGM Grand in Las Vegas. This was the

271

second time Kayla and Tom had met. Kayla didn't remember the first time because she was only four months old.

"'I first met your mom when she was your age,' Tom told Kayla.

"'Really?' Kayla was enthusiastic; she enjoyed learning fascinating tidbits about her mother.

"'You should have dropped by last night,' Tom said to us. 'I was wearing the ring. I wear it all the time.'

"'Really?' I said.

"'Yes," he nodded. 'Catherine Zeta-Jones was raving over it last night. She said she wanted a ring just like it. She and Michael Douglas came backstage after the show.'

"I had the ring custom-made for Tom in 1982 after we stopped seeing each other. I suppose you could call it a going-away gift; although at the time, I had visions of rekindling our relationship. The Fredericks Fine Jewelry appraisal certificate, which sits in a folder in my office, lists its value at $2,500. According to the inflation calculator, the piece is now worth $6,200. It is comprised of a large, gold dragon and forty-eight diamonds weighing one-and-a-half carats. Tom loved the symbol of the dragon. It wholly represented his essence. He would have loved the dragon china I'd bought for Dad."

"Do you think it's relevant that you gave your father dragon china and Tom a dragon ring?" Sharon asked.

"No. I think it's a coincidence, but I am sure there is a psychiatrist out there who would disagree," I laughed. "The dragon china was Chinese. The dragon ring was European, actually Welsh."

"Dragons are found in legends," Sharon added. "Both men have this myth-like, larger-than-life aura about them, and they have been prominent in your life."

"True, but I'm just a blip on the radar in their lives. I don't think Tom or my dad would call me significant."

"Really? Even your own father? He wanted you to move back to Atlanta."

"He hoped to control me, to mold me into the perfect southern belle. He wanted to say 'I told you so' about leaving Atlanta in the first place."

"Maybe he needed you to be the anchor in his life... since your adoptive mom was gone."

"I don't want to be anybody's anchor. When I look back, my dad was a speedboat jetting around, jumping over waves, socializing with other boaters. My mom was a lonely, stagnant anchor trapped at the bottom of a cold, dark sea."

I held Sharon's hand, "I'm glad I eventually tracked you down. It wasn't easy. It took a lot of detective work."

"That was 26 years ago. It's been a long time," she said.

"You're very important to me. Maybe I should call you 'Mom' instead of 'Sharon'? After all, you are my birthmother."

"That would be all right." Sharon smiled, and then gave me a hug. She had no other children and seemed happy to finally be a "parent."

"Have a safe trip back to D.C."

"I will," she said. "Good luck with the Hunter Moore trial. Next time we get together maybe you can tell me what you learned from your latest investigation."

"Latest investigation?"

"Yeah, the double murder–suicide... the devil worshipper who killed my dad... and your grandfather," Sharon replied.

"I have so much information," I was enthusiastic. "I even got into the devil worshipper's basement where the two bombs exploded."

"Really? That sounds scary," Sharon said.

"It was creepy. Why didn't you ask me about this three days ago?"

"I was afraid," she replied.

"Afraid?"

"I have mixed feelings about hearing the details. My father's death is still so painful."

"I understand," I said.

"But you can tell me next time, when we resume your life story. I think I need to know the truth."

"Okay. Next time," I said.

Sharon got out of the car. "Are you still in touch with… you know who? Is he still hiding you from his family?"

"My birthfather?" I nodded. "It's complicated."

"It sounds like there will be lots for us to discuss."

Sharon headed towards the front door of the hotel. Then, she turned. "I love you, Charlotte."

"I love you, too… Mom."

PART III
The Troll Slayer

"In spite of the risks, Laws took up the sword."
~ YES! MAGAZINE

"It's not an exaggeration to call Laws a leading expert on how much the internet hates women. She's a women's rights activist, former talk show host, and columnist, and she has a Ph.D. in social ethics. She's also regularly contacted by women from all over the country about what to do when their intimate pictures end up online. She's the revenge porn fixer, the Erin Brockovich of leaked nudes."
~ BUZZFEED

*"Charlotte Laws… a very appropriate last name.
Trying to get laws passed in a number of states."*
~ FOX NEWS

"If you care about women, you need this book. Charlotte Laws is the Erin Brockovich of 'revenge porn,' and she will change your life just like she changed mine. Buy this for your daughters, your sisters, your mother and yourself."
~ MANDY STADTMILLER, DEPUTY EDITOR, XOJANE

"THEY'RE GOING TO KILL YOU," Mandy screamed into the phone a week following Sharon's visit. "Oh my Lord, what are you going to do?"

"Calm down, Mandy. What are you talking about?" I asked.

"There are these two guys on Reddit. They say they're going to pick up Hunter after the charges against him are dropped, and the three of them will come after you. They know where you live."

"I'm sure they're just letting off steam."

"No. They sound serious. What if Hunter doesn't go to jail? You'll be a target."

Mandy was a highly emotional person. Frenzy was her best friend. Hysteria was her mode before and after lunch. I adored Mandy, but she viewed the world as a place of danger. She believed there was a spy in every parked car and a gun in every pocket. She lived in a world of *James Bond* and *Die Hard*, a mindset that may have originated from her time in Iran. My American perspective told me that women in that country balanced on pins and needles, always cognizant that one wrong move could prove fatal.

I had embraced my role as a calming force in Mandy's life, although I was never sure whether her panic was warranted. Was she the sane one? Should I have been worried? Maybe I was being stupid and reckless. I'd never alerted the FBI to personal threats because I didn't want to bother them. I appreciated that they had come to the aid of *Is Anyone Up?* victims and didn't think it was fair to request more of their time.

Mandy was right to worry about one thing: Moore's acquittal or release from prison. He had threatened to ruin my online reputation and to make my life miserable. I could visualize him devoting weeks or months to this obsession, assuming false identities, posting mean-spirited and purposely erroneous comments, targeting me on every website, sending viruses to my computer and commanding his devotees to follow his lead. I hoped he would go to jail—partly because I thought it was necessary for justice and would act as a deterrent for other revenge porn site operators—but also because it would give him and his followers time to grow up and shed their bitter and immature ethos. As they aged, I figured they'd come to the realization that life is not about harassment, hatred and misogyny. Harboring negative feelings is like a boomerang; it whips back and hits the instigator in the eye.

The Hunter Moore Arraignment

Hunter Moore's arraignment in Los Angeles was slated for February 7, 2014. Kayla and I attended together. Surprisingly, media attention was light that day, probably because Moore had already been through a press-filled arraignment in his hometown of Sacramento. He had been released to his parents on $100,000 bond, and the judge had banned him from the Internet. The injunction against online activity was no doubt painful for him because all of his power came from that medium. Without computer access, he could not communicate with the rest of "the family." He could not be "the father," the enraged and unpredictable cult leader with followers who would kill for him. Offline, Moore was just an unemployed, 28-year-old, "no name" living at home with his parents in a downscale suburb of Sacramento.

Moore had come to Los Angeles to say either "guilty" or "not guilty" with his attorney and his parents by his side. The proceeding was held in the same courtroom as the Evens arraignment. Moore had a full beard, and wore a gray button-down shirt and dark pants, covered by a coat. He seemed to be trying to hide his identity with sunglasses and a baseball cap, but he shed the camouflage in the courtroom. His mother wore a white blouse, black pants and gold earrings; and his father had on a brown jacket, jeans and cowboy boots.

As Kayla and I entered the room, Moore turned and glanced at us. Although it was clear that he recognized me, he was not about to let my presence ruffle him. He quickly shifted his eyes away, and for the rest of the hearing he fought any temptation to look back. Kayla and I sat a couple of rows behind him and to the right.

"Is that the lady sitting back there in the green?" Moore's attorney muttered, nodding in my direction.

Moore mumbled "uh-huh." Neither he nor his parents turned. Any curiosity they had about the woman who instigated the FBI investigation must have been squelched by pride.

"They're talking about you, Mom," Kayla whispered to me.

"I know," I whispered back.

During the proceeding, Moore's knee twitched. It jiggled up and down, back and forth, an outlet for the nervousness that was less conspicuous on his face.

When it was Moore's turn to stand before the judge, he was polite—just as Evens had been—saying "yes, your honor" and "no, your honor." Also, like Evens, he took a plea of "not guilty."

Following the proceeding, I asked the prosecutor why Moore still had a Twitter page. The judge had made it clear that his social media should be removed.

"He gets power and followers from that site," I told the prosecutor. "Those followers continue to harass me and the other victims."

The prosecutor then confronted Moore's attorney with this information, but he fired back, "Hunter doesn't want Twitter to come down because he plans to use the page for fundraising."

Clearly this cockamamie excuse had been contrived by Moore in advance. Unfortunately, the prosecutor did not have the chutzpah to press further.

At the elevators, Moore donned his disguise—the coat, glasses and backward-facing baseball cap—and when he got to the first floor, he jetted out of the courthouse door. He sprinted down the sidewalk like a mouse trying to outrun a stampede. It was an overreaction because the only person who wanted his photo was an *Inside Edition* reporter. Moore's desperation to avoid a camera was ironic. He seemed to think unclothed pictures of others were fair game, but a clothed picture of himself—well, that was an outrageous request. Rationality and equity were obviously not his strong suit.

Despite the lack of media at the courthouse, news outlets published articles about the arraignment; and as usual, an uptick in press led to online attacks against me.

I had endured waves of venom during the past two years. Backlash would happen, then subside, happen again, then subside. The cycles correlated with the media Moore received. Following a flurry of articles about "the most hated man," members of "the family" would be reminded of my role in their "daddy's" arrest and in my fight against revenge porn.

I felt like the goalie in a high-stakes hockey game. Social media was a bunch of folks skating around a rink, leisurely passing a puck back and forth; and then a whistle would sound and suddenly a group of strangers would launch an attack on me. They would whip their sticks in my face, spit at me, corner me and lunge in my direction, pressing me to the ice.

Following the arraignment, I found a flurry of vicious tweets on my feed. Some were aimed at me; some targeted Kayla.

"Dear Charlotte Laws, your daughter is a cock hungry slut and putting Hunter Moore in jail will not change that," said Sarazin.

Illush tweeted, "@CharlotteLaws What a worthless cunt, hope you and your slutty daughter die choking on a big fat cock. *spits in your face*"

Tony wrote, "Charlotte Laws is so fucking ugly. @Huntermoore #TheFamily."

Someone who went by the name "James#TheFamily" wrote, "@CharlotteLaws you'll never stop revenge porn! Your daughter is a fucking slut."

Heckeur said, "@CharlotteLaws you nasty whore," and Hans wrote, "@charlottelaws fuck you bitch," and Binks said, "Charlotte Laws is a useless butthole…"

Female members of "the family" also joined the hate fest.

Juice posted, "@CharlotteLaws you're a cunt, you should be banned from the Internet for your stupidity."

Ericka wrote, "Dude someone needs to backhand @CharlotteLaws…," and Halle tweeted, "@CharlotteLaws you're a dumb ugly bitch I hope you burn in hell."

Jilian said, "Fuck Charlotte Laws," and CuntPunch wrote, "#TheFamily should all spam charlotte laws just to get [her] suspended…"

Also, around this time, I fielded a number of "Charlie Evens phone calls." In other words, a few of the alleged hacker's former friends, classmates and acquaintances telephoned me to lend support to the cause or to give me their two cents on Evens. Some had been his close friends—or so they thought—until the day of his arrest; others never liked him.

"If a girl refused to go out with him," one of his former classmates told me, "he'd spread rumors about her all over school. He might say she's lesbian. He was disrespectful of women. Lots of people at Notre Dame thought he was a jerk. He had an arrogant, 'I'm untouchable' attitude."

A Victim Named Annie

Annie also contacted me. She was tentative, apologetic and fearful of Evens.

"I feel terrible. I think I'm the reason your daughter got targeted," she said. "Charlie Evens hacked me and my sister way back in October 2011, and I think he may have used my Facebook page to get to others. I'm Kayla's Facebook friend as well."

"Don't feel guilty," I replied. "It wasn't you. He got to Kayla through someone named Hayley."

Annie expressed relief, telling me that she had been one of Evens' closest friends.

"I knew I'd been hacked, but I didn't know who'd done it," she said. "My nude pictures were stolen from my email and put online. Plus, the hacker sent me a computer virus and threatening emails. I would never have suspected my friend, Charlie. He had a crush on me, and we hung out. We talked all the time."

"Wow," I said. "That's how he treats his friends?"

Annie had heard about Evens' arrest and texted him on the day of the arraignment. "Hey, what's going on?"

He called her back while leaving the courthouse. He did not recognize the phone number. They spoke for quite a while, despite the fact that "contact with victims" was a big no-no. It was contrary to the judge's order.

"He always seemed like a normal, silly kid," she told me. "He was charming in a dorky way. He was an uplifting, peaceful person with a hippie nature. Of course, some people told me there was something 'off' about him."

"He must have started hacking his own Facebook friends first, and then branched out to strangers," I said. "Now it makes sense. That's how he got into all those accounts."

Anne said that Evens confessed the whole disgusting truth to her on the phone, not a wise move for a guy facing 42 years in prison. Maybe he thought she'd remain loyal, laughing off the federal crimes and gross disloyalty. But instead she phoned me with her moral dilemma. She wanted my advice. I asked her to talk to Jed, lead agent for the FBI. Annie was hesitant to go that route; she feared Charlie would take revenge by derailing her new business or committing "God-knows-what-other" felonies against her. He was no longer a trusted confidante. He was suddenly a scary and creepy dude.

"I was completely fooled," she admitted. "He was the last person I would have expected. He flat out admitted he'd hacked into my accounts on a bunch of occasions."

Annie said that Evens seemed unaware of the severity of his crimes, claiming, "I just want to confess, face the consequences and go to prison. But, I've been advised not to... I've been hacking since I was 16. I'm addicted to drugs and alcohol, but my worst addiction is hacking. I'm great at manipulating people."

Evens also explained how he got linked with *Is Anyone Up?* Interestingly enough, he'd hacked Hunter Moore, but rather than get angry, Moore had responded, "Hey, do you want to hack for me?" Evens agreed on the spot.

After three lengthy conversations, I persuaded Annie to relay the details of her phone conversation to Jed. Jed then communicated her testimony to the prosecutor, who in turn hauled Evens back into court for breaching the judge's order (by talking to a victim).

The hearing for "the breach" was held on February 24, 2014 in Judge Dolly Gee's courtroom on Spring Street in Los Angeles. The room had a formal feel and a slight echo; the walls were comprised of wood paneling and cement tiles. Behind the judge's stand was a red curtain and a seal that said, "U.S. District Court, Central District of California."

Evens sat in an area reserved for defendants; he wore a blue, button-down shirt and a dark gray jacket. He was cleanly shaven and his hair was tidy. His mother, Jackie, sat in the audience section in a beige sweater and navy pants; she had a yellow purse in her lap. Her less-than-friendly glance in my direction told me that she was now aware of my identity. She knew I was not *just* a mom and writer, but also the instigator of the federal investigation.

It was decided that "the breach does not give rise for remand." In other words, the judge and lawyers agreed that Evens should not be thrown in jail—and his bail money revoked—since Annie had texted him first. Of course, she did not know she was his victim at the time; she found out during the call. Nevertheless, Evens was permitted to remain free on bond.

Sedate-Gate: A Scandal

Months passed, and in November 2014, I was blending my usual fruit and granola drink when Mandy called.

"Did you see the headlines?" She sounded out of breath.

"No," I replied.

"They need you. You have to come forward."

"What are you talking about, Mandy? Who needs me?"

"The women of the world. You can't desert them now."

"You're being over-dramatic again," I laughed. "Is there a new revenge porn website?"

Mandy, the quintessential feminist, phoned me regularly about cyber-scoundrels and their misogynistic cults. She was a thermometer, measuring online heat and backlash against females. There were repugnant trolls, sexist big-mouths and macho bloggers. No one could escape detection. Mandy was an Internet monitoring machine, a miniversion of the NSA. Plus, she bequeathed her homemade title—"the daily woman-hater"—on every deserving target.

"No, it's not a website," she replied. "This is different. You've got to stop the JELL-O pudding man."

"There's a JELL-O pudding man?" I was starting to think Mandy was one container short of a full Snack Pack.

"Bill Cosby," she said. "You told me your friend dated him. And that he drugged her years ago."

"What does that have to do with revenge porn?"

"Nothing," she said. "But they're saying nobody believed those women who came forward against him. You have to help them."

I hung up and searched the web to learn that Mandy was right. The women who made allegations about Bill Cosby back in 2005 had never been taken seriously. Sexism was apparently the broom that had swept their allegations under the collective American carpet. It took a male—comedian Hannibal Buress—to peel back the wrapper, to put the issue in the spotlight and make the public examine it. I hemmed and hawed, contemplating whether I should come forward with my 34-year-old secret. I had known the comedian for 35 years.

I had last seen Bill at the Paramount Theatre in Oakland, California on February 19, 2005. He was performing at the venue, and it was "between shows." I was accompanied by my husband and stepdaughter.

"Did I ever drug you?" he joked when I entered his dressing room.

His comment was meant to defuse tension because a woman had just come forward, saying she was drugged and raped by him. It was obvious that Bill was feeling uneasy about negative media attention. I wondered if his decision to hang out with me and my family one-on-one for 45 minutes was part "damage control." I was not his close friend; I was more of a friendly acquaintance. Perhaps "friendly acquaintances" can expect more attention when 34-year-old secrets are involved.

Bill knew that I knew. I could feel it. I had known the truth since that memorable night in 1981. Bill had drugged my close friend, Sandy, and then had sex with her.

Bill met Sandy in the casino at the Las Vegas Hilton around 1979 or 1980. He was gambling and asked her to join him. She was in her late teens or early twenties, thin and medium height with hazel eyes, freckles and straight brown hair that fell just below her shoulders. She routinely wore slinky, form-fitting dresses. Bill and Sandy immediately began a consensual intimate relationship. At the time, Sandy was sexually adventuresome, dating a number of men around town.

Sandy was not a would-be actress and had no major career aspirations, other than possible enrollment in the U.S. military. She did not date Bill with an eye toward professional advancement, and to my knowledge, he made no promises of this sort. She simply liked his company. She also came to appreciate the few hundred dollars he gave her following each date.

"I don't know why Bill always leaves me money. He gave me six hundred dollars last week," she told me. "He must think I'm a hooker. But I don't want to tell him the truth, because I like getting the cash."

Sandy had no job and lived in a downscale apartment in a dreggy section of town. Those extra dollars came in handy at rent time.

Sandy introduced me to Bill in 1980. I was 20 years old. The three of us sat alone in his dressing room at the Las Vegas Hilton. He coached me on my college plans. He was the incarnation of the wise and protective patriarch, a role he would play on a national scale when *The Cosby Show* launched in 1984, making Cliff Huxtable a household name. I particularly appreciated his commitment to causes and his down-to-earth nature. He was not only an incredible talent; he was a caring and generous soul.

"If you grow your hair down to your waist, I will give you $2,000," Bill told Sandy.

She did not react with enthusiasm. But then again, she was not a bubbly person. Her temperament was more like a panther: sleek and even-keeled.

Then he looked at me and smiled, "What's your favorite clothing store?"

"Suzy Creamcheese," I said.

"If you help Sandy grow her hair down to her waist," Bill said to me, "I will buy you $1,000 worth of clothes at Suzy Creamcheese."

I figured Bill had a "thing" for long hair in the same way that some men have a "thing" for feet.

Sandy never grew her hair. She was not motivated by money. But she did come to me one morning a year later to tell me that something bad had happened. Bill had drugged her. She was not angry. She was baffled, stunned, even shaken by the experience. Plus, she felt betrayed.

"Bill drugged me last night, and then had sex with me," Sandy confided. "I just don't understand it. It's not like I would have said no to *anything*."

He had given her two pills and said, "These will relax you." She trusted him and swallowed them. She figured they were vitamins or herbal medicine. They did not relax her; they flat-out knocked her unconscious.

"He didn't need to do it," she repeated. "I just don't understand why."

Did it turn him on to see a woman "out cold" or was this all a mistake? Maybe Sandy's body had reacted to the pills in a bizarre and unexpected way. I was willing to give Bill the benefit of the doubt, although Sandy felt his actions were intentional.

She did not view the encounter as rape, because she was already in an intimate relationship with him. I likewise did not categorize it as a sex crime, because it was Sandy's experience, and she had a right to define it any way she wished. I was only the bystander, the friend, the shoulder to cry on. Of course, now that I am older, I look back and realize that when a woman is unconscious, she cannot ever consent.

Sandy had no idea what happened to her that night. She knew it involved sex; she could tell by the way her body felt afterward. It never occurred to either of us that Bill might be drugging other women. We both assumed the encounter was a "one-off." After all, Bill was charming, intelligent, attractive and famous. He did not need to sedate women in order to secure dates. He could not possibly have a dark side.

I moved from Las Vegas in 1982 and fell out of touch with Sandy. But I stayed in touch with Bill. In fact, I hung out with him at least a dozen times over the years and even met three of his post-Sandy girl-friends. I learned that he kept multiple suites at the Las Vegas Hilton so he could "date" a handful of women at once. I witnessed him giving a thousand dollars to one girl after a tennis match; he clearly liked being a big spender.

One evening in the mid-1980s, Bill and I were alone in his dressing room.

"Have you seen Sandy?" I asked.

"No," he replied. "I haven't seen her in years."

It occurred to me that the "drugging date" may have been their last.

In an effort to elevate Sandy a few notches, I disclosed, "She was never a hooker. You probably thought she was."

"Really?" He was expressionless. I could not tell whether he already knew or was surprised.

"She needed the money for rent," I added. "That's why she never told you."

He nodded, indicating he understood and was copacetic with it.

In 2005, I had arrangements to attend Bill's show in Oakland and to go backstage with my family. But days prior, I got wind of the drugging and rape allegations against Bill. I was shocked and in a quandary. For the first time, I realized that Sandy's ordeal had *not* been a "one-off." Plus, I was a witness. I could corroborate this woman's story. But should I? Was it better to leave it to the courts and law enforcement? After all, I was not a victim. Bill had always treated me with respect. He had given me advice and been generous with his time. He had never offered *me* a pill.

I was also unclear how to handle the backstage mingle. Should I cancel? Should I question or confront him? Should I be polite? I chewed on this for hours, finally deciding to keep the arrangements.

After Bill tossed out his opening line, "Did I ever drug you?" I took a seat across from him in his Oakland dressing room. I introduced him to my husband, Charles, and my stepdaughter, Sibylla.

"What style do you think this is?" Bill asked in an upbeat way, alluding to the room's furnishings.

"Art Deco," Charles replied.

"What do you do, Sibylla?" Bill asked.

"I'm an astrologer," she replied.

"Sibylla is going to tell you if you're going to be a success," Charles said. Bill laughed.

"Charles is not only funny," I finally spoke. "He can recite entire Shakespearean plays."

"You like that, don't you?" Bill grinned at me. He loved the idea that poetry had swept me off my feet.

"You can make up anything at this point, and she'll think it's Shakespeare," Bill winked at Charles.

The conversational tone had been set; it was friendly and humorous. There would be no confrontation or interrogation. We calmly discussed politics and national news stories—except, of course, that certain news story about a certain comedian. It was the elephant in the Art Deco room. We also talked about the criminal justice system and Bill's favorite subject: education.

Ironically, Bill was concerned that certain reform schools might be pumping youngsters with drugs.

"Could you check into this for me?" Bill asked, since I wrote a newspaper column at the time.

I said, "Sure."

I did *not* say, "I know someone else who has been pumping youngsters with drugs!"

I was usually a rebel, outspoken and controversial; but on this particular evening, I opted to be pleasant. I gave Bill a friendly goodbye hug, still uncertain whether I should come forward. It was not long before a number of women corroborated the first woman's account about drugging and rape, and I assumed my testimony was not needed.

I assumed wrong.

I tried to reach out to Sandy to get further details of her story, but I was never able to track her down. Her full name is common, and some people aren't as easy as a Facebook search. But I never forgot the conversations we had, or the ones I had with Bill later.

Edmund Burke once intimated that bad things happen when good people do nothing. Since I wanted to be a good person and I did not want bad things to happen, I decided to go public with my story. I realized I was late. I realized I was not a victim myself. And I realized I did not help my sisters in 2005 when they needed me most. But I also realized that it is better to be late than silent.

I wrote an op-ed about my experiences. It was published in the online publication *Salon* on November 30, 2014.

Mandy immediately phoned. As usual, her words had a theatrical flair, "I'm speaking for all the women in the world... all the abandoned victims. We thank you for your confession."

Then I received a call from a 61-year-old stranger, Rosie. She had worked with Bill Cosby forty years prior as a copywriter in New York. She was privy to his less-than-above-board activities and said that lots of folks were witnesses. She felt that my story in *Salon* might prompt them to come forward.

"I'm not going to the media because no one will listen to me," she said. "You, on the other hand, are the Erin Brockovich of revenge porn. People take you seriously."

Rosie was friendly with Frank Scotti, the ex-NBC employee who was part of Bill's inner circle. Scotti went public in November 2014 about keeping guard outside the comedian's dressing room while he was "entertaining" young models. Scotti also helped Bill deliver checks to some of these women, allegedly to keep them quiet.

Frank possibly saved Rosie from rape. He spoke to her like a father one afternoon in the mid-1970s, revealing that he was Bill's pimp and "lookout."

"He has already given me the signal that he wants to jump you," Frank told Rosie. "Don't ever go into a room alone with him, and if you leave your tea on a table unattended, throw it out."

"What if I end up alone with him anyway?" she asked.

"Lock yourself in the bathroom," Frank advised. "He won't break down doors."

"At the time, I thought Frank was an idiot, that he was exaggerating, but I decided to take his advice," she told me on the phone in 2014.

Rosie almost got fired for refusing to deliver a script to Bill.

"He was yelling for the script, but I wouldn't take it to him," she said to me. "He was in that room alone. I didn't know what to do. There was nobody to go with me. I got a verbal reprimand later from my boss. Luckily, I got to keep my job."

"I will never forget Frank. He saved my life," she added.

Rosie also said she could corroborate ex-model Janice Dickinson's claim about being forced to remove the Bill Cosby rape story from her autobiography. Rosie became a witness by accident when she and her colleagues booked a recording studio in the Brill Building in New York City. The rooms were rented by the hour, and the previous clients—Bill Cosby's lawyer and Janice Dickinson's publisher—had gone over on their time. The door was slightly ajar, and Rosie could hear the lawyer inside threatening the publisher.

"I don't know who the attorney was," she said to me on the phone. "But he sounded like mafia. He said he would sue left and right. He would inconvenience them financially by suing over and over."

She added, "Then, I heard the attorney say to the publisher, 'I know where your kids go to school.'"

Rosie and her colleagues backed away from the incensed attorney as he emerged from the room.

"He demanded to know our names and where we lived," Rosie told me. "We were intimidated."

"If so many people knew about these things, why didn't anyone come forward? I can understand why victims didn't. But why not witnesses?" I asked.

"Bill Cosby was like a god in Manhattan," Rosie said. "He could attack your career, ruin your ability to get work. You didn't come forward. Plus, there was no such thing as a rape kit. There were no women's rights in those days."

Rosie and I said good-bye. From that day forward, I knew I needed to be ready, willing and able to help brick-and-mortar victims as well as those tormented by trolls in the cyber realm.

A Victim Named Suzy

"I wish Roger had just raped me," Suzy told me.
"Revenge porn is so much worse."

Days passed, and the Hunter Moore and Charlie Evens trial—which had been delayed by the defendants' attorneys—was finally drawing closer. The FBI provided me with a special login, password and website link so I could stay up-to-date on the process. I compiled a loose-leaf binder full of paperwork about status hearings, pretrial release conditions, courtroom minutes, protective orders for discovery, criminal history reports and case summaries. I also continued to help victims of online harassment, a time-consuming, but a soul-enhancing pastime. I averaged two to three callers per week.

Suzy's case was particularly disturbing.

She had given up on life. She picked up a dusty flip-flop from the floor of her next-door neighbor Gus' garage. Gus was a weathered old character who worked on cars when he wasn't toiling away at the nearby shipping warehouse. Suzy had often seen him tinkering under the hood of his latest vintage vehicle or revving up the engine.

She studied the discarded shoe in her hand. It was just like her. It had no direction, no purpose, no friends. Suzy felt alone even though she lived with 350,000 other people in New Orleans.

Suzy was trespassing that day. She knew Gus always left the pedestrian door of his garage unlocked, and she knew where he kept the key to his old Chevy. It was in a drawer under his workbench. She maneuvered past piles of junk: thrashed clothes, empty food containers and automotive tools. She even noticed the mate to the flip-flop; it was in the corner.

Suzy had no mate. She attributed her bad luck in the "love department" to being middle-aged and 195 pounds; and to having rough and wrinkled skin due to smoking. She was divorced with no children and had moved to Louisiana from Michigan with plans to start a new life.

Suzy remembered the night that changed her life—the night she was drugged.

She and her platonic friend, Roger, had been watching television, just as they did regularly. Maybe Roger was angry because she made him watch *Dance Moms*. Maybe he didn't like the stew she made for dinner. Maybe he needed fast cash. But, for whatever reason, he decided to pull a "Bill Cosby." He slipped something into her Coca-Cola. At least, this was her theory. While she was unconscious on the bed, Roger disrobed her and photographed her nude in hard-core poses. Suzy woke the next day with her clothes disheveled, and Roger was gone. She did not know what had happened. She phoned Roger; he did not answer. She left message after message.

He never returned the calls, and days later, his phone was disconnected. She went to his apartment, but it had been vacated. The landlord had no forwarding address.

Suzy was confused about Roger's disappearance, but did not think much of it until strangers began harassing her online. They emailed links to websites with obscene content, featuring *her*. There were dozens of crude, naked photos of her unconscious on the bed, legs apart, from every conceivable angle. She was a victim of ultimate betrayal. Suzy panicked, hyperventilating and running recklessly from room to room. She felt like an out-of-control vehicle veering over a cliff.

There was more bad news. The photos were labeled with Suzy's particulars: her full name, city, email address and ex-husband's name. Plus, the images seemed to be circulating around the world; trolls were posting and reposting the shots. Some of the hosting websites originated in the United Arab Emirates, Africa and the Netherlands—far away and impossible to control.

Commenters on these sites abused Suzy further. One called her "blubber butt," while another referred to her as "the thing." She was threatened with "Send me more nudes or I will load these onto more sites." She received an email: "Why don't you just go kill yourself, Honey." Suzy's self-esteem, which was already in the gutter, fell further; and she felt there was only one solution. The final one.

This is why she was in Gus' garage. She thought carbon monoxide poisoning was her best bet because it would kill swiftly and painlessly, and it would take no more than 15 minutes to kick in. Suzy prayed she would die because she knew an unsuccessful attempt might lead to paralysis, blindness, or dementia. She had learned this from an article.

Suzy taped a homemade sign to the outside of the garage. It read, "Danger. Do not enter." She was afraid Gus would come home from work, become overwhelmed by the gas and die. There was no reason for revenge porn to claim additional victims.

The sign saved Suzy.

A concerned neighbor saw the word "Danger" only minutes after it was posted and became curious. This woman entered the garage to investigate and found Suzy in the driver's seat of the Chevy with the engine running and the windows down.

"I read that you've tracked down men who violated women's personal privacy. And you've brought them to justice," Suzy phoned me a few days later. "I'm at my wit's end. Please help. I don't know what else to do."

She told me that she had gone to her local police department, who sent her away. "They said they don't handle this sort of thing and that it would be my word against Roger's."

"There isn't an anti-revenge porn law in Louisiana yet," I told her. "But there are definitely laws in your state against drugging women and undressing them."

"I'm seriously depressed. Roger was my closest friend."

Advising suicidal victims always made me nervous. Was I qualified for the job? Would I say the wrong thing? Could I make things worse? I had doubts and insecurities, so I routinely referred these callers to someone with the experience, usually Debbie, a licensed therapist who worked for the FBI. Counseling victims was her full-time job, plus she could fast-track a case to an agent who could launch an investigation.

"I can also put you in touch with a cyber-forensic lab," I told Suzy. "They might be able to track down Roger and trace IP addresses for the trolls who are resubmitting your photos."

Lastly, I connected Suzy with a law firm, so she could begin the process of legally changing her name. She wanted a new identity.

"I wish Roger had just raped me," Suzy told me. "Revenge porn is so much worse."

Suzy was not the first person to express this sentiment. The parents of Audrie Pott and the mother of Rehtaeh Parsons told me that sexual assault had *not* driven their daughters to suicide; they snapped weeks later when humiliating, nude photos surfaced and became public. It was revenge porn—not rape—that prompted these young girls to kill themselves.

"I'm the victim, yet I'm the one who has to pack up and move to a new city," Suzy said to me. "And what if those online criminals find out my new name? Those pictures will chase me for the rest of my life."

The Elusive Trial

It was time to get back to the Hunter Moore and Charlie Evens case. My final assignment was to gather together victims for the sentencing phase of the trial. The FBI and prosecutor's office wanted me to coordinate testimony, a difficult task because I needed to hide true identities from the press. No one wanted to be linked with nude photos. The hacked victims had to be in disguise with dark glasses, wigs or maybe Guy Fawkes Anonymous masks. I would have to sneak them into the courthouse, make them invisible to prying eyes and cameras—a fitting task, I suppose, for a former private eye and gate-crasher with "smart talent."

My list of phone numbers was ready. My calendar was clear. The victims and I were on high alert, anxious for the trial to begin, prepared to tell the judge about the humiliation and pain the defendants had caused. Revenge porn had led to depression, job losses, terminated family ties, attempted suicides—and even death. Hunter Moore and Charlie Evens had enjoyed ruining lives and constructing an online world of "pure evil."

The victims and I waited for the trial.

And we waited.

And waited.

But, as it goes with the court system, the date—which had already been changed twice—was changed a third time. Delay can be a shield for those without a defense. The prosecutor's office told me that it is routine for defendants to seek continuances. They look for excuses, even fire their attorneys at the last second. They hope to avoid the unavoidable, to escape the inescapable and to flee from the obvious. Hunter Moore and Charlie Evens are still trying to flee from the obvious.

The trial is currently set for March 24, 2015.

And my work as a troll slayer is not yet done.

Trial Update

T IS ONLY HOURS BEFORE this book is scheduled to go to press, and Hunter Moore—the man who might be described as the moral equivalent of a bed bug infestation—has unexpectedly pleaded guilty. This is quite a shift from the days when he adamantly denied stealing nudes and slammed women as nasty whores who deserve what they get. Of course, he probably still believes that last bit.

Moore has signed a plea agreement, confessing to the crimes of identity theft and hacking; and he faces two to seven years in prison, a fine of $500,000 and three years of supervised release following his sentence. Victim testimony is crucial if he is to receive more time behind bars, rather than less.

I constructed a Twitter post in search of additional witnesses, "If you're a victim of @HunterMoore, we can hide your identity from the press & public. Please testify at the sentencing. Contact me."

My announcement went viral; 15,000 blogs reposted it. I was bombarded with emails, tweets and phone calls.

As usual, Moore had supporters on Twitter. Codee said, "Hunter Moore is still the closest thing we've got to Jesus. Kinda bummed. #FreeHunterMoore." Renard tweeted, "Daddy's going to jail," and Cameron wrote, "@CharlotteLaws you're lame as hell. Lol."

But there were significantly more anti-RP tweets, many made by Moore's former disciples.

Alex said, "Ironic Hunter Moore getting shit from scene kids as he faces jail. The very group who participated in and perpetuated isanyoneup…" Mike wrote, "Mad props to @CharlotteLaws for her fight against Hunter Moore. There is no place for bullying and hate in our scene."

Chibbs said, "The human scum dumpster that is Hunter Moore is going to jail #dontdropthesoap." Troy wrote, "…From his mom's basement to a jail cell," and Mary stated, "If you are a woman and you like Hunter Moore you have turned your back on women, period. Go show a stranger your tits #lowselfesteem."

Sam wrote, "A whole lecture hall just applauded Hunter Moore going to jail. This is why I love warped tour kids," and Aaron tweeted, "…and to think I wanted to be like Hunter Moore 2 years ago."

Jeremey wrote, "Hunter Moore considered himself God about a year and a half ago. Within the blink of an eye he's 100% gone and forgotten," and Grandma Moses wrote, "I feel like the only ass Hunter Moore is about to get for the next few years isn't quite the kind he hacks into emails to steal…"

Adam Steinbaugh—a prominent victim advocate—wrote a humorous post, "The absolute last person I would ever want to piss off is @CharlotteLaws."

Jed told me that a plea agreement with Charlie Evens is imminent. Unfortunately, his confession will miss the publication deadline for this book.

"Now that Hunter Moore's going to prison, victims can get some closure," Mandy told me on the phone.

"Yes. So many people are recovering from P.M.S.S…. Post-Moore Stress Syndrome," I replied. "Finally, they can begin to heal."

Rebel in a Binder

POSTMODERNISM—a late-twentieth century movement—is about deconstruction, analysis, genre-blurring and peering at alternate angles. It is about upending the traditional and accepting iconoclasm. It dances with braided layers, nuanced themes and fractured complexities. This book embraces that radical structure, despite the fact that naysayers warned me that no one wants a "rebel in a binder."

"Readers have a comfort zone. You cannot combine your childhood experiences with your revenge porn fight," an editor from a major publishing house warned. "No one will read a book like that. You were not the same person at twenty that you are today."

Or am I?

Is the mother who fought against revenge porn simply an adult version of the life-crasher, described in Part II? Don't both incarnations require crashing through barriers? Is waging a battle against trolls much like asserting independence against old-money Atlanta? Is facing death threats and online sexism a little like being attacked by racists or ankle-kicked by Christian bullies?

My childhood stories are nestled in the center or womb of this book. My birthmother, Sharon, coaxes them out, as if she is opening a window for fresh air. She yearns for more oxygen, a new perspective, a new dimension to her life. She craves that which she missed after placing me for adoption: the warmth of parenthood. She has no other children and must know me, even though her husband has forbidden us to be in touch. She wants to know about my tragedies and triumphs, the adventures that define the "little Atlanta girl who could"—the daughter she only knows as the "Erin Brockovich of revenge porn."

Just as Sharon encourages me to reveal the first 22 years of my life, I encourage my own daughter, Kayla, to emerge from the womb called her bedroom after she becomes victimized by revenge porn. She feels humiliated, depressed and defeated, but I know her story needs to go public; it needs to be heard. It is the only way to protect other victims, to rid the world of the website called "pure evil," and to pass criminal laws. My daughter boldly steps forward, and I learn that she is a life-crasher, too…

…As well as a hero in the battle against revenge porn.

CONCLUSION

From Museum to Center Stage

"WHAT DOES THE ERIN BROCKOVICH of revenge porn want to tell the world?" Mandy asked when I told her about my memoir. "What are her words of wisdom? What did she learn from writing this book?"

"I don't think anyone wants me to synthesize the material and dole out advice," I replied.

"Yes, they do. Don't disappoint me, Charlotte." She hung up the phone.

Since this book is intentionally unorthodox, I figured there would be no harm in mixing my memoir with a touch of "how to" and self-reflection. I include the following information for Mandy, as thanks for being my friend and for courageously joining "Team Troll Slayer."

Penning *Rebel in High Heels* was much like transforming into a curator at Sharon's favorite art museum. I had to choose which collections to display and which to ignore. In the end, exhibitions (or life stories) were selected because they were meaningful to me or likely to be entertaining to an audience; and I knew if I was lucky, even my crazier antics would convey deeper messages.

Although the swirling universe is the true museum curator (since I don't believe that ideas can be *freely* absorbed or rejected), it is my hope that this book—which I was "determined" to write—will be a cause that leads to a positive effect for those "determined" to read it. Perhaps it will be a green light in people's lives or provide a ramp into the bold zone. Perhaps it will contribute to othercentrism (helping others), lessen violence in society—against human *and* nonhuman victims—or prompt a passion for perseverance. At the very least, it is a contribution to the marketplace of ideas.

I began this memoir under the assumption that Dad was the Captain Hook of my existence because he regularly flung verbal swipes in my direction with his barbed tongue. Yet, after reviewing my totality of experiences with him, I realize he was a gray area. Although he could make me walk the plank emotionally, he taught me how to dive for treasures beneath the sea, and he gave me confidence that I could achieve success.

The insights I gained while compiling this book partly revolve around the colorful and ostentatious pieces on my museum walls. Dad had always said that show business and its cronies—Las Vegas and Hollywood—were fantasy and superficiality. But he was wrong. Old-money Atlanta was the lie and the mirage; and so was the gold-plated bubble that wreathed my childhood until Mom's (attempted) suicide. Plus, there were other false doctrines that I fought in the South: blind faith in Christian truths, the superiority of the white race, and the moral perfection of preppiness and conservatism. Many of my show biz relationships were stronger than the connections I forged in Georgia. I spent a great deal more time with some entertainers than I did with my adoptive dad.

There were, of course, authentic people in my childhood: Aunt Helen and my "man maid" Richard Baker. They may have lacked sophistication, but they were real. Richard was a big shot in his family, although he didn't act like one. He had surpassed expectations: he worked as a servant, while his ancestors had been sold as slaves. Aunt Helen lived in a mobile home in Texas, dated truck drivers and ignored condescending stares by socialites. She didn't care what others thought. But, her sister, my adoptive mom, cared very much; and this led to her downfall.

Mom wanted to live up to the grand expectations of Atlanta and Dad, and lost herself in the process. She led an artificial life, filled with fake status and real fur. She sold her soul for a curtsey and a pointed pinky finger. Her biggest goal was to be a proper wife. This meant hanging as an ornament on Dad's arm. Unfortunately, ornaments are hollow and fragile. They are empty inside, and they break.

I was schizophrenic about Mom. I was initially scared of her after the attempted suicide; but, in my early twenties, I decided I would invite her to live with me if she regained full consciousness. I no longer saw her as an unsympathetic figure; she was an outcast and an underdog. She no longer fit into Atlanta society or Dad's carefully constructed world. She had no one, but me.

Although we were different, I could relate to her on one level: we'd both felt trapped. We were flames, confined inside the glass lantern called Atlanta. Mom unfortunately moved inward and extinguished herself. My wick was longer. I lashed out, scorching the container until it cracked and then making a bonfire out of the morals and mores I had come to despise.

Escaping from Georgia was both easy and difficult. It was in accordance with my rebel nature to barrel out of town, mowing down speed limit signs, veering off the narrow road, and forging my own path through wild lands. Plus, there was no one to keep me there. Richard Baker and Aunt Helen were no longer alive; and the only beings that I felt loved me in childhood were my dogs. Unfortunately, they were either dead or had been given away by Dad.

However, leaving Atlanta was difficult in that I had to survive. The game was no longer an easy win against Buddy. It was suddenly a life or death contest against the world, and I knew I could end up like Tween, hobbling along the shoulder of the road with empty pockets. Wild lands are given their name for a reason. They are wild and unpredictable, and I was unsure whether I could tame them.

Prior to stocking my museum, I was unaware of the link between philosophy and my other interests: gate-crashing, chip chatting, becoming the Erin Brockovich of revenge porn, working as a private eye, wangling a date with Tom Jones, tracking down my birthparents, and investigating hidden corridors in hotels and casinos. All require peering around rules, finding loopholes or looking outside the box. All are aided by smart talent and contempt for conformity. My aptitude in these areas partly compensated for feelings of intellectual inadequacy, but there were other advantages. I was able to go on tantalizing adventures, which led to insights. I was able to upend the status quo and throw myself into not-yet-mainstream causes. I was able to fight for victims and justice.

Lastly, I hope my museum will inspire you, the reader, to become a bigger star in your own life. You need not be afraid to take center stage, to foster your own beliefs (regardless of what the masses say), to persist toward your goals (even if they are unconventional) and to buck a flawed system. From the spotlight, you can venture into the bold zone and embark upon meaningful, othercentric missions. You can direct the action. You can decide the plot and theme of the play. It is unfulfilling to be a mere "seat filler" in someone else's life, or to labor as a forgotten prop master.

And when naysayers or Internet trolls extract their vaudeville hooks (as they will) and try to drag you behind the curtain, do not be afraid to resist. Security may even try to oust you from the theater, but remember… It's your party, and you can crash if you want to.

You can be a rebel in high heels.

Glossary

Alma Davis – Tom Jones' bodyguard in Las Vegas

Anne – Charlotte's childhood friend

Argyle Ike – Private investigator hired to keep tabs on Charlotte

Bathrobe Arne – Customer who hired a prostitute named Lynn to participate in an orgy

Bold Zone – A fierce mindset in which one tackles goals by taking calculated chances

Buddy (or Arthur) – Charlotte's brother

Charles – Charlotte's husband

Charlie Evens – Alleged hacker (who stole nude photos and sold them to Hunter Moore). He went by the fake name "Gary Jones."

Con Man – Swindler who tried to cheat Charlotte out of money in Las Vegas

Darla – Charlotte's Las Vegas friend who worked as a casino dealer

Fred Flintstone – Stranger who gifted Charlotte $7,700 in money and clothing when she was seventeen

Frosty – A woman who Charlotte met in Tom's dressing room. The word Frosty is Charlotte's synonym for "romantic rival."

Gary Jones – Fake name used by the hacker who stole photos and posted them on IAU

Helen (Aunt Helen) – Charlotte's adoptive aunt

Hunter Moore – Revenge porn site operator who called himself a "professional life ruiner"

Ike – See "Argyle Ike"

Jed – Lead FBI agent

John Moran – Tom Jones' advance man

Kayla Laws – Charlotte's daughter

Is Anyone Up? (IAU) – The most nefarious revenge porn website, which was run by Hunter Moore

Lloyd Greenfield – Tom Jones' manager

Lovett – The school Charlotte attended from first grade through high school

Lynn – Las Vegas prostitute

Magic Marvin – Magician at a childhood birthday party

Mandy – A revenge porn victim who became Charlotte's assistant and close friend

Mark Woodward – Tom Jones' son

Missy – Charlotte's nickname until she was 30 years old.

Othercentrism – A focus on helping others (humans and nonhumans)

Omniocracy – A government with representation for all living beings

Revenge Porn (RP) – The online distribution of nude and topless photos without consent in an effort to humiliate and hurt victims, mostly females.

Richard Baker – The Laws family housekeeper or "man maid."

Ricky – Sharon's husband

Sharon – The woman Charlotte met secretly for 26 years. Her full identity is revealed at the end of Part II.

Sherilyn – Charlotte's childhood friend

Snooty Hooty – Clothing boutique in Atlanta

Suzy Creamcheese – Clothing boutique in Las Vegas

Trolls – Online bullies who hurt and humiliate victims

Troll Slayer – Person who fights trolls

Tween – Charlotte's adoptive uncle

Some names and personal details in this book were changed in order to protect privacy.

Made in the USA
San Bernardino, CA
28 April 2015